Introduction

The Editor

This volume actually has two functions. First, of course, it acts as a "Proceedings," or a record of the Ninth Convention of RID. Second, and perhaps more importantly, it can be viewed as the first of a two-volume series on interpretation as cross-cultural mediation. As such, its value to the field increases. The issues addressed in San Diego and in this volume are timeless: Deaf people will always keep their culture and interpreters will always be mediating between this Deaf culture and the world at large.

The book opens and closes with the two addresses by Lane. Lane, of course, is the author of *When the Mind Hears*, a most important record of Deaf history in America. In his keynote speech, Lane makes some most cogent and important remarks about the nature of language and power. In his closing comments, he challenges RID to face certain issues of the future: to establish strong academic and theoretical roots in the cognitive and social sciences; to revise the evaluation system such that it can meet the most rigorous standards for mass testing; to lead the struggle for acceptance of American Sign Language in the U.S.; to take steps enhancing and enlarging the role of Deaf interpreters; to recruit new members. His comments, both opening and closing, are pertinent for every member of the organization: they serve as "brackets" for the contents of this book and they can serve as guidelines for the RID for years to come.

The *Proceedings* is organized into general divisions: cross-cultural mediation and issues of general interest. Within the cross-cultural section, authors address a broad variety of issues. Brislin, who taught the pre-convention course on training for cross-cultural experiences, gives an overview on a structured approach to cross-cultural encounters. His discussion of affective learning and values training can be used as a general framework within which to view all the rest of this section of the book. The next "paper" is not really a paper; it is the summary of three panel discussions by Deaf interpreters, Hearing interpreters who have Deaf parents, and Hearing interpreters who have Hearing parents. These panel discussions are available in video format in their entirety; only the flavor of these discussions can be captured on paper.

Rutherford's paper on Deaf humor is a close analysis of one means oppressed people have of releasing the hostility that results from oppression. This is an ideal example of the sorts of contributions that the social sciences, in this case anthropology, can make towards our understanding of the cultural nature of the interpreting task. Baker-Shenk's paper takes a political view of the relationships between Deaf people and interpreters. Because she asks us to look hard at our own complicity in the oppression of Deaf people, her views are not easily accommodated. Still, they have great value insofar as we engage in self-questioning.

Coppola's and Miller's and Mathews' papers both give us views from the Deaf community on interpreters. The former paper focuses on the experience of children who have Deaf parents. Miller and Mathews come from the point of view of Deaf adults. Both help us understand more about whom we work with. The following three papers, by Jones, Mathers and White, and Aramburo and McAllister, present us with invaluable views on Black Deaf and Black interpreters. They each present a challenge to the organization and to individual interpreters regarding our views and behaviors regarding the Black Community.

Atwood and Grey and Pokorny look at the issue of cross-cultural mediation from the stance of practicing interpreters. They present both theoretical and empirical issues which challenge us on a daily basis. Finally, Cavell and Wells offer a practical means through which student interpreters can learn to cope more successfully with cross-cultural conflicts.

In the section on "General Issues of Interpretation and Transliteration," the reader will find a variety of valuable papers. Isham's paper on message analysis and Fritsch Rudser's paper on linguistic changes in interpretation both have strong roots in the academic tradition. They are both solid analyses of specific issues related to the task. Scheibe and Hoza present some concrete suggestions relating to the problems of the educational interpreter trying to follow the Code of Ethics. In another paper relating to the Code of Ethics, DeMatteo, Veltri and Lee present another solid academic paper that has significant implications in the "real world" of the working interpreter: how the Code of Ethics applies in the mental health setting. Barber-Gonzales, Preston and Sanderson discuss some of the ways an agency can offer support to the working interpreter. Antosch's closing paper looks at language attitudes of both Deaf and Hearing communities throughout the history of Deaf people in America. Her paper challenges us to think through our own beliefs about ASL and about Deaf people.

In all, this *Proceedings* reflects RID's status as an organization of professionals. As Lane so vividly points out in his closing paper, "professionalism" does not mean "dehumanization." RID, because of who the individual members are and because of the nature of our task, will always remain a humane and concerned organization. At the same time, we are now able to take a mature stance in regard to our profession and to begin developing the theoretical and academic roots which will eventually help us to follow Deaf people into a broader acceptance in society.

The editor extends her special appreciation to Millie Brother and Sheila Jacobs for all their assistance in the preparation of a report on the panel discussions. This task was virtually impossible, and their warm-hearted spirit of cooperation made it easier. All the authors who made their contributions in a timely and cheerful fashion (including corrections and revisions) made this job a more pleasant one: thanks go to each of you. As usual, Susie Kaufman added her own special panache to the task of copy preparation; she is a joy to work with.

Keynote Address —
On Language, Power, and the Deaf

Harlan Lane

Language and power are so intimately related that an interpreter cannot translate a single word, cannot even appear on the scene, without communicating messages about group loyalty. Much of what the interpreter mediates between two cultures, explicitly and implicitly, is a struggle for power.

Our daily newspapers record the power struggle between the world's various language minorities and the language majorities that engulf each of them. French speakers protest their oppression in Canada, Breton speakers in France, Tamil speakers in India, Georgian speakers in the Soviet Union, Armenian speakers in Turkey, Turkish speakers in Denmark, Basque speakers in Spain (three people died in Basque separatist violence last week), Spanish speakers in the United States — the list goes on and on. Each entry on the list stands for lives taken and for countless more lives enfeebled by needless suffering and ineffectual education.

Listen to Cesar Chavez describe the common experience of Spanish-speaking children in the United States: "In class, one of my biggest problems was the language. Of course, we bitterly resented not being able to speak Spanish, but they insisted that we had to learn English. They said that if we were American, then we should speak the language, and if we wanted to speak Spanish, then we should go back to Mexico. When we spoke Spanish, the teacher swooped down on us. I remember the ruler whistling through the air as its edge came down sharply across my knuckles. It really hurt. Even out in the playground, speaking Spanish brought punishment. The principal had a special paddle that looked like a two-by-four with a handle on it. The wood was smooth from a lot of use. He would grab us, even the girls, put our head between his legs, and give it to us" (in Grosjean 1982).

Modern studies in multilingual countries such as Canada show that excluding minority teachers and their language from the schools and thus attempting to force the assimilation of minority children like Chavez carries heavy penalties. Educators do indeed become disciplinarians as they pursue the aggressive steps required to stop the child from using his or her primary language — grades are lowered, physical punishment is inflicted, friends are separated — and the school becomes a place of incarceration. An Alsatian student: "When I was in primary school it was forbidden to speak Alsatian both in and out of class. Children were punished if they were caught." An Arab student: "In my boarding school, the nuns forced us to speak French to one another, even when we were playing. We had a special dog collar that every violator of the rule had to wear."

Language oppression is not, however, a contemporary development. Language has long been an instrument of empire, used to create homogeneity and fealty to a central power, to minimize or eradicate diversity.

Queen Isabella of Spain, for example, ordered that her American colonies were to abandon their "crude barbaric tongues" in favor of Castilian Spanish, so they would become subject to God — and the crown! Under Charles II, the Indians were ordered to learn Spanish and "other good habits of reasonable men." They were to be schooled only in Castilian, which was to become the one and universal idiom, since "it belongs to the monarchs and conquerors." "This universal knowledge of Castilian," the decree continues, "is necessary in order to facilitate the governing and spiritual guidance of the Indians, in order that they may be understood by their superiors, conceive a love for the conquering nation, banish idolatry, and be civilized for purposes of business and commerce... The natives' inclination to retain their own language impedes their will to learn another and foreign language, an inclination accentuated by their somewhat malicious desire to hide their actions from the Spaniards and not answer them directly when they believe they can be evasive" (cited in Lane 1984).

Likewise, at the end of the Enlightenment, when the first French Republic supplanted the monarchy, its legislators were told: "Governments do not realize, or do not feel keenly enough, how much the annihilation of regional speech is necessary for education, the true knowledge of religion, the ready implementation of the law, national happiness and political tranquility... Federalism and superstition speak Breton; emigration and hate of the Republic speak German; the counterrevolution speaks Italian, and fanaticism speaks Basque." So much for "Liberty, Equality, Fraternity." The renowned *Encyclopedia* defined a patois as "a degenerate tongue such as is spoken in all the provinces....The language of France is spoken only in the capital (Certeau *et al.* 1975).

Few communities have as long and as tragic a history of language oppression, however, as deaf communities in the western world. Let us trace that history briefly and see where it has led us today. Many centuries went by before the world even recognized manual languages. At the dawn of deaf education in the seventeenth century, its founder in the German speaking world, Jan Conrad Amman, could write: "The breath of life resides in the voice. The voice is the interpreter of our hearts and expresses its affections and desires.... The voice is a living emanation of that spirit that God breathed into man when he created him a living soul." And because signers did not use voice, "What stupidity we find in most of these unfortunate deaf," Amman wrote; "how little they differ from animals" (cited in Lane 1984).

Civilization had to wait until the middle of the French Enlightenment before the education of deaf children was undertaken systematically using the language of the deaf. Even then, the founder of this education, the abbe de l'Epee, and his successor, the Abbé Sicard, thought their pupils' manual language to be without grammar or method and sought to reorganize it along the lines of French — articles, genders, and all. Said Abbé

Sicard: "We all know the kinds of sentences in use among the Negro tribes; well, those used by the deaf and dumb are even closer to nature, even more primitive" (Sicard 1790). It mattered not a whit that Pierre Desloges, in what was probably the first book ever published by a deaf man, had given a ringing defense of sign language, showing how it served the needs of the deaf community of Paris, so that "No event in Paris, in France, or in the four comers of the world lies outside the scope of their discussions." (See Lane and Philip 1984.)

The leading medical authority on the deaf in the following decades, resident physician at the National Institution for the Deaf in Paris, and the renowned teacher of the Wild Boy of Aveyron, Jean-Marc Itard, likewise vilified sign language as "that barbaric language without conjunctions, without any of the words that permit us to express abstract ideas, which provides only a vague collection of adjectives, nouns, and a few verbs, without determinate time and always in the infinitive" (cited in Lane 1976).

The decisive victory in the struggle to supplant the sign languages of the western world with majority languages was gained some decades later at the infamous Congress of Milan in 1880. In the opening address the Italian host enjoined the delegates to remember that living speech is the privilege of man, the sole and certain vehicle of thought, the gift of God, of which it has been truly said,

"Speech is the expression of the soul
As the soul is the expression of divine thought."

The congress of educators of the deaf, from which the deaf were excluded (although one slipped in), elected a rabid enemy of sign language as its president, an Italian priest named Giulio Tarra. "The kingdom of speech," Tarra began in what would prove to be a two-day peroration, "the kingdom of speech is a realm whose queen tolerates no rivals. Speech is jealous and wishes to be the absolute mistress. Like the true mother of the child placed in judgment before Solomon, speech wishes it all for her own — instruction, school, deaf-mute — without sharing; otherwise, she renounces all.... Let us have no illusions," Tarra continued. "To teach speech successfully we must have courage and with a resolute blow cut cleanly between speech and sign...., Who would dare say that these disconnected and crude signs that mechanically reproduce objects and actions are the elements of a language? I know that my pupils has only a few imperfect signs, the rudiments of an edifice that should not exist, a few crumbs of a bread that has no consistency and can never suffice for nourishing his soul, a soul that cries out for a moral and social existence."

The congress president eventually came to what he called his fundamental argument. "Oral speech is the sole power that can rekindle the light God breathed into man when, giving him a soul in a corporeal body, he gave him also a means of under-standing, of conceiving, and of expressing himself.... While, on the one hand, mimic signs are not sufficient to express the fullness of thought, on the other they enhance and glorify fantasy and all the faculties of the sense of imagination.... The fantastic language of signs exalts the senses and foments the passions, whereas speech elevates the mind much more naturally, with calm, prudence and truth and avoids the danger of exaggerating the sentiment expressed and provoking harmful mental impressions."

When a deaf-mute confesses an unjust act in sign, Tarra explained, the sensations accompanying the act are re-awakened. For example, when the deaf person confesses in sign language that he has been angry, the detestable passion returns to the sinner, which certainly does not aid his moral reform. In speech on the other hand, the penitent deaf-mute reflects on the evil he has committed and there is nothing to excite the passion again. Tarra ended by defying anyone to define in sign language the soul, faith, hope, charity, justice, virtue, the angels, God.... "No shape, no image, no design," Tarra concluded, "can reproduce these ideas. Speech alone, divine itself, is the right way to speak of divine matters."

All but the Americans voted for a resolution exalting the dominant oral language and disbarring the sign language whatever the nation:

> "1. The congress, considering the incontestable superiority of speech over signs, for restoring deaf-mutes to social life and for giving them greater facility in language, declares that the method of articulation should have preference over that of signs in the instruction and education of the deaf and dumb.

> 2. Considering that the simultaneous use of signs and speech has the disadvantage of injuring speech, lipreading, and precision of ideas, the congress declares that the pure oral method ought to be preferred."

In the closing moments of the congress, the French delegate cried from the podium, "*Vive la parole!*" This has been the slogan of hearing educators of t e deaf down to the present time. But an American deaf leader has written: "1880 was the year that saw the birth of the infamous Milan resolution that paved the way for foisting upon the deaf everywhere a loathed method; hypocritical in its claims, unnatural in its application, mind-deadening and soul-killing in its ultimate results" (Veditz 1933).

In the aftermath of Milan, "pure oralism" washed over Europe like a flood tide. Many people and schools were swept up in its advance. There is no single explanation for such tides in human affairs. In my history of the deaf, *When the Mind Hears*, I have discussed the confluence of nationalism, elitism, and commercialism that led to the Congress of Milan and to its deadly legacy. Another contributing cause was the educators' desire for total control of their classrooms, which cannot be had if the pupils sign and the teacher knows none. The teacher then becomes the linguistic outcast, the handicapped. Nor can he or she acquire the necessary skill in a year, or even two, any more than an Anglophone teacher can so rapidly prepare himself to teach in French. This understandable reluctance of hearing teachers to master a language radically different from their own continues to have the greatest weight in what are misrepresented as pedagogical decisions. There was a time when teachers of the deaf could not practice without a knowledge of their pupils' primary language. But the vast expansion of schools for the deaf in Europe and America late in the last century created more professional positions than there were educators and administrators fluent in sign. Increasingly, people with few ties to the deaf community dominated their education.

Teachers who used sign language were increasingly forced into retirement; whereas most teachers of the deaf had been deaf themselves, by the turn of the century only a handful were. Before Milan, American deaf teachers had founded the Florida School, the New Mexico School, the Kansas School, the Oregon School, the North Dakota School, and the Arizona School, among others. Many more deaf teachers taught in these and scores of other schools, and some developed widely-used teaching materials. Some published learned articles and appeared on the international deaf scene, shaping the future of their profession worldwide. Within a decade after Milan, however, the fraction of teachers who were deaf fell from one-half to one-quarter; by World War I it was down to a fifth, and most of the fifth were in the South teaching manual trades in just a few schools. Nowadays the fraction is about one-tenth (Lane 1980b).

With the forced retirement of signing teachers, and the quarantine and then graduation of the older signing students, sign language could be totally banished from the schools. There were twenty-six American institutions for the education of the deaf in 1867, and ASL was the language of instruction in all of them; by 1907 there were 139 schools for the deaf and ASL was allowed in none. The French figures provide a comparable glimpse of ruthless linguistic imperialism: in 1845, 160 schools for the deaf with FSL the accepted language; by the turn of the century, it was not allowed in a single French school.

Of course, the signing community protested. At the Convention of American Instructors of the Deaf in 1890, a decade after the Congress of Milan, there was this characteristic exchange:

A Hearing Principal: A teacher in a pure oral school who understands the sign language is out of place... He might demoralize the school in a very short time. Only insofar as he would suppress his inclination to use sign could he be useful...

Chair: I would like to hear from a deaf educator.

J. Schuyler Long, a Gallaudet graduate and superintendent of the Iowa School for the Deaf, rose to respond. He was a poet, a journalist, and author of the first pronouncing dictionary of American Sign Language, published in 1908. Long said: "The Chinese women bind their babies' feet to make them small; the Flathead Indians bind their babies' heads to make them flat. And the people who prevent the sign language being used in the education of the deaf...are denying the deaf their free mental growth through natural expression of their ideas, and are in the same class of criminals" (in CAID 1909).

At the dawn of this century, the first president of the National Association of the Deaf, Robert McGregor, cried out against the oppression of sign language in these words:

"What heinous crime have the deaf been guilty of that their language should be proscribed?....The utmost extreme to which tyranny can go when its mailed hand descends upon a conquered people is the proscription of their national language....By whom then are signs proscribed? By...educators of the deaf whose boast is that they do not understand signs and do not want to; by a few philanthropists who are otherwise ignorant of the language; by parents who do not understand the requisites to the happiness of their deaf children and are inspired with false fears by the educators and philanthropists....Worst of all, these (people) ignore the deaf themselves in their senseless and mischievous propaganda against signs. Professing to have no object in view but the benefit of the deaf, they exhibit an utter contempt for the opinions, the wishes, the desires of the deaf. And why should we not be consulted in a matter of such vital interest to us? This is a question no man has yet answered satisfactorily" (cited in Lane 1984).

But the deaf did not have — do not have — the final word. The final word, as always, came from their hearing benefactors. As the new century dawned on deaf education, a representative view was articulated by the principal of the Nebraska school. "The oral method has been weighed in the balance;" he wrote in the Alexander Graham Bell Association *Review,* "— and it may be believed weighed conscientiously and with all fairness — and it is not found wanting... (Experience) confirms the faith of those who practice...oral education of the deaf....be question of methods," he concluded, "is practically retired from the field of discussion" (AGB 1900).

Today, more than a century since the congress of Milan, the oppression of the languages of deaf communities in Europe and America continues unabated and in the crucial realm of education that oppression is becoming worse. The attempt to educate deaf children with teaching methods appropriate for hearing children continues to prove a failure, decade after decade. In a classroom where spoken and written English are the basic means of communication, deaf children are baffled and withdrawn, the more so as nine out of ten in the schools today became deaf before they could learn English at home. These children lack the knowledge of English and the skills of articulation and lipreading required to succeed: studies have shown that speech teachers find two-thirds of their own deaf pupils hard to understand or utterly unintelligible, and deaf high school students can lipread no better than the man in the street — that is, scarcely at all (Conrad 1979).

An educational disaster has thus resulted from using English to instruct deaf children: the average twelfth-grade deaf student reads at fourth-grade level and does arithmetic (his best subject) at sixth-grade level. Only one deaf adult in ten readily reads a newspaper or holds a professional post; most are employed in the obsolescent manual trades, and that is where we are consigning the futures of deaf children in large numbers. (See Conrad 1979; Jensema 1975; Trybus and Karchmer 1977; Wolk and Allen 1984; Schein and Delk 1974.)

Why this staggering and disastrous rate of English illiteracy among the deaf? The relation between language and power accounts for much of it. I submit, first, that the English illiteracy of the deaf, far from being the unwanted calamity educators claim, is in fact the state of affairs desired by the prevailing institutions. It is in the interest of the establishment, and especially deaf education, to undermine critical thought and the acquisition of bureaucratically acceptable language, because if the deaf had these abilities once again, as they did in the last century, they would once again enter the teaching profession in large numbers, reform that profession, and make obsolete the present teachers' training, endangering the employment of many.

The deaf are English-illiterate, further, because their own extensive language skills are not acknowledged in the school; they are demeaned or worse. Nothing is said of the manifold forms that deaf literacy takes: the narrative traditions, the poetry, the handshape games, the pantomime, and so on. The deaf are English-illiterate because the systematic oppression of sign language shuts out the most effective strategy for teaching a second language: namely, conduct a contrastive analysis of the student's first language skills and second language goals, and develop an instructional strategy based on that analysis.

The deaf are English-illiterate because the written language is taught orally and they are deaf, or it is taught using written English, which is just the language they do not know and are trying to learn; it is never taught nowadays using a language in which they are fluent. The deaf are English-illiterate because the middle class white style of language their hearing teachers present as the only correct English is quite alien to whatever English the deaf pupils have use for. The deaf are English-illiterate because the schools treat language as an acultural formal skill, whereas language accords with and reinforces a host of cultural patterns, including group loyalty, problem-solving, recreation, perception of space and time. The deaf are English-illiterate because standard English is presented as an aesthetic and moral norm, not as a practical necessity for rapid transfer of information. In this era of information technology, the price the deaf are paying for the alliance between language and power gets higher every day.

As a remedy, many leaders among the deaf minority are urging the revitalization of the residential schools for the deaf and the reintroduction of sign language and dear teachers in their classrooms — successful practices in the last century, when American deaf children studied all their subjects in their most fluent language, the American Sign Language of the Deaf. In a residential school with deaf teachers and a signing community, the deaf student is able not only to understand and respond to the instruction, but also to get help after class with coursework, to discuss local, national, and international events, to participate in student activities, to develop friendships with other deaf students (nearly all deaf people choose a deaf partner when marrying), to emulate older students and deaf teachers, to acquire self-respect as a deaf person.

Although none of these advantages is available to the deaf child in an ordinary public school, where sign language, deaf teachers, and a deaf community are absent, that is just where deaf children are being sent in large and growing numbers. More than half of the estimated 80,000 deaf schoolchildren in the United States have now been "mainstreamed" to some extent, and the specialized schools for the deaf they would have attended are starting to close.

Granted that the conditions in the local public school for the deaf child's social and emotional growth are quite poor. Is the child receiving a better education in the "three R's" there? Not at all. The first report cards on mainstreamed deaf children show no improvement in their blighted English or mathematics attributable to mainstreaming (even though the first to be mainstreamed were the children with the best speech and hearing) (Allen and Osborn 1984; Gregory *et al.* 1984).

The deaf children who do best in school are — note it well — the fortunate ten per cent who learned sign language as a native language from their deaf parents, the core of this linguistic minority. These "native signers" outperform their deaf classmates from hearing homes in most subjects, even in learning to read and write English. They are also better adjusted, better socialized, and have more positive attitudes (Mindel and Vernon 1971). The superior performance of deaf children of deaf parents highlights the changes that most need to be made in the education of deaf children, namely, a return to sign language, deaf teachers, and deaf administrators. These changes have long been advocated by the deaf community itself.

Unfortunately, the very professions created to serve the interests of the deaf have been totally at odds for over a century with what the deaf perceive as their interests. These professions have vainly pursued the assimilation of deaf children into the hearing majority at the expense of their individual growth; thus, many special educators embraced mainstreaming precisely because it would help to close the residential schools the deaf hold dear. In passing the Education for All Handicapped Children Act ten years ago, Congress was wiser, recognizing (in the words of the Supreme Court) that "regular classrooms simply would not be a suitable setting for the education of many handicapped children" and providing for alternative placements. But educators have largely ignored this provision of the act (Duncan 1984).

Confronted with a similar tragedy in England, members of the British National Union of the Deaf, rather more political than their American counterparts, have formally charged their government with a violation of the United Nations Convention on the Prevention and Punishment of the Crime of Genocide. That treaty prohibits inflicting mental harm on the children of an ethnic group, and it prohibits forcibly transferring them to another group. According to deaf leaders in Britain, mainstreaming will gravely injure "not only deaf children but deaf children's rightful language and culture." Their published *Charter of the Rights of the Deaf* asserts that "deaf schools are being effectively forced to close and therefore children of one ethnic/linguistic minority group, that is, deaf people, are being forcibly transferred to another group, that is hearing people."

To achieve intellectual and emotional maturity and full participation in society, most deaf children require an education conducted in their primary language, American Sign Language, with the participation of deaf adults, in the setting of a specialized school.

In the Bilingual Education Act of 1968, Americans institutionalized the premise that children are best educated, transitionally at least, in their most fluent language. The laws of most of the states soon came to require that schools acted with more than a certain percentage of children whose primary language is Navaho, or Chinese, or whatever language, must offer a portion of their instruction in that language. Yet it has never been possible to add American Sign Language, one of the more populous minority languages, to that list. Several possible reasons for the particularly severe oppression of sign language come to mind. One is that the hearing impairment of most users of ASL plays into the hands of the large segment of our society that would deal with social problems by medicalizing them. From this point of view, the hearing impairment of the signing community is more salient than its shared language. This is precisely the posture of our government, where the same agencies that support research and training for the education of retarded people do likewise for deaf people, and the agencies that address the needs of minority language groups refuse to have anything to do with the two million or so Americans who use some form of manual communication.

Yet another reason for the singular oppression of ASL must be its unexpected mode, manual and visual, giving rise to the well-known fallacious beliefs that ASL is inherently pictorial, concrete, and primitive. For example, in a recent book on thinking and language, the author remarks on "the crudity of sign language.... Even deaf and dumb humans who rely entirely on sign languages find it cumbersome to make complicated abstract statements because of a lick of subtle grammatical inflections (cited in Jarvella and Klein 1982).

Let us not dismiss the difference in modality of signed and spoken languages, just because it has been at the source of so much sign language oppression. I think we might have something to learn from turning the table on the English snobs and claiming: ASL is not only as good as any oral language, it's better!

The argument goes like this: our species, in common with all the mammals, is much concerned with three-dimensional space. In fulfilling our needs, both biological and social, we move about in space. Commonly, those movements are coordinated among the members of a pair or group of people, and they relate to an arrangement of people or objects. Consequently, much of human communication is explicitly about spatial arrays. "How do we get to the swimming pool from here?" "Where shall the interpreters stand?" "Where are you going to put the new couch?" "Where did you leave the car?" Countless similar everyday questions and their answers require us to talk about space.

But so spatial an animal are we, that we also choose to talk about nonspatial matters in spatial terms. Lists start at the top and end at the bottom. Political alignments range from right to left. The future is ahead of us, the past behind. Power relations extend from the high and mighty to the lowliest of us. Comparatives in general are expressed in spatial metaphors, above all other means.

Yet space inheres in language even deeper than metaphor. A doctoral student in my laboratory, Mordecai Rimor, finds that English speakers asked to rate the similarity of English verbs are guided most of all by a spatial principle: does the meaning of the verb entail translatory movement or fixed position? Thus, his subjects repeatedly rate the verb *giving* closer to the verb *pushing* than to the verb *giving up*, and the verb *standing* closer to the verb *waiting* than to the verb *walking*. As several linguists have also suggested recently, lexical semantics may be spatially based.

Let us see how adroit oral language really is, then, in this fundamental task of spatial description. How well does English convey arrangements and distances of people and things in three-dimensional space? Both literally and metaphorically, we will need to refer to left-right, in front-behind, and above-below. (See Levelt 1984.) I look at two adjacent people in the audience, say Dennis and his wife. In English I might say, "Dennis is to the left of his wife," but in that case I can also say he is on his wife's right, that is, "Dennis is to the right of his wife." So I have been quite unclear. Which is it? Is Dennis to the left or the right of his wife? Anna, who is seated behind them, disagrees with me; Dennis was never to the left of his wife. If you followed that and think that English is clear although complicated about left and right, try this one: arrange Dennis, his wife and Anna, so that Dennis is to the left of his wife, his wife is to the left of Anna, and Dennis is to the right of Anna. (Anyone who solves that by tomorrow come see me and I'll give you a pat on the back — from in front.)

I have tried to illustrate that in English we must give different accounts of the same array, depending on two things: first, the speaker's point of view, and, second, whether the speaker is using verbal pointing or intrinsic reference. Verbal pointing, called deixis, requires the English listener to know where the speaker is. The intrinsic system requires an interpretation of the scene and an intrinsic orientation. It applies to people and houses, but it will not work for trees, tables, or heaps. To illustrate, let's go for a picnic. If I ask you to put the little picnic table in front of the tree, you can comply with the instruction by putting it anywhere on the planet earth; I have been quite unclear.

There's a nearby racetrack and we take our seats at the start line. As they leave the gate, the only horse I can see is the horse closest to me, which is, of course, in front of the other horses — but he may be behind them as well especially if I bet on him. The rabbit that runs around the inside rail of the track is behind all the horses up to the turn even though it is always in front of all of them.

My horse loses and the sky darkens. "The sun is behind the clouds," you say. When the sun comes out from behind the clouds, is it then in front of the clouds? Of course not! So, the sun is always behind the clouds. Actually, the sun is only behind the clouds when there is no sun.

I have brought two balloons to the picnic and tie them to a branch, so that the red is above the green. You, however, are lying on your side on the grass, looking at the vault of heaven and the red is to the left of the green or to the right of the green, depending on which side you're lying on. Unless, of course, you can see the horizon, in which case the red is above the green. "My friend," I tell you, "there's a spider dangling above your head." You go to brush it away but where to swing? Is it close to you or far? Is it near your cheek or near the top of your head? Who knows?

Dennis is to the left of his wife. The table is in front of the tree. The black horse is in front of the others. There's a spider above your head. All of these sentences are ambiguous, but are like those we use all the time. Then we must be rather poor at communicating in English that most essential of human messages, spatial arrays. I decided to do an experiment.

I bought a doll house — my first — that came with a few pieces of plastic furniture and, most important, a picture on the box showing where to arrange the furniture in this split level home. There was a sofa, a TV, a stereo, a picnic table and two chairs, and a barbecue. A graduate student in my laboratory, Dana Ginsberg, and I asked pairs of English speakers to assist us, as follows. With the house set up and the furniture in a pile in front of it, one of the pair was to look at the box and tell the other where to place each item of furniture, in an effort to reproduce the arrangement shown in the photo on the box. We asked the furniture mover not to talk and we tape-recorded the speaker. Seven pieces of furniture to place in common ways — it should have been easy. Here is an *average* transcript from a graduate student, native speaker of English.

"Okay, Moti, we'll start with the table and chairs on the bottom floor. In front of the house, um, there's a patch of green, like a patio, and the round table goes in the —in the, uh, top corner of the pa — of the green square. Okay. And, in front of the — at — in front of the table — um, between the ladder and the table — goes one of the red chairs. Okay. And across from that red chair, on the other side of the table, goes the second red chair. Okay. Now, the barbe — the barbecue goes on the strip of patio between the green square and the house. Um, um, over to the left, almost in the left corner. Not quite. Okay, now let's go upstairs. Oh, excuse me, we have to go back downstairs, I forgot the record player. Now we're in the house, and as you face the house, it's a the the right — your right corner — okay, that's where the record player will go. Against the wall, well, against the wall in the corner. Okay? Now let's go upstairs, Moti. Okay. Now on the second floor — the floor's divided into a terrace and a bedroom and just where the terrace and the bedroom are divided there's no — there's a frame but no wall there and the couch or the little red seat goes in that frame, at an angle, so it's mostly in the room but it seems to stick out onto the terrace just a little bit. Okay. And the television goes — okay, the floor in that room is separated by — there's a little ridge that sticks out of the floor, so the couch is on one side of the ridge — the television goes in the area that's separated with the other side of the ridge — and it's facing so that the person who is sitting on the couch can't see the TV screen — in other words, the TV screen is facing into the — is facing out of the house. Okay. Sort of facing the ladder. Okay. So we're done."

Now, because American Sign Language is a spatial language, it can communicate arrangement and relative distance of things and people in quite a different way from English or, indeed, any oral language. This makes interpreting sign into oral language and vice versa unique among translation tasks in that interpreters must mediate between spatial and linear languages, utterly restructuring spatial discourse as they interpret from the one language into the other. American Sign Language, instead of conveying a spatial array by a linear chain of words, can map that spatial message right onto its surface form. Moreover, once ASL establishes a location for an object, it need not be re-established in order to refer to it. When I asked pairs of signers to do my experiment, they were not only quicker at it than English speakers, they followed a different strategy. Let me try to convey that by reading a transcript — not a translation — of their signing, prepared with the help of Judy Shepard-Kegl.

"Okay. Table, white, round. Table. Outside, okay, front-of-house, put-on green square flat-area. Put-there. Chairs, two-of-them, associated-with-table. Okay, table here chairs one-here one-here in-front. Now grill, cooking, you-know, black, hood-opens. Table here, here grill. Table here, round, chairs here, here, grill here. Now stereo — careful heavy. Now you-know living-room, wall, bookshelves on-wall, okay, there, corner, mirror. There, put-there. Now TV, hum, okay go upstairs, go-up steps, outside enter where finally roof, now TV — you-know dresser there, all-that, pictures, lamp there, put tv there. Now chair — folds-open like bed, red, white something, okay, that — go upstairs, see where TV, where dressers, then lamp, there put-there. Finish."

So is speech, in the words of the Milan resolution, "incontestably superior to sign," or is it the other way around? My point, of course, is that no language is superior to any other, and none is beneath you if you look up to it. Languages have evolved within communities in a way responsive to the needs of those communities. ASL is attuned to the needs of the signing community in the United States; English is not. And the effort to replace sign with English lo these last hundred years will get a chapter all its own in the history of human ignominy.

The renewed appreciation of cultural pluralism in our society today invites us to re-examine the assumption that others should speak as we do. Many Americans can recall their initial shock when they realized fully for the first time that other people were conducting their lives in an entirely different language. Perhaps that shock reflects a kind of egocentrism that it is in our mutual interest to overcome; for the growth of social consciousness, like that of the child, is largely a series of triumphs over egocentrism.

As I am not less but more when I recognize that the earth revolves around the sun and that man has evolved from the apes, so I am not less but more when I recognize that there are other languages, manual and oral, on a par with my own. This humility is the enemy of forced assimilation; it is the friend of bilingualism and mutual respect; it is the premise of interpreting.

Section One
—Cross-Cultural Mediation—

Close Intercultural Relationships: Benefits and Proper Preparation

Richard W. Brislin

Cross-cultural studies have a large number of intellectual attractions which can provide great amounts of satisfaction for its practitioners. There is the possibility of shedding new light from cross-cultural research on topics which have a long and well-established tradition within the behavioral sciences (e.g., perception, Deregowski, 1980). There is the possibility of integrating various pieces of data into a theoretical framework (e.g., the eco-cultural model, Berry, 1976). There is the possibility of contributing to the solution of methodological problems which pose difficulties to virtually any data-gathering effort (e.g., cross-cultural equivalence, Poortinga, 1979; Irvine and Carroll, 1980). There is the possibility of making a contribution to applied problems such as the adjustment of people to other cultures brought on by migration or other changes in people's lives (e.g., problems and prospects of culture contact, Taft, 1977).

In addition to these intellectual challenges, there are other benefits which are undoubtedly more affective in nature. Consider these seemingly unrelated observations:

a. Adolescents who have had a cross-cultural experience tend to, upon entering college, interact with others who have also had such an experience. The interaction and subsequent close relationships take place even though the two people may have had their experiences in very different parts of the world. This observation is attributed to John and Ruth Useem (1955; 1967), who have based their work on the concept of a "third culture" which is shared by people who have had extensive cross-cultural experiences.

b. Adults who return to their home country after an overseas assignment also seek out companions who have had a similar experience. Again, the relationship develops even though the people may not have worked in the same part of the world. In addition, they may not have had the same type of job. One may have been a teacher in India, and the other a businessperson in Sweden.

c. Scholars who attend sessions at conferences devoted to cross-cultural studies attend a variety of presentations outside of their specialties. In my observation, this range and variety of attendance is much greater than cross-specialization attendance at national or regional conferences devoted to general advances

within the behavioral and social sciences (e.g., any large conference such as the American Psychological Association's annual
convention). For instance, a specialist in cross-cultural studies of
perception will find stimulation in sessions on social psychology,
worker selection, Freudian concepts, and child socialization. The
research may have been carried out in different parts of the world
than those in which the perceptual specialist has worked.

d. A Black professional has told me that the Caucasians with whom
he is most comfortable, and who seem most comfortable interacting with him in a mutually respectful relationship, have had a long-
term experience in a country other than their own.

e. Language interpreters often find, as an attraction in their work,
that interacting with culturally different others is very stimulating.
Interpreters find their jobs more interesting as they learn that they
not only transmit information gained from their knowledge of languages, but also transmit information based on their knowledge of
culture and cultural differences. Like people who have had an
overseas assignment, language interpreters enjoy interaction with
others who have had extensive experience with culturally different
individuals.

What might be the underlying principle behind these five examples?
The people forming close relationships and benefitting from each other's
work do not necessarily have the same profession or professional specialization, nor do they necessarily have the shared experience of working in
the same part of the world. If there is some principle at work, it may
extend to one's relationships with members of sub-cultures within a large
country (example "d," above). Interacting extensively with deaf people
probably is as impactful as interacting in other countries or with members of minority groups within a country.

My hypothesis is that the underlying factor is a deep appreciation of
the concepts collectively called "culture" and "cultural relativity." A deep
appreciation of these concepts is acquired through first-hand experience
while living in a culture other than one's own. Most college graduates
learn enough about culture ("...ideas and their attached value.. ;" "...the
man-made part of the environment...") and cultural relativity to earn passing grades on a final exam. But there is a difference between this form of
cognitive understanding and the affective understanding which is developed through one's own trials and errors while adjusting to life in another
culture. Adjustment to another culture demands hands-on experience
with various conceptions of reality, various ideas and their values, and
various ways of meeting environmental demands. Often, an idea or behavior which is repugnant in one's own culture will be expressed as a normal,
respected way of meeting life's everyday needs. This type of encounter
with differences, and the consequent reflection it encourages about
behavior in one's own country, leads to insights about life which are
taken for granted by people who have not had the stimulation of a cross-
cultural experience. The affective experience which stems from cross-
cultural encounters causes a deeper type of understanding about culture

and about culture's influence than can be obtained in books alone. The element that is shared among people who have had a cross-cultural experience, then, is the affective learning stimulated by an encounter with cultural differences and the subsequent adjustment demands placed upon the people.

I should not claim originality for this hypothesis. It has been suggested by others, although never examined in an empirical study aimed at clarifying various aspects of cross-cultural learning. After a good deal of thinking about the experiences of Peace Corps Volunteers in the Philippines, Szanton (1966, pp. 51-52) came to this conclusion:

> After some while in the field, many PCV's did finally begin to accept emotionally the idea — and its extraordinary implications — that a people could be equally human, could be equally entitled to consideration, while at the same time they were significantly different in their values and behavior. Differences, in short, no longer implied inferiority. Differences, indeed, were to be respected. And to respect cultural differences meant first to understand them, which required one to take one's time, to empathize, to comprehend.

While discussing the influence of culture on one's own thinking and especially on one's judgments about others, Hall (1977, p. 212) also pointed to the insights which cross-cultural experiences can bring:

> Self-awareness and cultural awareness are inseparable, which means that transcending unconscious culture cannot be accomplished without some degree of self-awareness. Used properly, intercultural experiences can be a tremendous eye opener, providing a view of one's self seldom seen under normal conditions at home. Like all opportunities for growth and self-knowledge, the mere thought can be somewhat frightening.

Overcoming and learning from the fear may be part of the shared experience held by people who have engaged in extensive intercultural contact.

There is a relationship, I believe, between the intellectual challenges mentioned at the very beginning of this paper and the affective learning discussed thereafter. The people who are able to make the most creative advances in our collective intellectual understanding may be those who reflect and learn from their own cross-cultural experiences. The scholars who contribute to cross-cultural studies may gain insights from their comparisons of own-other culture differences and may integrate them into their research programs. Academic norms against presenting large amounts of autobiographical information prevent an extensive treatment of this hypothesis based on published sources. A few hints, however, exist. In responding to an invitation to deal explicitly with his own development as a cross-cultural researcher, Guthrie (1979, p. 365) pointed out that

> ...those who are adjusting well in an alien society are able to see a wide range of individual differences in members of the host

society and are able to describe, to some degree, the world as experienced by the host national.

While discussing his important multinational study of worker motivation, Hofstede (1980, p. 373) presented his opinion that "a deep and often painfully acquired empathy with other cultures is required before one becomes sensitive to the... relativity of our society's norms."

Interestingly, more analyses have been done on effects a cross-cultural experience has on an artist's creative output (Brislin, 1981, pp. 296-297).

Many great artists have developed creative products after participating in a cross-cultural experience. Paul Gauguin lived for many years in Tahiti and later incorporated various images in his paintings. Anton Dvorak visited the United States, learned themes from American folk music, and included variations of them in his "New World Symphony." In fact, he was so skillful that he may have donated a theme which has entered the American folk tradition. The tune for "Going Home," a well-known black spiritual, may have been collected by Dvorak, or he may have written it. If the latter is the case, it shows that he was able to learn the new musical forms so well that he could make a contribution which is now considered traditional. Henry James wrote specifically about the experiences of Americans who chose to live for long periods of time in Great Britain. Mark Twain (as analyzed by McCormack, 1980) experienced life in Hawaii as a liberation from bonds that stifled his creative potential. Contrasts between Hawaii and parts of the United States he knew allowed Twain to look upon his past with a fresh perspective. After his cross-cultural experience, he wrote his most successful novels.

What specific path might lead to the benefits?

Given that cross-cultural experiences can bring benefits, what might be the specific paths which lead to the positive outcomes? One could be the development of close interpersonal relationships with people from another culture. These might be either romantic in nature, or non-romantic as in the development of close, intimate friendships. The adjustments people must make to each other in the development of genuine romances and friendships will inevitably involve cultural differences. Just a few examples are adjustments concerning people's preferences (as well as their coping with cultural norms) concerning where they can go, what sorts of things they can discuss, what sorts of guidelines there are for developing the relationship, what aspects of the relationship are made explicit and which remain implicit, what the mutual obligations are, when various intimate exchanges are permissible, and so forth. While making these adjustments to cultural differences in friendships and romances, people experience the affective learning under discussion. Friendships and romances demand an openness, a willingness to share, a sensitivity to the feelings of others, and the acceptance of mutual obligations. All these elements demand the understanding and acceptance of cultural differences.

A romance or close friendship may also provide a specific vehicle through which the abstract concept called "culture" comes to life. It is one thing to read about culturally-influenced ideas and unfamiliar behaviors which meet environmental demands. It is another to actually encounter these firsthand as a person tries to understand and to react positively to another. The positive emotional bond found in romances and friendships is a motivating force to learn enough about cultural differences so that appropriate, helpful responses are possible.

The development of cross-cultural friendships as a vehicle for learning is a hypothesis in agreement with the published literature on positive intergroup relations. Intergroup contact is by no means an automatic guarantee of positive feelings. In making recommendations for the *type* of contact which can lead to favorable relations, different researchers have pointed to various factors which should be part of the contact situation (Allport, 1954; Cook, 1970; Riordan, 1978). The three most frequently cited conditions (Amir, 1969; Brislin, 1981) are that the contact involves people of equal status, that it allows for intimate exchanges, and that the people should be interested in achieving the same superordinate goal. Friendship usually involves equal status since similarities in background, age, education, and occupation can form the basis for the first meeting among people. Similarity in background and interests can also provide a basis for conversations. Intimacy then develops as people exchange personal information about their worries, goals, values, and life ambitions. As the relationship develops, the superordinate goal which demands the efforts of both participants is the continuation and advancement of the romance or friendship.

An investigation into cross-cultural friendships and romances

Given knowledge of the potential benefits but lacking information concerning how the benefits are accrued, a study was undertaken (Brislin, 1983) to investigate cross-cultural romances and friendships. Among the ideas investigated, a first cross-cultural romance or friendship was viewed as a hurdle. The "hurdle" could well be a specific manifestation of culture with its attendant component of fear (discussed by Hall, above). Once cleared, however, the richness of another culture is open for additional learning experiences. In this study, the formation of other friendships (above and beyond the first romance or friendship) was the operational definition of additional richness afforded by cross-cultural experiences. The study was carried out in Hawaii, New Jersey and Newfoundland, and among professionals whose jobs involve extensive cross-cultural contact. These samples were chosen since they varied in the amount of cross-cultural contact members were likely to have (high for Hawaii and the professionals; low for Newfoundland). The influence of education was investigated by sampling students from both a college and a technical school in New Jersey.

The major idea behind use of the term "cultural relativity" is that behavior can be judged only in the context of a specific culture with its unique norms and environmental demands. It is improper to make quick judgments based on standards acquired in one's own culture. A recently investigated phenomenon within social psychology may be relevant. Ross (1977) has pointed out that people too often employ a "fundamental attribution error" of attributing trait explanations to the behavior of others. For example, we see someone give an impassioned speech. There is a tendency to view that person as an "activist" and perhaps as "emotional," both trait explanations. People do *not* take the extra time to discover what other explanations may account for the behavior. It may well be that the individual is giving his first public speech, and that he has been brought to an emotional peak due to recent budget cuts in a social program to which he has dedicated twenty years of his life. These other explanations are called "situational" since they involve factors outside of the personality of the individual himself. If the *speaker himself* was asked about *his own* behavior, he would give the situational reasons. He has quick access to these factors in contrast to the observer who only has access to the emotional speech. One reason for the frequency of trait attributions is that they are easy to make and do not demand the extra work of discovering possible situational explanations. In addition, there is a widely used language to describe traits (e.g., aggressive, sociable, dominant), but no widely used set of terms to describe situational factors (Jones, 1979).

The fundamental attribution error, then, involves the tendency to over-attribute traits to the observed behavior of others and to downplay situational factors. This is an especially frequent problem in cross-cultural encounters, as Taylor and Jaggi (1974) have discussed. People from one culture will inevitably observe many unfamiliar behaviors while living in another culture, and they will be motivated to explain the behaviors. Based on the research which has led to the concept called the fundamental attribution error, traits will too often enter into the explanations of the behaviors observed in the other culture. Upon observing poverty, for example, a trait explanation would be that the people are lazy and do not have the drive to raise themselves by their own bootstraps. This explanation ignores situational factors such as opportunities for employment and existence of strong class systems which place limits on social mobility.

Cross-cultural experiences, however, may lead to a breakdown in the fundamental attribution error through a greater appreciation of cultural relativity. If people do indeed enter into intimate contact, then they must engage in some thinking from the *others'* point of view. The people would inevitably learn about some of the less visible situational factors and would incorporate these into their explanations.

The hypothesis that one intercultural contact acts as a hurdle which, if transcended, leads to another was clearly supported. There were significant differences in the number of additional friends and intimate discussants for those reporting a romance or close, long friendship. The interpretive problems here stem from plausible alternative hypotheses. One could be called "gregariousness." Perhaps a person who likes to be with others happens to come into contact with a group of people which includes other-culture members. That person then interacts with people from other cultures and later may form a close bond with one or two. Another alternative hypothesis could be called "active tolerance." Perhaps some people are very tolerant of diversity and actually enjoy meeting many people who have obviously different backgrounds, such as those from other cultures, and they may later form close bonds with a few.

These are important rival explanations. Even though the hurdle hypothesis is being defended, the alternatives should not be dismissed out of hand. I am sure that some intercultural romances and friendships do indeed proceed according to the two alternative scenarios, and future research might more closely compare the various ways people enter into cross-cultural contact. For the present study, I am concerned only with demonstrating that the alternatives do not completely account for the obtained data.

Two additional pieces of information were available. One was the number of other occupations held by the friends and intimate discussants listed by each respondent. If the gregariousness hypothesis was operative, different classifications of respondents might show interaction with lots of different people in various occupations (e.g., students with secretaries, businesspeople with physicians). However, there were no differences in the "number of others' occupations" for people who reported intercultural romances and/or friendships compared to people who did not. The other additional piece of information was the relative status level of the other people listed by each respondent. The "active tolerance" hypothesis would suggest that some people would be interacting with others regardless of their relative job status (e.g., students with gas station attendants, college teachers with store clerks). Again, however, there were no differences comparing people who had an intercultural friendship and/or romance with people who did not. While certainly in need of further analysis, the hurdle hypothesis seems safe for the moment. In everyday language, the hurdle hypothesis might operate like this. A person has the one romance or friendship, and says: "Whew!! That was a good experience. Maybe all those people who told me to stay away from those others and to stick to my own group weren't entirely correct. I would have other such relationships with different kinds of people if given the chance."

The hypothesis linking intercultural experiences to situational explanations of behavior received reasonable support. The relationship was statistically significant or close-to-significant in three samples (Hawaii, New Jersey College, Newfoundland), with ceiling effects interfering with the relationship in the other two. The ceiling effects seem related to formal education and to an expressed interest in the subject matter. At the technical school, the sample with the least amount of formal education in academic (as opposed to specific job skills) material, there were very few situational explanations from anybody. In the professional sample, there were large numbers of such explanations, the most for any of the five samples. Given that there were so many situational explanations among the professionals, the ceiling effect here means that it was difficult to distinguish among them based on the measure of romances/friendships. The basic finding about situational explanations constitutes another basis for the observation, referred to earlier in the paper, that people with diverse experiences in different parts of the world later interact with each other back in their home countries. The sharing of situational explanations may well provide the basis for intelligent discussions since such explanations stem from a culturally relative respect for others in contrast to trait explanations (e.g., laziness, aggressiveness, etc.).

There are also many explanations of prejudice and intercultural contact in Hawaii, but this finding is much like a good-news, bad-news joke. There are many reasons given, some situational, but many of them are the less sophisticated trait explanations. Perhaps the "contact intensity" concept is useful to apply here. If a person had experienced a great deal of intercultural contact, not all of it could possibly be positive. When thinking about reasons for prejudice or intimate contact, one of the negative experiences may come to mind. For instance, an individual may have been physically attacked by a member from another cultural group. While the situational explanations of "was pressured by peers," or "reaction to past discrimination" may come to mind, it is hardly surprising that the trait explanations of "hostile" or "aggressive" are listed.

The professionals show what can be done with analyzed cross-cultural contact. As a whole, they did best on the situational explanation task. As a whole, they also had large amounts of cross-cultural interaction but have also had various opportunities to examine their experiences as part of their jobs. This suggests that people in Hawaii have a learning experience waiting to happen. Careful analysis of their cross-cultural interaction may lead to insights. To Hofstede's suggestion about painfully acquired empathy (p. 20), then, I would add that a careful analysis of the cross-cultural experiences is necessary before the empathy is attained to the highest degree possible. Techniques from the field known as cross-cultural training or cross-cultural orientation programs (e.g., Gudykunst, Hammer, and Wiseman, 1977; Brislin, 1981) are likely to help in this educational process. This is the topic which will be discussed next.

Cross-cultural training

The general goal of cross-cultural training programs is to prepare people to live and work in a culture other than their own (Brislin and Pedersen, 1976; Landis and Brislin, 1983); or to prepare people to interact extensively with culturally different others within their own country. The people for whom such training is prepared are usually about to participate in a cross-cultural experience that can be identified by such role labels as: foreign student, overseas businessman, missionary, technical assistance advisor, diplomat, Peace Corps Volunteer, teacher in a school about to be desegregated, language interpreter, and so forth. Three major assumptions that seem to be implicitly accepted by practitioners of cross-cultural training are:

1) there are enough commonalities in cross-cultural encounters (e. g., culture shock, need to interpret unfamiliar interpersonal

cues) that lessons learned from one type of audience can be used in planning for another type;

2) information and experiences can be conveyed in training that will make adjustment to another culture easier since trainees can use the relevant information when faced with an actual problematic situation;

3) training programs are efficient substitutes for other means of learning about international contact. For example, extensive travel and residence abroad are often cited as the best preparation for effective cross-cultural interaction. Yet these methods are too time-consuming, too inefficient, and too expensive for widespread use.

Cross-cultural training programs take different forms depending upon the background, skills, and interests of the program director, the resources available and the perceived needs of the trainees. Experiential training, one of five general types, is probably the most impactful. This type is characterized by two factors: it involves the intense feelings and emotion of the participants as well as their cognitions; and it demands more participation by trainees in terms of what actually happens during the program than other types. These two factors can be explained by briefly examining the nature of experiential training and then by contrasting it with the four other methods from a five-part typology developed by Brislin (1979). (Other typologies are the four-part system of Triandis (1977) and the six-part organization by Gudykunst, Hammer, and Wiseman (1977). The three typologies are quite similar and all have an experiential component.)

In experiential training, people actively participate in realistic simulations of other cultures. Sometimes called "total immersion," this approach involves all the senses of the participants and their total cooperation in satisfying their everyday needs. For instance, contract teachers about to work in Micronesia have been trained in rural parts of Hawaii (Trifonovitch, 1973). There, they (a) provided their own food, (b) planned daily activities based on tides and sun rather than clocks, (c) rationed the available water, (d) made their own entertainment, and so forth. The point, of course, is that such activities are performed on a day-today basis by Micronesians and that outsiders must understand the behaviors to interact effectively in Micronesia. The advantage of the techniques is that the relation to reality is greater than any of the other approaches. The disadvantages are the expanse of preparations and the danger that some people will not be able to cope with such an intense experience.

There are other, less complex, experiential techniques that can be incorporated into orientation programs. Role playing is the most common approach. Trainees take the part of various individuals involved in a cross-cultural encounter, and they develop a short scene that incorporates a problematic issue. These often fit the criterion of experiential training since the participants determine what's done in role playing and since the role plays can be emotional if they deal with sensitive topics.

The other four types are as follows:

1) in *cognitive training,* participants receive factual information about other cultures on such topics as food, climate, customs, and religion. Materials are prepared by the training staff;

2) in *attribution training,* participants again receive facts, but they are from the point of view of people in the other culture. Again, such training is based on materials prepared by the staff;

3) in *self-awareness training,* participants learn about widely shared opinions, attitudes, and values that are held by members of their own culture. Such training often is based on group discussion, and participants talk about their own experiences, but it does not incorporate the intense involvement typical of experiential training;

4) in *behavior modification,* participants examine their own thoughts and actions according to well-established principles of learning. For instance, participants might list their cognitions and potential behaviors that may interfere with a successful cross-cultural experience. They would then be asked to substitute positive cognitions and behaviors that would lead to the successful attainment of the participants' own goals. Such training would involve the participants in determining what happens during the program, since each participant has different goals and different cognitions regarding these goals. But this type of analysis does not involve the intensity of emotion and feelings that mark experiential training.

The entire typology is not perfect. The major reason is that a situation which is emotion-arousing to one person is not arousing to another. In cognitive training, for example, a "fact" presented by a trainer might trigger a reminder of one trainee's recent emotional experience, and the trainee might become quite upset. Or, if certain trainees have previously engaged in long-term survival training such as that conducted by the military, they may not be emotionally aroused by experiential training. The typology, however, probably explains the levels of emotional involvement and individual input of most people who participate in cross-cultural training.

Experiential cross-cultural training can be summarized in terms of the advantages, disadvantages, and unknowns of the methods. In an idealized training program, an advantage is that the relation to reality can be greater than other methods. Participants can test themselves in training, can learn about the effects of their behavior, and can modify their responses if they are not functional. Participants can learn to understand another culture in terms of emotions and feelings since they have to deal with the (simulated) situation for twenty-four hours a day. They have to satisfy their needs on the basis of what the culture provides. Ideally, participants will be motivated by their experience to study the other culture after the simulated experience ends. They might become involved enough to ask: "I faced this problem; how do the people themselves deal with it?"

They then could study the available materials (probably ethnographic) to find the answer.

One aspect of experiential training can be considered an advantage or a disadvantage, depending upon one's perspective. Trainees will inevitably complain and hostilities will rise to the surface. This can be considered an advantage if trainers view the actual cross-cultural assignment as frustration-inducing. Complaints and hostilities can be dealt with during training rather than during the actual assignment. This state of affairs is a disadvantage if trainers dislike constantly dealing with people's complaints and frustrations. I am aware of many skilled trainers who have left the field of cross-cultural orientation because they grew tired of being the target of hostility.

Other disadvantages are that the method is very time-consuming and sometimes expensive. Trainers usually have to stay with the participants during the entire length of the program, or risk being the target of obvious complaints. This means that trainers can get no other work done and also have to make arrangements for their absence from their own families. Expenses can take the form of preparation time, which is greater than for other methods, and rental fees for the site of the training.

Finally, any experiential training runs the risk of affecting a given participant so much that s/he becomes upset and dysfunctional. Trainers then worry whether such participants would have been better off if they had *not* participated in training. There is no generalization that can help deal with this problem. When trainers choose experiential techniques, not all participants will react in ways that trainers feel are desirable (McClelland, 1978).

Unknowns of experiential training include the desirable length of such programs, the amount of structure by the trainers, and the amount of generalization about the experiences which the trainer should offer. Programs can be too short to create much of an effect, or so long that participants become bored. To further complicate the issue, boredom might be desirable since some cultures do not have the number and types of entertainment forms to which trainees are accustomed.

A recent approach to cross-cultural training

Ever since becoming involved in cross-cultural training (about 1972), I have tried to imagine programs which combine the advantages of experiential training while avoiding the negative aspects reviewed here. Specifically, I have tried to imagine programs which engage the emotions and interests of participants while avoiding the hostilities which occur when participants' emotions are stimulated but not dealt with effectively. Recently, colleagues and I have devised a set of training materials organized around 100 critical incidents (Brislin, Cushner, Cherrie, and Yong, 1986). The following is a detailed description of a training workshop based on this recent approach, along with rationale for key assumptions.

The workshop is designed for people who live in countries other than the one in which they hold citizenship; or for people who interact extensively with different ethnic groups within their own country. The workshop provides participants with experiences, knowledge, and coping skills so that they can interpret and benefit from the specific interactions they will have with people from varied cultural backgrounds. The general term for encounters which take place either in other countries, or with ethnic minority groups within a country, is "cross-cultural interaction."

Goals:

1. To provide participants with a framework for understanding the cultural differences they will encounter.

2. To encourage participants to look at these cross-cultural encounters as opportunities for growth.

3. To provide participants with information, experiences, and coping skills so that they are not delibitated by the "culture shock" phenomenon.

4. To encourage participants to form support groups during their cross-cultural experiences so that they can help each other deal with any difficulties which arise.

5. To encourage participants to think about the commonalities in cross-cultural experiences. Such a perspective allows them to benefit from interactions with others who hold seemingly different jobs. For instance, overseas business people have experiences similar to those of foreign students and multicultural counselors. Building bridges across these jobs allows for mutual enrichment.

Method:

Workshop participants examine and discuss 100 critical incidents gathered from the experiences of people who have had extensive intercultural contact. Each incident deals with a problem which most participants will eventually face, or which they will help others face, during actual cross-cultural interactions. Each incident names the people involved, tells a story about them, and ends with a miscommunication or misunderstanding between people from different cultural backgrounds. Participants then choose among four or five alternate explanations. More than one of the explanations can be "correct" in the sense that they help to explain the incident. Participants make judgments about all the explanations since actual cross-cultural interaction involves the development of correct explanations as well as the rejection of incorrect ones. Each of these explanations is then discussed.

Here is an example of an incident:

Learning the Ropes

Helen Connor had been working in a Japanese company involved in marketing cameras. She had been there for two years and was well-respected by her colleagues. In fact, she was so respected that she often was asked to work with new employees of the firm as these younger employees "learned the ropes. One recent and young employee, Hideo Tanaka, was assigned to develop a marketing scheme for a new model of camera. He worked quite hard on it, but the scheme was not accepted by his superiors because of industry-wide economic conditions. Helen Connor and Hideo Tanaka happened to be working at nearby desks when the news of the non-acceptance was transmitted from company executives. Hideo Tanaka said very little at that point. That evening, however, Helen and Hideo happened to be at the bar. Hideo had been drinking and vigorously criticized his superiors at work. Helen concluded that Hideo was a very aggressive Japanese male and that she would have difficulty working with him again in the future.

Which alternative provides an accurate statement about Helen's conclusion?

1. Helen was making an inappropriate judgment about Hideo's traits based on behavior that she observed.

2. Since, in Japan, decorum in public is highly valued, Helen reasonably concluded that Hideo's vigorous criticism in the bar marks him as a difficult co-worker.

3. Company executives had failed to tell Helen and Hideo about economic conditions, and consequently Helen should be upset with the executives, not Hideo.

4. Helen felt that Hideo was attacking her personally.

Rationales:

1) You chose number 1. This is the best answer. When observing the behavior of others, a very common error is to make conclusions about the traits or qualities of those others. Here, those judgments (called attributions) are that Hideo is aggressive and hard to work with. There is much less a tendency to take into account the immediate factors in the situation which could also cause the behavior, such as the frustration upon hearing bad news. Interestingly, if Helen had been asked to interpret *her own* behavior had she gotten angry, she would undoubtedly have said something like, "Well, wouldn't you be angry if a plan you had worked hard on ended up being rejected?" In addition, vigorous behavior in bars is an acceptable outlet in Japan. People are not supposed to make permanent conclusions about others based on the "bar behavior" they see. But in analyzing the behavior of others, there is much less tendency to take into account such immediate factors of the situation or social context. This error — making trait judgments about others and not taking situational factors into account has been called the fundamental attribution error and is probably more prevalent in cross-cultural encounters, since there is so much behavior that is new and different to sojourners. When abroad, sojourners often make more attributions about people and events than they would in their own countries. Even though Helen

had been in Japan for two years, there will still be many new experiences that demand judgments or attributions from her.

2) You chose number 2. Certainly a common observation about Japan is that decorum is highly valued. Yet people do become angry and upset. Rather than jumping to a conclusion it is usually better to go beyond the common observation (in this case the frequently noted value placed on proper decorum) and to analyze in more detail the specific instance. If a person has been exposed only to the common observation, then he/she is ill-prepared for behaviors (which will inevitably be encountered on a long sojourn) which are at odds with the general observation. An important point is that vigorous behavior in bars is an acceptable outlet in Japan. Permanent conclusions should not be made based on "bar behavior," Japanese hosts tell us. Please choose again.

3) You chose number 3. Helen and Hideo, if they are capable professionals, should know about industry-wide conditions on their own. While Hideo might be expected to take into account these conditions before his reaction to the non-acceptance of his plan, a highly abstract and non-immediate thought like "industry-wide conditions" rarely wipes out the frustration of seeing hard work leading to no visible reward. Please choose again.

4) You chose number 4. This could be part of the interpretation. There is a strong tendency on the part of people, upon seeing the negative behavior of others, to wonder if they somehow were involved. Since Helen had been working with Hideo, such feelings would be natural. During cross-cultural experiences, this tendency is probably stronger. Since Helen and Hideo have not worked for a long time together and are still learning things about each other, Helen is not going to be able to interpret readily all of Hideo's actions. Since she is not intimately knowledgeable about Japanese culture after two years there, she will be motivated to wonder even more if she somehow is personally involved. Because of felt personal involvement, any of Helen's final conclusions will be even more intense. There is another explanation which focuses on a mistake Helen could be making in her thinking. Please try to identify this additional explanation.

Note that, even though the setting is Japan, almost all the issues raised are general to the cross-cultural experience. These include over-reacting to colorful incidents, the trait-situation distinction, avoiding stereotypes, going beyond easy generalizations, acceptable outlets for aggressive feelings, feeling personally attacked, and so forth. All of the incidents bring up such commonalities.

Incidents are of three broad types:

1) people's emotional experiences brought about by encounters with cultural differences;

2) knowledge areas which differ across cultures and which must be understood so that cross-cultural mistakes can be avoided;

3) the basis of cultural differences, such as differences in the ways people make judgments about the behavior they observe. For instance, the same behavior might be considered polite in one culture but rude in another. This broad focus helps participants interpret a wide range of specific behaviors.

Each of the 100 incidents was validated by asking sixty experts to give their interpretations of the reasons for miscommunication or misunderstanding. These sixty people have lived in many different countries for long periods of time, holding down a wide variety of jobs. Many have contributed to our understanding of cultural differences through their professional writings.

Advantages of working with critical incidents:

1) The incidents, since they depict real people attempting to make a good cross-cultural adjustment, are inherently interesting. Workshop participants want to know what happened to the people depicted in the incidents.

2) The incidents capture actual problems which the participants will eventually experience.

3) Any of the critical incidents can form the basis of role play scenarios should participants want to actually "play out" the encounters during the workshop. They can role play select incidents and then discuss their reactions.

4) A great deal of information about people's cross-cultural experiences is contained in the discussions of the various explanations of the incidents.

5) Participants can retain the 100 incidents so that they can be referred to after the workshop so as to help in the interpretation of actual cross-cultural encounters.

Thematic organizations of the 100 incidents:

The three broad areas referred to under "Method" (p. 30) contain eighteen thematic areas, each of which is developed in five or six of the critical incidents. These eighteen themes, when understood by workshop participants, provide a framework which allows them to interpret the various encounters they will have during their cross-cultural interactions. Essays are available which examine each theme.

A. People's emotional experiences brought about by encounters with cultural differences:

1. *Anxiety.* Since people will encounter many unfamiliar demands, they will be anxious about whether or not their behavior is appropriate.

2. *Disconfirmed expectancies.* People may become upset not because of the exact set of situations they encounter in the host culture, but because those situations differ from those which they expected.
3. *Belonging.* People want to feel accepted by others and want to feel "at home," but they often cannot since they have the status of outsiders.
4. *Ambiguity.* The messages people receive in other cultures are often unclear.
5. *Confrontation with one's prejudice.* People discover that previous attitudes they learned during their socialization in their own countries simply are not useful when interacting in another culture.

B. **Knowledge areas:**
6. *Work.* Many cultural differences are encountered in the work place, such as attitudes toward creative effort and the proper relationship between on-task time and social interaction.
7. *Time and space.* Varying attitudes exist regarding the importance of being "on time" to meetings, as well as the proper spatial orientation people adopt when inter-acting with each other.
8. *Language.* Perhaps the most obvious problem to overcome in crossing cultural boundaries is that of language differences. Attitudes toward language use, and the difficulties of learning language as it is actually spoken rather than "read from a book," are part of this knowledge area.
9. *Roles.* Sojourners are accustomed to a set of generalizations regarding who plays what roles, or performs various sets of related behaviors, because of long experience in their own culture. Examples of roles are the family provider, the boss, the volunteer, the leader, and so forth. Large differences exist with respect to the occupants of these roles, and how the roles are enacted, in other cultures.
10. *Importance of the group and the importance of the individual.* All people act at times because of their individual interests, and other times because of their membership in groups. The relative emphasis on individual and group allegiances varies from culture to culture.
11. *Rituals and superstitions.* All cultures have rituals to meet the needs of people as they cope with life's everyday demands, and people in all cultures engage in behaviors that outsiders can easily call "superstitions."
12. *Hierarchies: class and status.* The relative importance placed on class distinctions, and the markers of high versus low status, differ from culture to culture.
13. *Values.* People's experiences with broad areas such as religion, economics, politics, aesthetics, and interpersonal relationships become internalized. Understanding these internalized views, called values, is critical in cross-cultural adjustment.

C. Bases of cultural differences:

14. *Categorization.* Since not all pieces of information can be attended to, people group bits of information into categories for more efficient organization. People in different cultures place the same individual elements into different categories (e.g., who is a friend, what a good worker does), causing confusion for people accustomed to any one given set of categories.

15. *Differentiation.* One result of increased interest in, or importance of, a certain knowledge area is that more and more information is *differentiated* within that area such that new categories are formed. Example are the types of obligations which accompany various types of interpersonal relationships, and the various ways to overcome red tape. If outsiders do not differentiate information in the same manner as hosts, they may be treated as naive or ignorant.

16. *Ingroup-outgroup distinction.* Ingroups refer to people with whom interaction is sought. Outgroup members are held at a distance and are often the targets of rejection. People entering another culture have to be sensitive to the fact that they will often be outgroup members, and that there are some behaviors associated with ingroup membership in which they will never participate.

17. *Change and growth, as well as the possibility for self-improvement, involve new learning styles.* Even though people desire change and improvement, the style in which they best learn new information differs from culture to culture.

18. *Attribution.* People observe the behavior of others, and they also reflect upon their own behavior. Judgments about the *causes* of behavior are called attributions. The same behavior, such as a suggestion for how a proposal can be improved, may be judged as helpful in one culture but insulting in another.

It is hoped that this approach to training best mimics what happens to people during actual cross-cultural experiences. Most people enter these experiences with no expectations that events will be much different than they have beer: in their own culture. Instead, they are faced with a series of encounters they find puzzling and upsetting, such as those depicted in the 100 incidents. At that point people became interested and ask, "What is going on?" Then, people may be willing to study the thematic organization for an understanding of cross-cultural experiences as reviewed immediately above. Without the actual experiences, or the substitute represented by the critical incidents, my fear is that a direct assignment to study the thematic organization will be an overly abstract exercise, no better and no worse than any college-type assignment which a professor requires as part of a course for credit. If interest and excitement is generated by the 100 incidents, the mere mention of the explanatory framework should motivate participants to study it carefully.

Panel Discussions on Cross-Cultural Issues

[This was a first for RID conventions (or any other organization in deafness): three panels met to talk about biculturalism and bilingualism for Deaf people and for Hearing people. The panels were organized by Sheila Jacobs (California) and, given the outcome, PAID members owe Ms. Jacobs a great debt of gratitude. For many people, these panels were the high point of the week.

Because of the nature of the interaction and because of space constraints, it would have been impossible to reproduce exactly what happened. Fortunately, the sessions were videotaped and will be available for purchase What we present in this volume is a summary of the interactions, which we hope will be stimulating for both those of us who were witness to these very special events and for those who missed them. ED.]

Three panels took place: one of Deaf people (DP), one of Hearing people who had Deaf parents (HDP), and one of Hearing people who had Hearing parents (HHP). Each contributed a particular perspective on particular issues that concern them. The single theme that bound the groups more than any other was: we are not all alike! The aim of the panels was to present varying views and experiences in crossing cultural boundaries. It was pointed out that culture, in the final analysis, informs and guides our gut-level reactions as to what is right, what is comfortable, and what is "normal." It is easy for hearing people to miss the significance of Deaf Culture, because the words and values sound the same: friendship, loyalty, and the like. As one person said, "It's different for Deaf people." Making room for all these legitimate differences is the focus of all three panels.

Panel — Deaf people

Moderator: *Theresa Smith (Washington)*
Panel: *M.J. Bienvenu (Maryland)*
  Dennis Schemenauer (California)
  Mark Hoshi (Washington)

Shifting away from what schools taught ("being good at English means you are intelligent") to what was intuitively right (identity as a Deaf person) causes much confusion and even pain. The conflicts may be magnified in the case of DP whose parents and cultural upbringing are identified with the hearing world. The question was asked: what are the things that DP value? The primary answer was: ASL. We resent HP who mess around with our language! As Kannapell (1980) pointed out, this is the one thing that is in our control, that is truly ours.

Other values include the residential school experience, importance of friendships with other DP, loyalty to DP, and the importance of clear, easy communication. It is easy for HP to miss the point of residential school often, a HP reacts with pain at the thought of a child' being reared separately from her family. For DP, however, the comfort and ease of communication experienced in residential school far outweighs any loss of closeness with a hearing family. (Note that the notion of "family" has different significance to different sub-cultures, depending on the experience.)

In examining where hearing and deaf values conflict, a strong point was made about the use of the term "hearing-impaired." This is definitely a "hearing" word, which often is insulting to DP, who are proud and comfortable with their identity as Deaf. HP — specifically interpreters — who want to be involved with Deaf people are subject to an unspoken "checklist." DP want to know and understand why any HP has become involved with this language and this community. Attitude is the crucial factor. HP often inadvertently "take over " in a relationship with DP. Since the world is full of sound, HP rarely can help bringing their values with them ("Your hearing aid is squealing"; "You're shuffling your feet"; "They just announced that the plane will be late.") Worse, still, is the HP/interpreter who openly oppresses DP: "You need to learn English."

DP have had a lifetime of being told by hearing educators that English is the most important thing for them to learn. Yet, if deaf children learned and were taught in ASL, they would learn much more content matter, rather than being hung up on the form of what they learned (English). Since HP control education, DP inevitably lose these educational battles. Humor is a major means of relieving the resulting pressure and hostility; DP often tease HP as a means of "testing" attitudes, as well as a means of keeping the out-group out.

DHP (Deaf people who had hearing parents) often feel torn between the two cultures: they maintain values on both sides and feel the risk of being rejected by both. Indeed, many DHP feel oppressed by DDP. This is an issue which has been magnified by the interest in working with "native" Deaf signers. yet it seems that the question of "attitude" is again the most crucial: those DP who refuse to accept the notion of Deaf culture or who resist the notion that DP have been oppressed are resented and even rejected by DP who have made this leap. For DP who share the culture and the language, they have more in common than anything that separates them.

Panel — Hearing People Who Had Deaf Parents

Moderator: *Millie Brother (California)*
Panel: *Gary Sanderson (California)*
   Millie Stansfield (California)
   Anna Witter-Merithew (North Carolina)

The shift from "home" to "professional" interpreting is not an easy one. In the past, training programs and the RID itself have been less than sensitive in aiding HDP to make this transition a smooth one. The motivations of HDP's entering the field as professional interpreters have been varied. The single theme that seemed consistent was the accidental nature of their involvement. Circumstances, rather than conscious planning, seems to lead HDP's to the field.

HDP's often suffer as a result of certain myths that surround their upbringing. Many — Deaf and Hearing alike — assume that these people have "inherited" superlative ASL skills. Yet their parents represent the wide variety of Deaf communication preferences (ASL, PSE, oral) that we all know exists in the Deaf Community. The panel strongly expressed their wish for respect for all Deaf people's communication styles and their wish to feel comfortable with their own parents' communication styles.

HDP's often feel the need to hide any negative aspects of growing up in a Deaf family, for any express ion of the negative will reflect badly on their Deaf parents. Out of guilt, then, they have allowed or encouraged "outsiders" to believe that their childhoods were idyllic. In fact, Deaf parents are like all others: they are loving and they make mistakes.

Sometimes some HDP's feel guilty because they can hear and they fear being the "wrong" kind of hearing person; sometimes they feel alienated from the hearing world because their parents are viewed as "freaks": sometimes they feel angry at the hearing world for oppressing their parents and siblings.

Panel — Hearing People who had Hearing Parents

Moderator: *Charlotte Toothman (California)*

Panel: *Craig Anderson (Massachusetts)*
Theresa Smith (Washington)
Jenna Cassell (California)

"This group (HHP) approached the learning of sign language as becoming bi-lingual, without realizing that they would encounter a second culture as well. Much of this discussion focussed on the question of panel members' "discovery" that they had become bi-cultural. The emphasis here was clear: becoming bi-cultural had changed and expanded reality for these people in some positive and permanent ways. Yet they are still aware that they are "outsiders," and are constantly aware that many Deaf (and Hearing) people assume they can never learn to do the job properly.

Many times, Deaf and HDP's look cynically at HHP's, feeling that they can (and will) leave the field whenever they want to. It is true that HHP's have chosen the field, usually as adults. Yet, the feeling was that HHP's have made what was characterized as an "irrevocable" shift in their lifestyles. Even though HHP's chose to be involved in the Deaf Community, every interpreter, whatever their background and motivation for becoming professional, chooses to stay or to leave.

The panel seemed to agree with the notion that those HHP's who come to the field were "marginal" in the Hearing world to begin with. That is, in order to choose a bi-cultural identity (of any sort) requires a special sort of personality. HHP's, in leaving behind their mono-cultural identities, feel anxious, frustrated, and sometimes paranoid. Yet they come to this painful experience as adults; HDP's experience the conflicts earlier, as children, and therefore deal with them differently. These differences in reactions to bi-cultural conflicts provide the potential for creative problem-solving.

Funny in Deaf — Not in Hearing*

Susan B. Rutherford

There is an incident in the Broadway play, "Children of a Lesser God," that speaks directly to my subject. For the reader who may not be familiar with the play, the action concerns the relationship of James, a hearing man, and Sarah, a Deaf woman. At one point James boasts of how funny he is. Sarah snaps back her disagreement: "You're funny in hearing," she signs, "not in Deaf."

That one line reveals much — both about humor and about the two cultures I am concerned with here. The focus of this paper is on the text of a joke reflecting the other side of the coin — funny in Deaf, not in hearing.

Bascom (1965) teaches us that "amusement is, obviously, one of the functions of folklore, and an important one; but even this statement cannot be accepted today as a complete answer, for it is apparent that beneath a great deal of humor lies a deeper meaning" (p. 285). My study of this text was based on the belief that through an examination of a community's folklore one can find a reflection of its culture, and it is perhaps through the humor of the group, and its unselfconscious release of anxieties, that one can get closest to the essence of the community. As Dundes (1973) aptly puts it, "It is what makes people laugh that reveals the soul of that people" (p 611).

The joke in question has a long history in the American Deaf community. Quite often it's the first joke cited when informants are asked for an example of a "deaf" joke. Further, it is often referred to as a joke hearing people would not understand. My discussion is based on 13 texts and informant analyses collected in American Sign Language (ASL) on videotape. The following is an English translation[1] of one collected text:

One time a man, a Deaf person, was driving along and stopped at some train tracks because the crossing signal gates were down but there was no train going by. So he waited for a long time for a train to go by, but nothing. The person decided then to get out of the car and walk to the control booth where there was a man who controlled the railroad gates. He was sitting there talking on the phone. The Deaf man wrote in his very best way (elegantly), "Please b-u-t," and handed the paper to the controller. The controller looked back at the Deaf person quizzically, "Please but? Huh?" He didn't understand that.

If you are a nonsigner, you would not find the joke funny at all. The punch line is a play on sign. There is a substitution of one of the parameters of ASL, similar to the substitution of a letter in a spoken word that creates a play on that word.

* Reproduced by permission of the American Folklore Society from *Journal of American Folklore* 96:381, 1983. Not for further reproduction.

The sign used for "open the railroad crossing gate" was the /G/ hand shape classifier, as follows: the movement resembles an actual crossing gate being raised and lowered. The palm orientation is inward, palms facing each other.

The ASL lexical equivalent for the English word "but" has the sane parameters as the above classifier for railroad crossing gate, with the exception of palm orientation: the palms are facing outward.

Thus, the punch line, "Please b-u-t," is an obvious punlike play between the phonological similarities of the two signs. The play is on the intended idea: "Please, open the gate and let me pass." The substitution of the one phonological element of palm orientation would be similar to the substitution in: "The Reverend Spooner had a great affection, or so he said, for 'our queer old dean'" (Koestler, 1964, p. 64).

Whether "Please b-u-t" is a true pun is debatable. There is a change in meaning from "open the railroad gates to "but"; however, the new statement does not make equal sense with the new meaning. A true pun would generally evoke a double meaning with the phonological play where both meanings are perceived simultaneously. As we can see with the previous examples, "Our queer old dean" and "Our dear old queen," each statement makes sense. Compare this with the two meanings in the joke: "Please, open the railroad crossing gate" and "Please, b-u-t." The latter does not make equal sense.

The play is also one step removed. Since the person telling the joke writes the English word b-u-t, but does not use the sign "but," the play is actually with the English gloss.

But even many people who are fluent in sign and who understand and enjoy the play between sign and gloss do not fully appreciate the joke. That this happens is evidence of the more important fact of the cultural specificity of humor, for here, the lack of appreciation does not stem from "not getting it," but from a lack of a shared cultural experience. I was witness to a clear instance of this cultural difference at a workshop that I was conducting at a San Francisco Bay Area Deaf community service agency. The audience was mixed. There were Deaf people and there were hearing people. The hearing people included nonsigners, fluent signers, and native signers (children of Deaf parents). We were discussing culture, particularly Deaf culture, and I mentioned humor as being culturally specific. One of the participants asked if I would tell a Deaf joke. This is not my skill, but a Deaf friend — and master comedienne — consented. I include a translation of her text as one of the variations I collected:

There is a Deaf man driving along in his car. He is hurrying to get home because his wife will get very angry if he is late. He then comes to a railroad crossing and the gates are down. He waits as the train passes. The train is long past and still the gates are down. The man waits and waits and is thinking of how his wife is going to yell if he's late. The Deaf man then gets out of his car and proceeds to the control booth at the crossing, where there is a person who is in charge of all the controls. The Deaf man takes out his pencil and paper and tries to think of the English words to put on the paper requesting that the gates be raised. He thinks and thinks (in sign) and says to himself, ah ha, and writes the words, "Please b-u-t," and hands the paper to the hearing gatekeeper. The gatekeeper does not understand and says, "Huh?"

Of the Deaf and hearing signers who understood the play on the sign, there was a definite qualitative difference in the laughter, which broke along Deaf and hearing lines. The Deaf response was much more intense.

Why the difference, especially since this is a very old joke and many of the Deaf individuals had heard it over and over again? Why funnier to Deaf than to hearing?

Consider again the cultural specificity of humor. The reason that humor is culturally specific for a group is more than just language; it is a matter of experience. It becomes clear that the one thing not held in common by the native hearing signers and the Deaf signers is the experience of being Deaf with all its cultural implications. The experience of being a Deaf person in the hearing world is one that is fraught with daily communication frustration, as well as societal prejudices and the collective oppression of Deaf people. These are not part of a hearing person's life experiences. Hearing signers, through professional or familial ties, are generally aware to one degree or another of the frustrations and injustices Deaf people face. However, this awareness is usually on a more cognitive level, not on a deep, affective level.

Although a general level of awareness of deafness is increasing among the hearing world, it is not widely understood that there is a culture of Deaf people It is a common misconception that Deaf people are an isolated, handicapped group of people. Whereas this may be the case for some, it is not the case for all. The American Deaf community is a group of deaf and hard-of-hearing individuals share a common language and culture. In the United States there are two million people who are "audiometrically deaf" (Schein and Delk 1974, p. 17); that is, they are physically unable to perceive the sounds of speech. The Deaf community, however, numbers approximately 500,000. Membership in this cultural group is based more on "attitudinal deafness" (Baker and Padden 1978, p. 1) than on the actual degree of hearing loss. By attitudinal deafness we mean that an individual has, on the basis of certain characteristics, identified himself as a member of the community and is accepted by other members.

Use of ASL is the major identifying characteristic of members of the Deaf community (Stokoe 1970, pp. 27-41). Thus, individuals who are deaf but do not use ASL are not considered members of the Deaf community.

Another cultural characteristic of the community is its 85-95 per cent endogamous marriage rate (Rainer *et al.* 1963, p. 17). Deaf people tend to marry other Deaf almost exclusively. Still another characteristic, the existence of a formal societal structure within the culture, can be seen in the numerous Deaf organizations — local, state, national, and international. Of particular note are the National Association of the Deaf (established in 1880) and the World Federation of the Deaf, which involve themselves with the problems of the Deaf on national and international levels, respectively. There is also an American Athletic Association of the Deaf, which organizes Deaf sports and sends representatives to the World Deaf Olympics.

The Deaf community is a tight-knit one, and there are national fraternal orders, sororities and alumni associations, as well as numerous religious organizations and community social groups (Meadow 1972, p. 24). There are articles of material culture such as telecommunication devices (TDD's) and flashing light signaling devices to take the place of doorbells, clock alarms, and telephone rings. There are even sound-activated signal lights to alert parents to a baby's cry.

Ten per cent of the Deaf community's population are members of Deaf families whose principal language is ASL. The remaining 90 percent of the population are born to hearing families and are consequently potential members of a cultural group different from that of their own parents. State-operated residential schools for the Deaf are the primary places where enculturation of these children takes place (Meadow, p.24). There, through peers from Deaf families and through Deaf adult staff, if present, this process is carried on — informally, often surreptitiously and without the official sanction of the educational establishment.

One important characteristic to note regarding this culture is that it is a bilingual diglossic community Its members are a minority functioning within a larger society. Their language continuum ranges from ASL to English with many varieties of pidgin in between (Stokoe, 1970, p. 27; Woodward, 1973, p 191). The "we" and "they" dichotomy of this minority group is roughly: "we" are Deaf "they" are hearing; "we" identify with ASL, "they," English.[2]

If we look at the manifest content of the joke we see that the issue is one of communication or the lack thereof. It is also making fun of Deaf English.[3] Like the stilted expression of many whose knowledge of a second language is rudimentary, the language variety referred to as "Deaf English" is also characterized by simpler structure and over-generalizations of the grammatical rules of English. For example, if "walk" becomes "walked," why then doesn't "go" become "goed"? If more than one "mouse" is "mice," why is the plural of "house" not "hice"? Another aspect of Deaf English is the substitution of the English gloss for an ASL sign In the joke, the Deaf person is unable to find the right English words. In this case the right "words" are "open the railroad gate." Trying his or her best, groping for the right words, the Deaf person falls into an English gloss of ASL sign, which is identical in all respects but one. The punlike play is between the phonological similarity of the two signs.

Although perhaps not a true pun, the joke does present one frame of reference, "open the railroad crossing gates," and then switches to another, "but," provoking what Koestler terms a bisociative act, as a true pun would. Koestler (1964) sees this bisociative act as "the perceiving of a situation or idea...in two self-connected but habitually incompatible frames of reference" (p. 35). With the connecting of the dissimilar frames of reference an insight into the similarity between the two previously incompatible worlds is revealed. It is this resolution, according to Koestler, that makes us laugh or find something funny. It is my belief that two bisociative acts are at work here: one centering on ASL phonological similarity and the other on the English gloss substitution.

Of the informant analyses that went beyond the description of the play on sign, all referred to the Deaf person's problem with English. To quote a few: "The joke makes fun of Deaf people's English and their problems with writing"; "Deaf people always are having trouble with English"; "English is always a problem, you know that. So it's just a way of making fun of it."

One informant went further:

> You have to understand both languages in order to understand the joke. The joke makes fun of the Deaf person. You see Deaf people write down what they say. There are many possible English word choices. The Deaf person in the joke thinks what he/she wants to say in sign and then ends up writing English gloss. The Deaf person is writing so the hearing person can understand, but really, in sign it is not funny. The joke makes fun of Deaf English and the writing problems, which "they" blame on the influence of sign language. People blame sign language, so we have jokes that blame sign language. We laugh at that.

This is not only an insightful analysis, but a clear illustration of "we" and "they."

Herskovits (1948) reminds us that "the folklore of a people cannot be understood without an understanding of the culture to which it belongs" (p. 418). Considering how much of our socialization and education depend on language, we cannot understand the culture of Deaf people without understanding the educational system that controls the enculturation and linguistic development of the Deaf individual.

In 1817, after visiting a school for the Deaf in Paris, a hearing minister, the Reverend Thomas Gallaudet, together with a French Deaf teacher, Laurent Clerc, established the first school for the Deaf in America. Because the school they established was a residential one, deaf children who were previously isolated were able to gather together and form a community; this created the essential environment for the natural development of a language.

The educational approach that Gallaudet and Clerc used was called the "Combined Method." The children were schooled in the French Sign Language that the two men brought from France, as well as in speech.[4] In general, this combined oral and manual method was the standard approach in Deaf Education until the 1860's when the "Oral Method" took hold.

The Oral Method's emphasis is on speech only. Sign language is forbidden both in and out of the classroom, since Oral proponents postulate that to allow signing would hinder a Deaf person's development of speech. He would become lazy. The effort is to "normalize" a Deaf child so he can be like a hearing person. In fact, a look at old Deaf Education texts reveals references to teaching the child to hear. Children who failed at the oral method were often thought to be stupid and would be sent to a Manual or Combined program. It was this shift to the oral method that began what some refer to as "The Hundred Years' War" or "The Oral-Manual Controversy."

There had been an early acceptance of Deaf educators in Deaf Education in the mid-1800's. As the shift to oralism took hold, this acceptance of Deaf teachers, as well as of Deaf administrators being involved in the decision-making process, began to wane. In fact, many of the Deaf schools that were founded by Deaf people gradually were taken over by hearing administrators.

By 1880, an International Conference of Teachers of the Deaf held in Milan, Italy, resolved to settle the Oral-Manual conflict. The following was the result:

> The congress, considering the incontestable superiority of speech over signing in restoring the deaf mute to society, and in giving him a more perfect knowledge of language, declares that the oral method ought to be preferred to that of signs for the education of the deaf and dumb (Gordon, p. xvi).

Notably, there were no Deaf persons in attendance or involved in drafting the resolution.

While the Oral-Manual struggle was going on, changes were taking place in the Deaf population. Medical advances were lessening the incidence of deafness due to childhood disease, while at the same time ensuring the survival of babies who were born deaf due to prematurity. The result was an increase in perlingually deaf children — those who become deaf before acquiring language. For the perlingually Deaf individual, the learning of spoken English is a particularly arduous task. Fant (1972) created an analogy for hearing people which is worth quoting:

> Suppose, for example, you were in a sound-proof glass booth, equipped only with a pad and pencil. Outside the booth is your instructor who speaks, reads, and writes only Japanese. How long would it take for you to learn Japanese. How well would you learn it? (p. v).

Orwell went so far as to say that if you control the language you control the people. When a people are dependent exclusively on a visual mode to acquire language, the suppression of a visual form of language is double oppressive. "Please b-u-t is funny as a bilingual play, but again as Bascom (1965) asserts, "It is apparent that beneath a great deal of humor lies a deeper meaning" (p. 285). The deeper meaning here is a crystallized reflection of a historical and sociological experience of the Deaf. It is a picture of lack of control, lack of self-determination, negation of identity, stifled development, blocked communication, external control characterized by benevolent paternalism and authoritarianism, and one of general conflict with the majority culture.

This joke, which has been described as an "old chestnut" by a senior member of the community, is also often referred to as "a joke hearing people wouldn't understand." In Mother Wit from the Laughing Barrel, Dundes (1973) states that "it is really in the in-group jokes and understanding that a group tests the solidarity of its members. Those who understand are 'with it'; those who do not understand are not 'with it'" (p. 611). With the explicit statement that a hearing person would not understand the joke, there is an overt definition of in-group/out-group — those who are "with it" and those who are not.

We know from the content of the joke that the gate controller is hearing, as the Deaf man must communicate with him through written notes. Frequently, however, within the telling there are embellishments such as depicting him in a derogatory fashion, talking on and on and occasionally indifferent to the Deaf man's presence. Just as Basso (1979) observes that in Western Apache folkloric tradition the portrayal of "'the Whiteman' serves as a conspicuous vehicle for conceptions that define and characterize what 'the Indian' is not" (p. 5), so we may suggest that the hearing man here serves the same purpose. This is especially true when the hearing man illustrates his indifference to Deaf people and his penchant for speech. In the joke frame, slurred images of hearing people are safely expressed. The aggression against the majority culture is safely masked by the humor.

Dundes (1973) suggests "sources of anxiety make the best subjects for humor," noting that "race prejudice" is a common theme in Negro jokes" (p. 612). Similarly, "Please b-u-t" focuses on miscommunication and an ambiguous linguistic situation, both of which are daily sources of anxiety within the Deaf community. Dundes continues, "On the other hand, much humor is entirely intragroup rather than intergroup, and one often finds one Negro group making fun of another" (p. 612). As we have discussed earlier, informant analyses attest to the fact that "Please b-u-t" is also making fun of Deaf people and their misuse of English.

Martineau (1972) suggests that when the in-group humor is disparaging toward an out-group, as in the derogatory depictions of the hearing controller, it may serve to increase morale and solidify the in-group, and/or to introduce and foster a hostile disposition toward the out-group (p. 116). The former function is certainly fulfilled by this joke, and I would suggest that the latter is also a possible function for some of the tellers of this joke. Martineau also suggests four functions of in-group humor that is disparaging to the in-group:

1) to control in-group behavior;

2) to solidify the in-group;

3) to introduce or foster conflict already present in the group; and

4) to foster demoralization and social disintegration of the group.

The latter two do not seem to be as relevant in this situation. Based on my observations and informant analyses, the first two functions do seem to have some validity. The joke-teller displays the proper behavior and attitude of the Deaf man in the joke, thus reaffirming group behavioral norms and attitudes. A common occurrence of Deaf and hearing interaction is dramatized, illustrating sources of mutual anxiety, and this serves to rally the group around a pair of solidarity and demonstrate what is "Deaf" and what is not.

Douglas (1968) asserts that jokes mirror the incongruity in society. Jokes are anti-structure — an attack on the established order. By joking in a play frame, the resultant disruption challenges the social order on a symbolic level and reaffirms order on a social level (p. 361).

Further, Feinberg (1978) suggests that word play is aggression against conformity, especially, with reference to puns, a rebellion against linguistic conformity. When the language is distorted, it represents a revolt, albeit playful, against the rigidity of language (p. 106). Given the history of linguistic rigidity imposed on the Deaf individual by the majority culture, it is apparent that "Please b-u-t," as a playful linguistic distortion, serves as a particularly satisfying source of rebellion. This is especially true for those who must walk daily the linguistic tightrope between both worlds.

Douglas (1968), accepting Freud's analysis that the joke is an attack on control, states, "Since its form consists of a victorious tilting of un-control against control, it is an image of the leveling of hierarchy, the triumph of intimacy over formality and unofficial values over official ones" (p. 365). In the real world, the Deaf community has at least begun to level that hierarchy by identifying what it believes to be the major root of its problems. As one Deaf writer states, "Deaf people have been repressed, restrained and frustrated in their search for an adequate education and an equal opportunity for a meaningful life" (Jacobs, p. 2). The greatest handicap for the Deaf individual is not the inability to hear, but the ignorance of the hearing world. As Jacobs states, "Many parents and educators fail to realize the critical need for communication" (p. 12).

"Please b-u-t" symbolically captures the essence of the Deaf situation perfectly: the gates block the way for the Deaf person's own goods It may be reasonable to expect such protection for a while, but the obstruction remains beyond a reasonable time. This parallels the experience of many Deaf individuals within the education system.

In control of the situation, of course, is a hearing person, often portrayed talking on the telephone and indifferent to the Deaf person's situation. This is perhaps as close to a Deaf stereotype of a hearing person as we can get.

Frustration mounts as the Deaf person's way continues to be blocked. He is expected to arrive home no matter what, or his authoritarian wife will be angry. The Deaf person is caught: he has to play the game the hearing way, which for him carries built-in failure, but at the same time he is expected to succeed. This double-bind situation aggravates the frustration and erodes the self-esteem of the individual

When he gives the hearing gatekeeper the written English note, the gatekeeper does not understand. It should be noted here that speech therapists often tell a deaf child how well he speaks. While the child may be relatively proficient in the realm of Deaf speech, it is not uncommon that in the outside world the child will be unable to make his speech understood The majority culture — the hearing world — does not understand him.

The Deaf person in the joke, as one informant states, "writes his very best" and is still not understood. The slap at hearing control and education is obvious. The Deaf person does his best to communicate as the hearing world has taught him, but communication breaks down. It is, however, a key point, underlining Jacobs' point about an uninformed hearing world, that it is the hearing gatekeeper who fails to grasp the true situation.

The joke serves a second purpose, which sheds light on another source of anxiety. Since this joke is for the bilingual, it may serve as an additional source of group solidarity and identification for those who have to interact with the hearing world more than their more isolated fellows (who may not have an equal grasp of English). The greater the command of English a Deaf individual has, the more likely he is to be in conflict with himself.

If "we" use ASL and "they" use English, what happens to the "we" when we use English? Ambivalent feelings about self spring from such situations. The message is that it's not good to be too "hearing." There is a sign, THINK HEARING, used as a derogatory identification of such people; the concept is directly analogous to calling a Black person an "Oreo."

What compounds these ambivalent feelings is that many Deaf people themselves do not recognize that ASL is a real language, having been carefully schooled by the dominant culture to think the contrary. Because Deaf people operate linguistically on a continuum between two languages, using many different varieties as the situation demands (Stokoe, 1970, p. 27; Markowicz and Woodward pp. 1-15) the possibility exists for greater ambivalence about their own language. Hence, anxiety can crop up when the Deaf attempt to define what they use. Often you will hear an informant say that he signs English or that ASL is really a simplified English. Bilingual play can serve as a mediating factor for the bilingual person who has to function between both languages, mediating the languages and the associated linguistic identity, which is often blurred. By looking at what "we" are and what "we" are not through a vehicle such as "Please b-u-t," a reaffirmation of what "Deaf" is occurs.

"To understand laughter," Bergson (1911) tells us, "We must put it back into its natural environment, which is society, and above all we must determine the utility of its function, which is a social one. Laughter," he continues, "must answer to certain requirements of life in common. It must have a social signification" (p. 7). The joke is still told, is still laughed at, and still serves a purpose today for the simple fact that the conflicts still exist. There are anxieties related to communication with the hearing world. There is ambiguity with reference to linguistic identity. The decision-makers in Deaf education are still predominantly hearing, still paternalistic. The programs for training teachers of the Deaf still, for the most part, either are based on oral methods, or focus on artificial sign systems based on English. Although improving, the majority culture remains largely uninformed.

Fry (1963) states that "a metaphor allows us to treat a psychological phenomenon as a concrete entity and allows us to gather together items of humor, wit, comedy, etc., into one circumscribed object for contemplation" (p. 35). This joke is a metaphor for the language situation of the community, the experience of the community within the hearing world and the search of the individual for identity. In each of these dimensions, the way is externally blocked. The language is dismissed; the culture is not recognized; and the individual is prevented from gaining true acceptance on any formal level within the hearing world. Thus, the joke reflects the very real conflict that exists between two cultures — hearing and Deaf — and at the same time serves as an aggressive outlet against the majority as well as a vehicle to reaffirm the group identity of the Deaf minority. "Please b-u-t" will continue to be an "old chestnut" as long as the indifference continues and the gates remain down.

Notes

Parts of this paper were first presented at the American Folklore Society annual meeting in San Antonio, October, 1981 and at the California Folklore Society annual meeting at Davis, California, April 1982.

I would like to gratefully acknowledge all of the people who contributed to the collection, discussion, and/or analysis of the texts, particularly Ben Bahan, Dr. Byron Burnes, Olin Fortney, Leo M. Jacobs, Freda Norman, Carlene Canady-Pederson, Marie Phillips, Lillian Quartermus, and Howie Seago. Special thanks go to Ella Mae Lentz whose guidance, support, and friendship has been invaluable to this "outsider."

1. All translations of texts are my own.

2. The Deaf community has faced and continues to face the same kind of linguistic and cultural oppressions as other minority groups. Without a voice in the decision-making process, self-determination for the community has been an impossibility. As Woodward (1982) points out, the Deaf community has three additional pressures that other minority groups do not have. First, there is the necessity to overcome the negative stereotype that accompanies a label of medical pathology. Secondly, the majority of the community's members are of a different cultural group than their parents and, thus, do not get cultural reinforcement in the home as do other minority children. And thirdly, the community's language differs in channel structure as well as code structure from that of the majority culture, which makes the language oppression doubly severe.

3. For additional discussion of "Deaf English," see Meadow (1980) and Charrow (1975b).

4. For further historical discussion see Lane (1977), Cannon (1980), and Bender (1970).

Characteristics of Oppressed and Oppressor Peoples: Their Effect on the Interpreting Context

Charlotte Baker-Shenk

Both spoken language interpreters and signed language interpreters function as mediators between members of different linguistic and cultural groups. However, signed language interpreters additionally function as mediators between members of the powerful majority (hearing) and members of an oppressed minority (deaf). And most signed language interpreters, by virtue of their hearing status, are members of that powerful majority. These basic facts are of critical importance for understanding the context in which interpreters work, and they need to be examined openly if we are to get beyond the mutual hurting and confusion that permeate the field of signed language interpreting.

Introduction

This paper will describe some of the painful realities that make up the context in which interpreters work — including the attitudes and behaviors of deaf people toward interpreters, and the attitudes and behaviors of interpreters toward deaf people. It is often hard for us to talk about these things without becoming very emotional, even angry or hurt. We usually are not neutral on these issues. I am not, and I often become internally upset when giving a presentation on my understanding of these realities. Unfortunately, sometimes I become self-righteous and oppressive to some people. That is not what I want to do, but it is a real temptation for me — like the arrogance of a recent convert or someone who just stopped smoking. So I begin this paper with that confession, earnestly desiring to communicate non-offensively but honestly, and hoping to communicate with your hearts as well as your heads.

The "language" I will be using to discuss these issues may seem strange to some of you. It is the language of power that Harlan Lane refers to in his paper. This language divides people into two categories: the oppressed and the oppressors. In this country, people who are white, middle class, hearing, and heterosexual often find that this language seems too sharp, too "black and white." They do not see things this way. Yet this language is very familiar to people in many other countries in Latin America, in South Africa, and in the Philippines; it is also more familiar to some groups of people in this country, like Black people and Deaf people. Some women have also used this language to describe their experience.

I begin with the assumption that everyone has experienced being oppressed, that is, hurt by someone putting you down, making you feel inferior, or unfairly denying some opportunity to you. I also assume that all of us have oppressed other people, that we have made others feel inferior, perhaps taking advantage of someone else's problems, or trying to make ourselves look good at the expense of others. In both cases, we may not use the language of oppression to describe our experience, but we have experienced what oppression is.

Some groups or classes of people are oppressed. In many countries, such as El Salvador and Guatemala, poor peasants are oppressed by the wealthy and powerful people of those countries. In the United States, Black people and Native American Indians have been and are oppressed by groups of White people. Some of you might want to argue that signed language interpreters are an oppressed group. What I want to focus on in this paper is the oppression of the deaf minority by the powerful hearing majority.

There are four basic points I want to make:

1) that deaf people are a highly oppressed group who show many of the same characteristics seen in other oppressed people of the world;

2) that interpreters, by virtue of their "hearing heritage" and the context in which they work, run a serious risk of behaving in an oppressive manner;

3) that many of the conflicts that interpreters face can be better understood by analyzing them in terms of power and control, and by remembering the oppressed condition of deaf people;

4) that understanding these conflicts in this way can encourage deaf and hearing people to become more trusting and trustworthy, and hence, help resolve the tensions.

Minority oppression

What does it mean, in concrete terms, to say that someone is a member of an oppressed minority group?

It means you suffer because the dominant group denigrates your self-worth, your abilities, your intelligence, and your right to be different and affirmed in your difference. It means having neither power in the institutions that impact your life, nor opportunities for self-determination. It often means a denial of your language, its worth or your opportunities to use it, and a denigration of your culture. (Consider the experience of Black, Hispanic, and Native American Indian people in the United States.) It frequently means receiving a poor quality education, and then facing a lack of jobs and opportunities for job advancement. It often results in discrimination in housing, bank loans, and medical services.

What does it mean, in concrete terms, to say that a deaf person is a member of an oppressed minority?

It means having your teachers and counselors tell you that you have no language, that American Sign Language (ASL) is not a language, that Deaf people don't have a "culture." It means a denigration of ASL as less intelligent and less than fully human and an intolerance of and prohibition against its use in your schools. It generally means having teachers who cannot communicate with you and hence, cannot help you learn — while at the same time you are blamed for your poor academic performance. It means being deeply aware that hearing people view your group as being less intelligent, emotionally and behaviorally deviant, and incapable of self-determination. It means being told that you cannot make mature and intelligent decisions on your own, that you need hearing people to help you. It means receiving a poor quality education, and then a lack of jobs or opportunities for job advancement, and a lower average income. It also means not having decision- and policy-making power in the educational, medical, rehabilitation, and social service institutions that are supposedly serving you.

What lies behind this oppression of minority groups?

How does it happen?

Goffman (1963), a well-known sociologist, explains that oppressed minorities tend to have a *stigma*; they are stigmatized. This stigma is a "deeply discrediting trait" seen as a defect in the persons who have it. That is, as a rule, people develop expectations about the way others should act and what they should look like. Those people who are members of the dominant power group in society also develop such expectations about the way others should appear, behave, and think — using themselves as the standard (Higgins, 1980, p. 123). And then when some people do not measure up to these supposed "standards," they are reduced in our minds from a whole and usual person to a tainted, discounted one" (Goffman, 1963, p. 3). This is what characteristically happens to Black people, deaf people, and homosexuals, among others.

Unfortunately, those dominant group members who create and control the larger social world often treat this perceived "defect" or "failing" as an overriding, all-encompassing characteristic of the person who has it (Higgins, 1980). That is, all of the individual differences among such persons are overlooked, and all of the persons with this "defect" are viewed as if they were all the same. So the Black man who shines shoes and the Black man who has a Ph.D. in engineering are seen as the same — because they are both Black. Of course, members of the minority group have very different perceptions about themselves and are quite aware of their individual differences. Similarly, deaf people know that they are a diverse group, even i-hen hearing people lump them all together in classrooms or in their speeches.

The next oppressive phenomenon that happens is that the "defect" spreads (Goode, 1978; Higgins, 1980). That is, because of the original "defect" or difference, other additional negative characteristics are attributed to the minority group. For example, because Black people are black, they are then stereotyped as lazy, intellectually inferior, irresponsible, etc. Similarly, many hearing people assume that since Deaf people are deaf and hence, "don't use our language properly," they are intellectually inferior. Explaining this hearing view, Lane (1980a) writes "Only two kinds of people, after all, fail to use your language properly: foreigners and retardates." Since deaf people are clearly not foreigners, they must be retarded.

This defect "spread" can also be seen in the semi-humorous stories of deaf people being led by,the hand to the appropriate gate at the airport (as if they can't find it themselves) or even being driven to the gate on a personal transport car (as if they cannot walk). Similarly, deaf people have been described in the clinical and educational literature as ego-centric, easily irritable, and impulsive (Levine, 1956), dependent and lacking in empathy (Altshuler, 1974), immature, rigid rather than flexible, exploitative of others, and abusive of relationships (Hurwitz, 1967). A prominent speaker at the 1971 International Ecumenical Seminar on Pastoral Care of the Deaf, Father A. van Uden, adds another example to the list: "It seems evident that it is more difficult for deaf children than for hearing children to attain authentic, selfless love."

Characteristics of oppressed people

What is the impact of this stigmatization and negative stereotyping on members of the oppressed minority?

Goffman (1963), Freire (1970), a Brazilian sociologist and educator who has worked closely with poor people in several countries, and Ben Schowe (1979), a deaf thinker and author, have each described the way oppressed people feel about the trait or different feature which stigma-tizes them. Goffman describes this feeling as *ambivalence*, noting that stigmatized people tend to both embrace the feature that makes them dif-ferent, viewing it as an essential part of their identity, and also to degrade themselves and other group members because of the feature that makes them different. The latter shows an acceptance of the majority view; the former is seen in such one-liners as "Black is beautiful," "I'm gay and proud," and "Ain't I a woman," as well as the signed assertion "I'm deaf," in which the movement of the sign DEAF is large and emphatic with one cheek puffed out. Schowe notes that positive identification with the stig-matizing feature leads to "group solidarity" whereas negative identifica-tion with the feature leads to "self-hatred."

Freire also talks about this ambivalence and calls it an *existential duality*. On the one hand, oppressed people desire to break away from the oppressor, to become free and self-determining, to speak and act on their own thoughts, to have choices, to break their silence. For example, women of the past several decades have claimed their right to work out-side the home and to run for public office. Homosexuals have been aban-doning their silence, their so-called "closet," demanding acceptance of their difference and freedom from previous sanctions against them.

Oppressed people's desire for freedom is also seen in their expres-sions of resentment and even hatred toward the oppressor, as well as their fantasies of revenge. These expressions show their desire to get out from under the foot that's stomping on them and denying their freedom.

On the other hand, oppressed people often wish to be like the oppres-sor. They have internalized the dominant group's values and way of thinking about their (oppressor's) own superiority. The oppressed feel an irresistible attraction to the oppressors and their way of life; they want to imitate and follow them. Black people have desired big cars, big houses, and big TV's. Women have worn suits and ties and sought to be powerful executives. Deaf people have told each other sound-based puns.

This ambivalence is personally felt by some group members more than others. Members also may change in how strongly they experience one pole or the other. For example, one product of the Black Liberation movement of the 1960's and '70's was that some Black people who used to straighten their hair, smile, try to "talk White" and fit in began to proclaim "Black is beautiful," wearing Afros and dashikis, and publicly delighting in their own dialect (rappin', jivin', gettin' down, etc.) — which was then copied by certain members of the White majority. Similarly, some deaf people who used to pretend that they understood what a hearing person was saying and who used to watch hearing people out of the corners of their eyes to find out when it was time to laugh are now insisting on their right to understand and to be Deaf. Some are now saying "Don't bother me with your sound-based jokes — or your songs."

Freire observes that oppressed people tend to parrot the words of the oppressor: they call themselves ignorant, lazy, sick, unproductive, and inferior. They lack self-confidence and also distrust their fellow group members who, of course, are thought to share the same inferiority. Sussman (1976), a deaf psychologist, notes that an individual's self-concept is largely defined by how others view him or her. And he reports what are the findings of numerous studies: deaf people have negative self-concepts, pronounced feelings of inferiority, and low overall self-esteem.

Freire finds another characteristic of oppressed people to be "horizontal violence." Oppressed people tend to vent their frustrations and despair on their peers in an aggressive, often violent way. Black rioters have often burned down the homes and businesses of other Black people rather than the White people who are the source of their rage. Oppressed people usually feel unable to strike back at the oppressor, and instead strike out against their own people — where it is more safe to do so.

Another characteristic of oppressed people is called a "slave consciousness" or "fatalistic attitude" (Freire, 1970, 1973). The oppressed person becomes docile and passive toward their oppressive situation, feeling "I can't do anything about it." The person simply adapts.

Another characteristic of oppressed people is their diffuse, magical belief in the power and invulnerability of the oppressor (Freire, 1970). The powerful oppressors never make mistakes in English. They have everything they want. They easily get jobs and make money. In fact, life is easy for them.

Oppressed people believe deeply that they need the oppressors for their own survival (Freire, 1970). They are emotionally dependent on them. They need the oppressors to do things for them which they feel incapable of doing themselves. Thus, they experience a deep "fear of freedom" when confronted with the possibility of "liberation." They also resist their own movement toward liberation because they fear it will lead to greater repression by the oppressor. Thus, one deaf administrator at Gallaudet College last year told me that it was best to accept silently the official 1984 Gallaudet interpreting policy which forbade the use of ASL because things might get worse if we said anything.

In summary, the following are said to be characteristics of oppressed peoples:

- ambivalence between either embracing the feature which makes them different as a positive and essential aspect of their identity (resulting in group solidarity) or degrading themselves and other group members because of the feature (resulting in self-hatred) Another way to describe the ambivalence is as an existential duality in which the oppressed person both wants to break free from the oppressor and to become more like the oppressor.

- self-deprecation, parroting the negative evaluations of the oppressor; lack of self-confidence

- a basic distrust of oneself and one's peers due to a felt inferiority

- horizontal violence

- passivity, adaptation, fatalism

- emotional dependence on the oppressor

- a fear of freedom (losing the dependence) or of backlash (worse repression)

What I have read (e.g., Higgins, 1980; Schowe, 1979; Sussman, 1976; Berrigan, 1983; Padden, 1980; Glickman, 1984) and what I have observed over the past ten years suggests to me that the preceding descriptions of oppressed people are parallel in many ways to the experience and attitudes of many deaf people. In fact, during the past two years, I have seen some deaf individuals and groups analyze themselves along these lines. This is not to say that the preceding analysis fully and accurately characterizes deaf people. However, the apparent parallels do warrant our serious attention, especially toward the ways they help us understand how deaf people express themselves and how they interact with hearing people.

Characteristics of oppressor people

What behaviors and attitudes characterize members of the oppressor group?

The oppressor group is the dominant power group. As stated earlier, members of this group believe that their way of acting and being is the "best way, the "appropriate way, the "cultured" or "intelligent" way. The stigmatization of minority groups means that the ways in which they are different are viewed as inappropriate and inferior by the dominant group.

So a first characteristic of the oppressor group is their pejorative view of the oppressed. They view these minority people (who they, of course, do not call "oppressed") as inferior, not capable people, not trustworthy people, etc., etc.

Because the dominant group believes they are superior to the oppressed, they automatically assume that the oppressed want to change and to become like them. Hearing people often assume that deaf people don't want to be deaf, and that they would do anything they could to change and become hearing people. Thus, these hearing people are shocked to see that many deaf adults don't use their hearing aids. Similarly, hearing people often refuse to accept the possibility that deaf people would choose to remain deaf, even if a "miracle" operation could change them.

Furthermore, if deaf people reject efforts to make them more like hearing people, they are viewed as misguided children who cannot make proper decisions for themselves. This position was clearly articulated by a hearing doctor, Ménière, at the Paris school for deaf students (cited in Lane, 1984, p. 134):

> The deaf believe that they are our equals in all respects. We should be generous and not destroy that illusion. But whatever they believe, deafness is an infirmity and we should repair it whether the person who has it is disturbed by it or not.

The egoism of the dominant, oppressor group leads them to insist on their own importance, exhibiting a "take charge" attitude ("I know what's best for you," "I know what's needed here"), and a desire for constant control (to make sure things work out "right" — and that they stay in power!).

Another characteristic of the dominant, oppressor group is their paternalism toward the oppressed. "Those poor people need me; I'll take care of them." "I'm doing all these things to help them out." However, in fact, oppressors want to maintain the dependence of the oppressed; it re-affirms their superiority and makes them feel good about themselves (Higgins, 1980). And, as Lane (in this volume) adds, the dependence of the oppressed maintains the jobs of the oppressors.

Along with the paternalism comes what's called a strongly "possessive consciousness" (Freire, 1970). "These things are mine; they are under my control." This underlying consciousness is heard in phrases like "*My* deaf people" or "*My* deaf students."

A curious characteristic of oppressors is the desire for approval and even gratitude from the oppressed for their own behavior. We need them to tell us we're okay, that we're doing a good job, that we're good people. Poor people should be grateful for the tidbits we give them (even though the rules of our system often keep them in poverty and us on top).

Finally, one other important characteristic of the dominant, oppressor group is their fearful and angry reaction to attempts by the oppressed to become free. They perceive the liberation of the oppressed as taking away their own (oppressor's) freedom. When deaf people insist that teachers of deaf children should be skilled in ASL, hearing teachers become threatened and angry. They fear their loss of control, the control they maintain by using their own language instead of deaf people's. Liberation for the oppressed means a new sharing of power taking power away from the oppressors and sharing it more justly with the oppressed. The resultant loss of power feels oppressive to the oppressor (Freire, 1970).

Relevance to interpreting

How do these characteristics of oppressed people and oppressor people help us understand the many tensions and conflicts that interpreters experience in their work?

The first obvious insight concerns the recognition that most interpreters are hearing people, and that they are automatically members of the powerful dominant group in the eyes of deaf people. So all of the ways that deaf people think and feel about oppressors influences the way deaf people deal with the hearing people that they are using the interpreter to communicate with. Similarly, interpreters, when they interact with deaf people, run a clear risk of being highly influenced by the way oppressors think and feel about oppressed people.

Let us look at some specific situations to see how these things can happen. (Please understand that we are now considering general trends. There are always exceptions to everything.)

How many of you interpreters regularly get explicit feedback on your interpreting performance from deaf people? (RID audience response: 'Very, very few.") Why do you think deaf people are willing to sit without protest through an interpreted presentation that they clearly don't understand? Why don't deaf people ask for clarification when they don't understand?

Asking deaf people these questions reveals that they are used to not understanding, and that they blame themselves. Always the assumption is that the hearing speaker is smart and is being clear, but that it is the deaf persons' fault for not understanding, presumably because they are intellectually inferior. Often, the interpreter is at least partially at fault for the confusion, but deaf people still most often blame themselves. Why do they sit through it without protest? That is where the passivity and fatalism is seen — "there's nothing to be done about it; we can't change or improve our condition. Besides, we don't want to look even more stupid by drawing attention to our problems."

Many deaf people "code-switch" within a discourse or even within a sentence. That is, they switch back and forth between more ASL-like signing and more English-like signing. Why does this happen? Some deaf people say they are worried about looking dumb if they use ASL. Or they don't trust the interpreter's ability to understand them. Many deaf people today feel ambivalent about ASL — "Is it really a language? Really equal to English, or inferior? Can it handle all the things I need to say in this context? Yes, I'm more comfortable using AS,L, but what are those other people thinking about me? Yes, I m more comfortable using ASL, but I'm supposed to be using English." Deaf people's learned ambivalence about their language is a frequent source of confusion in the interpreting situation.

Or, how many of you interpreters feel that deaf people expect too much of you? You are supposed to be able to handle any and everything, no matter what time of day, how long the session is, or how mixed the linguistic preferences of the deaf group are. You are also supposed to understand everyone, deaf and hearing, to have perfect English, and make everything work out right. How many of you can relate to that somewhat exaggerated description?! (Audience response: pained laughter, many hands raised.)

These pressures you feel are part of what was meant earlier concerning oppressed people's belief in the pervasive, magical powers of the oppressor group. You are not seen as vulnerable. You are the powerful. You can make things go the way you want them to.

These are just a few examples of common problems that can be better understood by considering the characteristic ways that oppressed people think and act. I am hoping that you will do the same sort of analysis with the many other problems that you experience as interpreters, and see how it may be helpful to you.

I'd like to turn the tables a bit to consider what some of the common behaviors of interpreters may be communicating to deaf people. What do these behaviors mean in the context of deaf people's experience of oppression?

It's fair to say that the majority of hearing people who work as "interpreters are far from fluent in ASL and that most of them transliterate rather than interpret. What does it communicate to deaf people when "interpreters" don't know and don't use ASL — even when that's the preferred mode of communication for the deaf person? Is it telling them that ASL is not worth learning? Or that it is not really a language? Not a viable and respectable means of communication? Is it telling them that it is always deaf people's responsibility to adapt their communication to fit hearing people's, and in this case, interpreters' preferences?

What does it communicate to deaf people when "interpreters" say, "Oh, I know ASL," but then simply don't use signs for English words such as "is," "are," and past tense "-ed" — and feel debased by hearing people who treat their language so casually, and presume to know things that they don't? Or worse, are deaf people made even more confused by these false comments of hearing people — who are supposed to be the models of intelligence and power?

What does it communicate to deaf people when interpreters make up signs? (Would a native German-speaking interpreter make up a word in English when s/he didn't know an English equivalent for a German word?!) Does it tell them that "you deaf people don't own your language? We powerful hearing people can change it any way we please"? Or, does it tell them that their language is impoverished and that deaf people are incapable of deriving vocabulary to meet their own needs?

What does it communicate to deaf people when interpreters teach signs to deaf people? Or worse, what does it communicate to deaf people when interpreters correct deaf people's signs? Does it say that hearing people can take control over even this most basic part of deaf people's identity — their language? And that hearing people have the right to criticize how deaf people use their own language?

What does it communicate to deaf people when interpreters use all those artificially invented, initialized signs? Does it tell deaf people that their language isn't good enough, that it needs to be improved — i.e. to become more like English? (Imagine that some foreigner comes in and begins to change some of the vowels and consonants in your words to make them more like German. And you end up with words like "tsong" instead of "song." How would you feel? But also imagine that you were raised to believe that Germans are superior people and that you should try to be like Germans. Now aren't you confused when that foreigner comes in and attempts to change your language?)

What does it communicate to deaf people when an interpreter in a restaurant tells them admonishingly, "Lower your voice!"? Are interpreters responsible for the social behavior of deaf people? Do interpreters have the authority, like parents with children, to make deaf people behave according to the norms of hearing society?

As I reflect on all of these questions, I see that the theme of "interpreter control" occurs again and again. These examples also suggest the presence of paternalism and a pejorative view of deaf people shown in a lack of respect for their language and linguistic rights. Again, these are just a few of the conflict situations that can be analyzed in this way — i.e., in light of oppressed/oppressor power struggles in the deaf community.

In closing, this paper has presented some hard realities quite candidly, and it may have angered some of you. I hope, no matter what kind of response you feel today, that you will consider these things in your heart. I hope you will continue to talk with deaf people and with other interpreters about these issues. I also hope that you will find this way of analyzing the interaction of deaf and hearing people in terms of the dynamics of oppression and power helpful both personally and professionally, as it has been for me. I continue to struggle daily with my own impulses and my understanding of these things.

Afterword

Some thoughts on interpreting models

Perhaps we also need to take a second look at the basic interpreting model that many professionals now adhere to which views the interpreter as a machine — one who simply transmits the messages of one party to the other and vice versa. Although the interpreter may make "cultural adjustments" to accurately convey the messages of each party, still both parties are on their own; they alone must take responsibility for their interaction. The model assumes two "equals" who use the interpreter "machine" because they don't share a common language.

Yet, if the previous discussion of oppressed peoples fits even only approximately the experience and attitudes of deaf people, then we can see that the deaf person and the hearing person are not approaching their interaction as equals. In fact, it is unrealistic and naive for the hearing interpreter to make such an assumption and proceed on that basis.

Furthermore, is it really appropriate (and humane) for interpreters to make a unilateral decision about how they will handle every event, based on a machine model? Isn't that "more of the same" — hearing people deciding on how the deaf person should act (this time telling them to "take charge")? Let me be quick to throw in my "two cents" and say that this analysis does not mean we should return to the "old days" of interpreter paternalism and implied superiority ("they need me). We need more creative alternatives than the pendulum swing from interpreter paternalism to interpreter machine offers. We need a more humane model which is sensitive to the socio-political realities of the deaf community — which neither exploits those realities (paternalism model) nor ignores them (machine model).

To me, in fact, the first step needed is a painstaking examination of the ways in which hearing interpreters' behavior reinforces the old myths and keeps in place the oppression that causes the resultant attitudes/behaviors of deaf people.

Some may argue that until the oppressive paternalism is weeded out of the interpreting field, we had better keep the interpreter machine model, because it limits the damage that the interpreter can do. Perhaps this is true. Little progress can be made in developing a more humane model until interpreters become trustworthy.

In the interim, perhaps we could establish at the local level "dialogue teams" composed of deaf and hearing consumers of varying perspectives and interpreters of varying backgrounds who could reflect on these issues at regular intervals, give each other feedback, raise questions, and jointly work out problems. Perhaps these dialogues would facilitate the development of a more humane model of interpreting, which could be continuously modified as the community continuously changes.

Acknowledgements

This paper much benefitted from pre-RID conversations with several colleagues — Betty Colonomos, M.J. Bienvenu, Dennis Cokely, and especially Bill Isham. All interpretations, of course, are my own.

Exploration of Cross-Cultural Barriers: Hearing Children and Deaf Parents

Frank Coppola

Introduction

The focus of this paper is on providing an increased awareness of families of deaf parents and hearing children. We approached approximately twenty families in three upstate New York cities (Buffalo, Rochester and Syracuse). We conducted interviews and videotaped in people's homes. We feel that this method of production is superior to studio taping because the more casual atmosphere encourages more candid responses. Questions in the interview related to four primary issues:

1) interpreting,
2) the role of hearing children in the deaf community,
3) communication among family members, and
4) the role of deaf parents in the hearing community.

Findings

1. Interpreting

We asked young hearing children of deaf parents to interpret questions for their parents. We wanted to focus on the interpreting process and the linguistic competencies of the children. Young children often lack the skills to effectively interpret for their parents. Very few children felt comfortable in their role as interpreter and often resented being asked to interpret.

Parents would often prefer simultaneous interpretation; however, most children were unable to perform at this level. Parents often ask their children to assume tremendous responsibilities at a young age, consequently exposing their children to important family business. Parents tend to feel that their children should be willing to help and so cannot understand why their children resent interpreting for them.

Some participants felt the task of interpreting from an early age made them more responsible later in adult life. One hearing child of deaf parents felt more comfortable using sign language as his mode of communication during the interview. Perhaps this is because while he was growing up, all nuclear members of his family were deaf and no spoken English was used in his home. Later, while interviewing more families where no spoken English was used, it became apparent that there were two categories of these families having hearing-impaired children and deaf parents: one in which English was spoken in the household either by siblings or hearing aunts and uncles; the other in which no spoken language was used in the house.

2. The role of hearing children in the deaf community

Deaf people, whether parents or not, often view young hearing children of deaf parents as integral members of the deaf community. Parents bring their children to community events, bowling tournaments, golf tournaments, Christmas parties, and the like. As these children approach adulthood and develop stronger ties in the hearing community, their membership in the deaf community may move to a more peripheral status.

Participants with deaf siblings often felt a closer tie with the deaf community and experienced fewer of the frustrations caused by their bi-cultural identity. Hearing children of deaf parents who were not professionals in the field of deafness often felt totally removed from the deaf culture, except for their interactions with their parents. Those hearing children of deaf parents who are professionals in the field of deafness had more interaction with the deaf community, and presumably feel stronger ties with the community.

3. Communication among family members

Most hearing children of deaf parents learn to sign at a very early age. Yet, most parents feel that they cannot compete with their children's auditorily stimulated world; radio, television, friends and other hearing family members bombard these children with the sounds of spoken language.

Often the hearing children's linguistic competency in English supersedes their sign language capabilities. Parents may feel frustrated as they watch their hearing children easily communicate with a language they themselves have yet to master. Similarly, hearing children of deaf parents frequently feel frustrated as they try to understand the semantics of their parents' gestural language.

4. The role of deaf parents in the hearing community

We feel this issue is the most important of the four. Deaf parents frequently have limited access to their children's lives in the hearing world. Parents may feel overwhelmed by the hearing culture and often are reluctant to participate in their child's involvement with the hearing world. Some parents do not wish to attend PTA meetings, and school assemblies because they often have difficulty understanding what is happening. These are only examples; such reluctance is not limited to the academic lives of their children and often extend to the child's daily routine.

Parents often do not realize they have the right to request interpreting services. Contributing to this problem, children are sometimes reluctant to encourage their parents participation in the hearing world, fearing that they will be embarrassed by their parents' deafness.

Conclusion

As the rubella population approaches adulthood, they will be marrying and having children. Various statistics have shown that between 83% and 92% of these children will be born with normal hearing. Limited research has been done related to these families. Consequently, very few professionals in the field of deafness truly understand the complex nature and special concerns of these families. More research needs to be done with families of hearing children and deaf parents. Support groups need to be established as a way for the families to share their feelings and frustrations.

Warning! Crossing Cultures can be Hazardous to Your Health: A Look at Communication between Deaf and Hearing Cultures

Mary Beth Miller and Deborah Matthews

The Registry of Interpreters for the Deaf (RID) has seen many changes in its short history, many of which have been good. Yet, RID cannot be everywhere at once. The San Diego convention provided an opportunity for sharing both our achievements and our concerns, and for consideration of the future. The area we look at in this paper is how culture affects interpretation and the interpreting process.

To lay the foundation for our discussion, we begin with definitions. The first definition is "hearing-impaired." This is an umbrella term which covers hard-of-hearing and deaf people from birth to age eighty. It is too broad a term to accurately describe anyone. For example, if someone should lose her hearing quite by accident, she might experience a hearing loss (become "hearing-impaired"); she would not, however, become "Deaf." The Deaf mind and soul are the focus of this paper. The term "hearing-impaired" gives false hope for some sort of cure. By using "hearing-impaired," we soften the blow to parents of deaf children. "Deaf" seems *too* permanent. Other disabled groups have a single "label," i.e., blind, physically disabled, cerebral palsy, etc. and do not labor under "softer" labels such as visually-impaired, facially-impaired, and the like.

For a working definition of "Deaf," we use the following: persons who could not hear and understand speech and who had lost (or never had that ability prior to 19 years of age" (Schein and Delk, 1974, p. 2). All others who may fall into "hearing-impaired" are called "hard-of-hearing." For the rest of the paper, we discuss only Deaf people. "The deaf community is a group of people who live in a particular location, share the common goals of its members, and in various ways, work toward achieving these goals. A deaf community may include persons who are not themselves Deaf, but who actively support the goals of the community and work with Deaf people to achieve them" (Padden, 1980, p. 92). So, for our purposes, we use the term Deaf" as a cultural term. The culture of deaf people involves many areas, but our primary focus will be on the language of the culture, American Sign Language.

Although elaborate definitions are not necessary, we will mention "hearing" people and "hearing culture," as this is the group from which we get most of our interpreters. The primary language for this group is English. Still another group, interpreters, professionals in deafness, hearing parents of deaf children, and hearing children of oral deaf parents create a third culture we will call "hearing bi-cultural." According to Jacobs (1980), there are two groups of hearing people who could be included in this new hearing bi-culture. He states:

The first traditional group seems to regard the handicap first, and deaf persons as individuals second. Thus, their efforts have been mainly to conquer deafness by concentrating on the normalizing of deaf youngsters so they can "speak and listen" like hearing children, at the cost of their many other needs. They seem to be much more clinical and standoffish in their attitude, and to regard deaf people more like case studies than as human beings.

The second group has an entirely different attitude, they are more interested in deaf persons as individuals in their own right than in their deafness. They socialize much more often with deaf people and gain empathy that the first group does not seem to possess. Modern emphasis on Total Communication and realistic practicum methods, which include interaction not only with deaf children but also with local deaf communities, is producing an increasing number of hearing professionals in the second category, for which we are grateful. (Jacobs, 1980, p. 2)

Deaf culture has been in existence for over 200 years, but had not been recognized until linguists began studying ASL. Deaf people finally do have the dignity of recognition as a group with its own language and its own culture. "Culture" should not be misunderstood. We are not talking about ethnic cultures. To speak of the culture of the American Indians is to comment on their language, clothing, eating habits, religious beliefs and their ways of living. Deaf culture is not any different from hearing culture in the sense of how we live, work, dress and eat. Our religious beliefs are the same as any other cultural group. We have a culture because we have our own language, American Sign Language. Although ASL is the primary language of the community, members may choose not to use a "pure" form of the language. Deaf people will use ASL in conversations with deaf friends, club meetings and culturally-related activities. When deaf people are involved in community affairs which involve hearing people who use English, they may choose a variety of Signed English. Language use at the community level is flexible, but within the cultural group, language use is more restricted. Deaf people may accept, respect and even use English on the community level; yet they prefer the language of their cultural group. Deaf people feel a strong identification with ASL as their cultural basis of identity, but when involved in community activities will use another language which enables them to communicate with those who are not deaf.

In recent months, we have had innumerable discussions with culturally deaf members of the deaf community about themselves as consumers of interpreting services, their knowledge of the interpreting process and what they expect from an interpreter. We have been able to identify responses into a few general categories, as follows:

Deaf consumers

1. *Excellent Consumer* — knows the role of and how to use an interpreter; is skilled in getting interpreters out of "sticky" situations; enjoys working with skilled interpreters; refuses less qualified

interpreters; uses support of qualified interpreters to assist him/herself in professional growth.

2. *Misunderstood Consumer* — expects interpreter to take care of everything; explains everything to interpreter beforehand so that s/he can "handle it"; expects interpreter to become a friend; has never been trained in the use of an interpreter.

3. *Frustrated Consumer* — desperately in need of an interpreter; will accept anyone with signing skills; afraid to give feedback for fear of losing interpreting "privileges"; cannot tell if the interpreter is doing the job or not, because has never experienced a qualified interpreter; doesn't know to use the system to get what s/he wants.

4. *Abusive Consumer* — constantly frustrated; becomes a constant and chronic complainer; criticizes interpreters harshly; interpreters often decline to work with this person; lacks the ability to provide constructive criticism.

5. *Naive Consumer* — this person rarely uses an interpreter; has no idea of a consumer's role or that of an interpreter.

Hearing interpreters

1. *Sorry sorry Charlie* — always say "sorry" I can't keep up with the speaker; "sorry" I can't fingerspell; "sorry" I missed that sign, can you please repeat?

2. *Know-it-all Helen* — knows everything; gets involved in discussions about deafness with hearing consumers; dominates interpreting situations; usually has little contact with culturally deaf people.

3. *Mental Block Martha* — has attitude, "I can't learn ASL"; prefers "more comfortable" signs; expects deaf consumer to adapt and adjust to her skills.

4. *The Professional Interpreter* — focuses on deaf consumers as individuals; has goal in his/her work to facilitate the communication process; always tries to improve his/her skills; keeps up with current literature and research; encourages other interpreters; maintains at least some interest in community aside from interpreting; considered good role models; generally in great demand.

From these groups of deaf consumers, the major complaints are:

1. The interpreters don't understand me. I have to change my communication' to compensate for their lack of skills.

2. I understand my interpreter, but s/he can't voice for me.

3. My interpreter seems bored with work (apparent reference to lack of facial expression).

4. My interpreter uses signs I've never seen before (hasn't learned local signs?).

Why do these problems arise? Explanations from consumers range from "I can't work with an interpreter" to "That interpreter isn't one of us." Further explanation into the phrase "one of us" reveals that the interpreter is not knowledgeable about deaf culture.

What are the reasons for these problems? Some possibilities are:

1. Individuals taking a course in ASL are actually getting a form of signed English.

2. Instructors are not qualified to teach ASL and deaf culture; common misconception that anyone who can sign can also teach; lack of formal training.

3. Instructors who, although qualified to teach ASL and deaf culture, feel resistant to teaching for fear of losing privacy for their culture or fear of hearing.

4. Interpreters not getting enough visual training are therefore unable to "read" the deaf consumer.

5. The RID evaluation process does not place equal weight on expressive and receptive skills, i.e., it is possible for someone with strong signing skills but weak receptive to obtain a CSC level of certification. (Is this a form of cultural discrimination?)

6. Interpreters new to an area are rarely encouraged to take "local signs" courses, or observe for a time before interpreting.

7. There is no opportunity or encouragement for interpreters to be re-evaluated once certification expires.

8. Interpreters have not accepted differences between deaf and hearing cultures.

9. Deaf consumers are still in an outdated mode: "Hearing people cannot learn ASL; therefore they can never understand our culture.'

10. When hearing people do become fluent in ASL, deaf consumers feel threatened and experience a lack of privacy.

11. There is a serious lack of educational forums for deaf consumers to keep current on the growth of the interpreting profession.

12. Hearing and deaf consumers are unaware of the process of becoming an interpreter and its strengths and weaknesses; they could become more active in the process.

Conclusions

We have been looking at several aspects of communication from a cultural perspective — some problems, their sources, and their effect on communication. It is easy to become overwhelmed with the negative aspects. We would be remiss if we didn't offer some possible solutions.

1. First, and probably foremost, we would include deaf culture from the first day of ASL teaching.

2. Encourage students to insist on qualified instructors and inquire about a teacher's background.

3. Encourage interpreter training programs to include a segment on deaf culture.

4. Provide educational forums for hearing and deaf consumers as well as interpreters and sign language instructors to enlighten all parties about the field of interpreting, thereby calming any fears, clearing up any misconceptions and encouraging a cultural exchange.

5. Encourage RID to re-evaluate its evaluation process, placing equal weight on sign-to-voice and voice-to-sign.

6. Encourage local RID chapters to establish "local sign" courses to help new interpreters become familiar with new signs.

7. Encourage RID to re-evaluate interpreters whose certification has expired.

8. Encourage deaf consumers to take active roles in RID — as local supporting members, RSC interpreters, etc.

We hope this paper gives readers an added perspective on cultures as it relates to interpreting. As with all foreign languages, one cannot learn the vocabulary and ignore the culture. Additionally, it is our goal for interpreters to have an increased awareness of culture in the interpreting process.

Issues Involving Black Interpreters and Black Deaf

Phillip A. Jones

This paper deals with the dynamics of Deaf and Hearing cultural groups as they influence and interrelate with racially-based majority and minority groups. More specifically, this paper focuses on issues I feel are most relevant to Black interpreters and Black Deaf people. I attempt to describe the situation as it exists or has existed within the interpreting profession. I present information from the perspectives of Black interpreters and Black Deaf people. This information focuses not on solving the perceived problems, but more on stating the problems and how they may have come about. (This paper does have the purpose of improving and enhancing our profession; please keep this in mind while reading occasionally blunt, but sincere feelings expressed by minority persons.)

Differing definitions of "majority" and "minority" arose during the RID convention in San Diego. Typically, White Americans comprise the majority group in the U.S., and the word "majority" seems too non-committal. Therefore, I use the term "White" to refer to this majority group. Most of my research and information about minority groups relate to Black Americans specifically. Hence, I use the term "Black" to refer to the minority group. I believe, however, that the statements I make about Black interpreters and Deaf groups also pertain to other classic minority groups: Mexican-Americans, Puerto Ricans, Asian-Pacific Americans, and Native Americans. Despite these remarks, I hope that the reader will not conclude that I believe that *all* White people belong to the majority group and that *all* Blacks to the minority group.

Because we work in a profession which is overwhelmingly White, comparisons of Deaf and Hearing communities all too often describe primarily White communities. Linguistic and sociological studies, as well as more informal conversations, have centered on these issues and topics as they relate to the majority group. On the one hand, this is understandable, since most Americans are White; yet, it is highly unacceptable to me on other grounds. Let me list some issues which come to mind:

1) numbers, or per cent of population, are not an adequate criterion for degree of concern. If they were, less concern would likely have been given to deafness-related issues. Of course, we all likely agree that we do not wish to lessen societal concerns with deafness, based on the small numbers of people involved. The same issue applies to any other minority, such as Blacks;

2) many Black Deaf, especially those from what can be called more typical Black cultures and environments, have indicated explicitly or subtly to me that they prefer Black interpreters, sometimes even when such interpreters are judged to have less skill by (commonly elite) White interpreter criteria;

3) Black interpreters I have met over the years have expressed feelings of frustration related to the interpreting profession. Though these feelings could benefit White interpreters if they were aware of them, many Black interpreters are unwilling or feel unable to share these feelings. This situation encouraged me to devise a questionnaire for Black and Hispanic interpreters, based on the sentiments I was hearing. According to the responses, Black interpreters seem to feel that: a) the field of interpreting is "not nearly concerned enough" about minorities; b) the interpreting profession does not encourage Black interpreters; and c) that classroom training was not geared to adequate preparation of Black prospective interpreters to interpret for Black Deaf individuals;

4) Black interpreters, I feel, may be penalized in our profession for being mono-dialectal, in some ways similar to the way that Deaf people often are. That is, a Black interpreter fluent only in Black English would probably be evaluated less favorably than a White interpreter who is mono-dialectal in Standard English, a dialect which approaches, if not is identical to, the dialect of most White Americans. Based on the questionnaire completed by Black interpreters, I believe that many Black interpreters are fearful of the reality of this claim.

Black people being judged by White norms is an important issue as evidenced by a relevant situation which recently came up in Chicago. I addressed a group of Black and White interpreters and Deaf consumers at a recent workshop. One Black Deaf person stated that she has difficulty lipreading White Hearing people, but not nearly as much trouble with Black Hearing people. Then, a White Deaf person stood up and said her situation was exactly the opposite: relative ease in lipreading White Hearing people and relative difficulty with Black Hearing people. Would this Black Deaf woman, being evaluated for an RSC, be considered "unskilled" in this area? Would a Black (Hearing) interpreter likewise be penalized for strengths in his or her culture and language? These are timely questions the field of interpretation needs to address.

One renowned sociologist who has done extensive research on the differences of culture, society and styles of Blacks and Whites states that:

Clearly, the notion that American society is "culturally pluralist" is an impotent one if it merely *acknowledges* that people of different groups have different cultural patterns and perspectives. A culturally pluralistic society must find ways to *incorporate* these into the system. (Kochman, 1981, p. 62)

It seems that we professionals working in an area involving the Deaf minority group acknowledge Deaf people's culture and encourage its incorporation into "the American way." But we tend not to do the same with the Black minority.

We often do not acknowledge that cultural differences exist, as evidenced by our lack of public actions: lack of mention, lack of research, and, according to Black interpreters themselves, lack of concern. Having made very little progress with regard to acknowledging the cultural and linguistic differences of Blacks and Whites in a professionally meaningful way — a state of affairs I find embarrassing, since we lag behind most American professions in this regard — we surely are not practically equipped to incorporate these cultural and dialectal differences into the "structure" which now exists.

Kochman also states that "cultural differences among Blacks and Whites are often treated as an irritant, not otherwise receiving the attention they deserve" (Kochman, p. 160). In fact, he says, "there still exists a social etiquette that considers it impolite to discuss minority-group differences in public" (p. 11). This negative and unspoken rule of etiquette seems to supersede the personality of traits of successful culture-crossing which Brislin (this volume) discusses. That is, in the Black/White context, even though an open-minded White person has a sense of humor, positive self-concept and creativity, she still has little to help her deal with racial issues, since it is taboo to discuss such issues.

My hope is that our profession will start to discuss these differences and similarities for the good of our profession. This so-called etiquette thwarts progress toward providing more mutual understanding among interpreters, providing better interpreting services to Black consumers, Deaf and Hearing, and increasing the number of Black interpreters.

Interrelationships

Before we can effectively improve situations and contexts involving Black interpreters and Black Deaf people, we need to have a better understanding of these four groups:
- White Deaf,
- White (Hearing) interpreters,
- Black (Hearing) interpreters, and
- Black Deaf.

I will discuss each in turn.

White Deaf

There is little doubt that most White Deaf people are familiar with, and feel most comfortable with, interpreting situations in which their interpreter is also White. But when a White Deaf person is presented with a Black interpreter, especially for the first time, the approach to that interpreter tends to be different. White Deaf consumers will typically assume the Black interpreter is less skilled. They also tend to express or exhibit more surprise if that interpreter *is* skilled. White Deaf consumers typically spend more time long *at* the Black interpreter, when they should be looking *for* the message. If White Deaf people recalled how they feel when Hearing people treat them similarly, because of their audiological deafness, maybe they would be more apt to curtail such offensive behaviors.

Contact between White Deaf and Black Deaf individuals seems to occur largely as a result of geographical factors. In racially segmented, large cities like Chicago or Los Angeles, the two groups rarely converge. (I am sure we can all think of situations where this is not the case, but keep in mind that I am speaking in generalizations.) In other cities, there may be more contact because of smaller size and attempts at integration.

Even though it is true that Black Deaf people are subjected to similar kinds of inequities and frustrations as White Deaf in a Hearing-dominated society (see Hairston and Smith, 1983), pre-judgments among White Deaf toward Black Deaf is a reality for many, despite the common factor of deafness.

White Interpreters

Just as White Deaf people imagine interpreters as White, so the reverse is true: when White interpreters imagine Deaf people, they imagine them as White. Both of these groups may even go so far as to think that the Deaf Community starts and stops there. Let's take an example.

For the past few years, I have become increasingly aware that my White Deaf and White interpreter friends believe that the "Deaf center" in Los Angeles is the San Fernando Valley, specifically in Northridge, a predominantly White middle-class area. Lately, I have been pointing out to them that:

a) most Deaf people in Los Angeles do not reside in the Valley;
b) there are other so-called "Deaf centers';
c) the Deaf who live in the Valley are no better than other Deaf; and
d) they are exhibiting subtle aspects of White supremacy when they state or believe such.

Without going into further detail, I hope that the reader becomes cognizant of the possible dangers of this oppressive way of thinking.

I do not believe that this is an isolated occurrence. I would venture to say that this type of thought would be prevalent in other racially mixed cities across the United States. As such, this attitude echoes tendencies which have recurred throughout history. Since racism has such a strong basis in history, the goal of equal status for all is highly unlikely to come true. It also makes the dream of respect for cultural differences difficult, though still not impossible.

Racial arrangements in society, I feel, are a strong reason for the fact that nearly all interpreter training programs are in White middle-class areas. In these locations, they are best able to serve White Deaf people, and much less able to serve other communities conveniently.

The relationship of White interpreters and Black Deaf people is one of particular relevance to the interpreting situation. Various White interpreter friends of mine have expressed or exhibited discomfort, apprehension, and sometimes even fear of working in situations involving Black consumers. Some of these concerns may be justified. For example, in Chicago, White interpreters have been overtly intimidated by community Blacks. Yet, some interpreters handle such situations better than others. Those interpreters knowledgeable and familiar with Black culture are able to do their job successfully (Donna Reiter, personal communication). In another part of the country, New York City, one White interpreter was warned about the dangers of accepting assignments in Harlem and the South Bronx. She accepted them anyway, and found the paranoia of her fellow White interpreter colleagues totally unfounded (Nancy Frishberg, personal communication).

With education and a willingness on the part of White interpreters to understand and be comfortable with other races — who, contrary to common belief, are not "out to get you" — I see no reason why White interpreters cannot enter these communities to do their professional jobs, especially in the daytime.

Since there are so few Black interpreters at the present time, the relationship between White interpreters and Black consumers needs to be enhanced. I see progress in this regard, e.g., cross-cultural training for Black and White interpreters (Brislin, current volume). Cross-cultural training, though, will be most challenging because White interpreters often feel they understand Black people already. After all, many Whites have Black friends and colleagues, may have grown up with Blacks, and so on. Regardless, I contend that "exposure to Black people does not necessarily lead to understanding the thoughts, feelings and frustrations of Black interpreters.

Interpreters, especially Whites, are in a more privileged position, and may need to be made aware of the following:

...there is in fact no such thing as different races, not scientifically speaking. Despite all the years of investigating and charting...scientists have found no biological characteristics that belong exclusively to any one group of the world's people. Separate races do not exist. All we are left with are the scientifically meaningless variations of skin colour.... Yet there is racial inequality — inequality of treatment as between black and white people. So we see that distinctions based on "race" (i.e., skin colour) can only be understood as social distinctions. (Worswick and Hamilton, 1982, p. 1)

Obviously, as a profession, we do not allow distinctions based on biological factors, but it is perceived that we do indeed make distinctions and treat groups of people differently, based on socially, culturally and linguistically motivated criteria. The relationship between White interpreters and Black Deaf people also leads to my concern about our professional image. Presently in North American society, we apparently strive for racial balance. As a society, we Americans consciously want to achieve racial equality, particularly since inequality has been so prevalent in the past. I strongly feel that a basically "lily-White" profession does not enhance our image and will work against the very things we are trying to achieve.

White interpreters, just as do White Deaf, often exhibit what I consider condescending attitudes toward Black interpreters. This is evident by their surprise at our signing and interpreting skills. The amazement could be taken as a compliment, but all the while it is a slap in the face. It is an over-reaction that singles out Black interpreters as different and may take the form of patronization. I and many other minority interpreters are not preoccupied with becoming associated with an elite interpreting group and definitely do not set out to become tokens. Being members of a minority group ourselves, we tend to be in the field much because of a "natural" understanding and feeling for another minority group.

Black Interpreters and Black Deaf.

The following diagram (Fig. 1) shows possible contacts Black interpreters and Black Deaf people have with White Deaf and White interpreters.

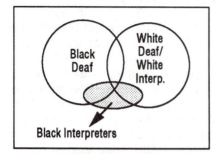

Figure 1: Possible contacts   **Figure 2: Necessary contacts**

More specifically, it reveals the "structure" to be the following:
a) A White Deaf consumer will invariably have a White interpreter and a White interpreter will invariably interpret for White Deaf individuals some time during his or her interpreting career (the likelihood of a White Deaf person never utilizing a White interpreter is so negligible that it hardly warrants mention);
b) A white Deaf person may or may not have contact with Black Deaf persons;
c) White interpreters may or may not have contact with Black Deaf persons;
d) White Deaf and White interpreters may or may not have contact with a Black interpreter;
e) Black interpreters may have contact with any of the three other categories;
f) Black Deaf may never have contact with any of the other groups.

Since the contacts a Black interpreter may make are to a significant degree voluntary, this structure is less important for present purposes than the next. Consider Figure 2 *(above)* which points out the number of contacts which must take place in the profession. I will discuss each one and some implications.

As with the "possible contacts," it is virtually impossible for White Deaf and White interpreters not to have contact. More interesting is the necessary contact of Black interpreters and Black Deaf groups, each with regard to the other two groups.

Black interpreters, as the diagram indicates, are the only group which necessarily must exist within other groups. That is, it is impossible for Black interpreters to "exist" away from White Deaf persons and White interpreters. This situation is inevitable for Black interpreters, as the vast majority of sign language and interpreting classes take place in predominantly White environments and are mostly taught by Whites. Let's take an example where this scenario might *not* be the case.

Only one sign language interpreter training program in the United

States has predominantly minority group students. At Los Angeles Southwest College, 96% of all students are Black. (The college is located in a primarily Black residential area of the city.) Even these interpreting students, who plan to work with Black Deaf populations, must have extensive contact with White Deaf and White interpreters.

These students, who happen also to have a Black teacher, become quite used to conversing and interpreting in situations involving Blacks. This is no different from White interpreting students who learn from White trainers. The crucial difference, though, is that these Black students, as with Black interpreters, must become familiar with White Deaf and interpreters as well. Two reasons for this come to mind:

a) nearly all sign language study materials, interpreter training materials, and evaluation tapes will include only or mostly White Deaf persons;
b) R.I.D. evaluators, as the present situation stands, are and have been White. Furthermore, they typically have a different subculture and dialect than these Black students.

This additional responsibility of Black interpreters who intend to work with minority Deaf groups is further aggravated by other factors. Based on answers to the questionnaire of Black and Hispanic interpreters from around the country, the vast majority of Black interpreters feel that their classroom training was and is not geared to preparing them adequately to interpret in situations with Black Deaf individuals. Similarly, most feel that their White teachers are not adequately knowledgeable of Black people and their culture to teach them, showing "appropriate" sensitivity. Those who did had Black or Jewish teachers.

So as not to paint a totally negative picture, I must admit that we do often encourage minorities and give positive strokes to some minority group members with certain characteristics. We applaud those persons who show cultural and personal traits more aligned with people of the majority group, i.e., those of many middle-class, usually White persons. We may applaud such likenesses as mannerisms, dress, associations, dialect, and so on. This, of course, is a natural thing to do. But the question is whether we should hold this cultural group as the "ideal" just because it represents the majority White group. This display of acceptance shows little regard or respect for the equally valid culture of Blacks. Black culture is not inferior, just as Deaf culture is not; it is only different.

Baker-Shenk (this volume) discusses the phenomenon of minority group members wanting to be like majority group people. She states it in terms of oppressed people often wanting to be like their oppressors. One of her examples — which, by the way, I found particularly offensive — was Blacks having big cars. I do not believe that Blacks own big cars or that Black interpreters take on behaviors and cultural traits similar to Whites for the reasons Baker-Shenk gave. Rather, it is more because Black people desire to attain, achieve, and possess what we rightfully deserve and have earned.

It is also interesting to note that one characteristic of oppressor people Baker-Shenk discussed is true; that is the case of Black and White interpreters. One Black interpreter stated on the questionnaire that "Other interpreters can't wait to say, 'I'm tired of losing jobs to black

interpreters because the black consumer prefers a black interpreter.'"
This is a good example of the characteristic of oppressor people who
have an angry reaction to sharing power with oppressed people, power
in this case being employment opportunities and money.

To summarize how many minority interpreters feel, I cite the following comments one Hispanic/Black interpreter made on the questionnaire:

> I want to state that I know full well what it is like to have (White)
> people appraise me on the basis of my color and culture accord-
> ing to their own misconceptions. I refuse to let myself fall into
> their own stupid "mental categorizing" .... My experience has
> been that if you do "good enough" and really facilitate communi-
> cation, then you are "fine." (Not what they expected, but I'm not
> looking to be invited for dinner, just respected, and paid!)

This interpreter points out clearly that she, as a minority interpreter,
feels that:

a) White interpreters have misconceptions about minority interpreters;
b) the issue of interpreting skills has an additional relevance for minority
interpreters;
c) minority interpreters are apparently not especially interested in White
approval;
d) minority interpreters want to be respected for competent work done;
e) minority interpreters are "just like everybody else" in that they want
to be paid.

Referring back to Figure 2, we see that the category Black Deaf stands
alone — Black Deaf people have no *necessary* contacts with White Deaf,
White interpreters, or Black interpreters. Black Deaf people are a double
minority and hence are more oppressed than White Deaf persons in our
society. If one ventured into the heart of many Black neighborhoods,
unfortunately it would not be uncommon to find Black Deaf people with
none of these contacts, whether social or professional. I have found this
to be the case in Los Angeles; even in this large city, many Black Deaf
people have never seen a minimally proficient signer or interpreter.

I believe that this is a serious reflection on our profession. Again, we
seem to be consciously or unconsciously neglecting a large number of
Deaf people who as a group have historically been discriminated against.
Hopefully, one day we will start to see change in this regard.

It is interesting to note that virtually all of the Black interpreters who
completed the questionnaire for Black and Hispanic interpreters have
expressed the desire to have a racial classroom make-up that is rather
evenly balanced with Whites (or majority group) and Black (or minority
group) members. Similarly, I would like to see an interpreting profession
which exhibits more balance.

Acknowledgments

I would like to thank the following for their ideas and moral support:
Dr. Tom Humphries; Ken Rust; the Chicago group; the Alberta, Canada
group; and minority interpreters who took the chance to express their
feelings.

Cross-Cultural Cross-Racial Mediation

Carla Mathers and Paula White

Introduction

Deafpride is a private, non-profit, community-based organization in Washington, D.C., which works for the human rights of all deaf persons and their families. The organization brings together deaf and hearing people and provides opportunities for them to develop their potential as advocates. There is a special emphasis on the skill development of minority group deaf persons and their families. Deafpride's main concern is to foster a national voice of deaf minority group citizens.

The nation's capital is unique in that the majority of the population are Black. Conversely, the majority of the interpreters who work in the city are White. With such a dichotomy, cultural mediation becomes a basic factor to consider for the professional interpreter and coordinator. This paper explores minority group interpreting issues within a majority culture using a cross-cultural/cross-racial mediation model. The model also applies to interactions between interpreters and consumers who are racially and ethnically similar but of different cultural groups.

The interpreting staff of Deafpride, Inc. has developed a four-step mediation model for interpreters. The model provides interpreters with skills for identifying potential conflicts and proposes strategies for mediation and resolution. This model can be applied to *any* cultural interaction; however, our paper will focus on the most pervasive cross-cultural encounter in Washington, D.C.: minority interpreting in a majority culture. Within this genre, there are two specific targets for concern: the dynamics faced by a White interpreter working in predominantly Black assignments and the Black interpreter in a predominantly White interpreting community.

The model

The model we are proposing borrows heavily from cross-cultural counseling theory. It is intended as a mechanism or tool for interpreters to identify their values, attitudes, biases and experiences in order to determine whether these may be disrupting the communication event. Much of the model will be recognized as a "common sense" approach to observing and understanding interpersonal dynamics. It is, in a sense, a consciousness-raising technique which encourages introspection to identify one's cultural biases and to accept and respect cultural differences.

To make sure that we are understood and that we all are working from the same knowledge, we would like to clarify the terms we use throughout this paper. People in our society enjoy notable differences in class, race, and culture. Society places positive or negative values on these differences through its value system. We operate on these values, which are ingrained through experience, unconsciously, and often without regard to individual differences. The experience of being raised in a specific culture at a specific time forms our attitudes. An *attitude* is defined as a mental position, feeling, or emotion toward a fact or a state. People are a product of their experiences and if one's experiences toward a particular class, race, or culture are negative, attitudes are also in danger of being negative. The interpreter mediating between cultures must know their attitudes lest their interpretation be affected. It is not the interpreter's place to make value judgments; it is therefore more crucial for interpreters to know their values to avoid possible conflicts.

In our role as mediators, we are the filter or lens through which our clients understand each other. Our attitudes can affect their perceptions of each other even if we are unaware of such projections. *To mediate* means to be a bridge between, to be in the middle, or to be a means by which; it is this function we serve as interpreters and coordinators. When we interpret, we are already mediating between two cultures; however, the deaf culture is the only one we know of which doesn't have an inherent ethnic component. The context is further complicated for interpreters when ethnicity is added, regardless of its nature. The risk of cultural misinterpretation and affected job performance is increased.

The final concept we define is the *cross-racial encounter*. Problems arise when our attitudes become barriers to our work, when we see what we expect to see and not what is truly operating in a situation. Knowledge of culture, race, and class differences is to be used as a guide for expectations, not as a prescription for behavior. Problems arise when two people of different racial backgrounds meet and their behavior or assumptions are guided too strictly by their expectations. People assume that if one is of a particular race, one automatically identifies with that culture These assumptions can impede effective communication and interpretation.

In this paper we focus on the dynamics of being a White interpreter in a city with a Black majority; however, we believe this model will be applicable to any cross-cultural interaction. The full model is in the Appendix. Figure 1 shows the basic steps one follows in using the model.

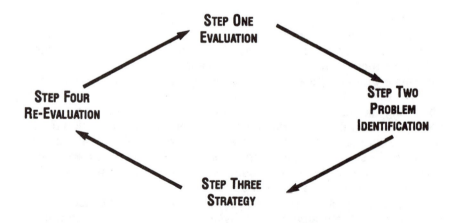

Figure 1: Cross-Cultural Mediation Model

Step One: Evaluation

The model is applied when an interpreter encounters a situation which is uncomfortable for no readily identifiable reason. In Step One, the comfort level of the assignment is assessed. Ideally, the interpreter and the consumer will both feel comfortable in the interaction and the model would be unnecessary. If, however, the interpreter, the consumer or both feel uneasy, the model applies.

Step Two: Problem Identification

Step Two allows interpreters to analyze their background, experiences, and values to determine whether the discomfort stems from these sources. Whatever knowledge of the culture or expectations its members may have that the interpreter is aware of will be considered here. For example, an interpreter was sent to a Baptist church in a predominantly Black neighborhood; the interpreter was asked to leave because she was wearing slacks In the interpreter's background, slacks were acceptable and appropriate in her church. Religion is a dimension of culture and formal dress is a requisite for attending certain churches. The expectations the interpreter held for the assignment did not coincide with those of the clients.

Significant experiences one has had with cultural groups provide valuable insight into what interpreters can expect from an assignment. The previous scenario can be used to guide the interpreter in accepting future assignments. The coordinator can also use the information to apprise future interpreters about specific requirements. Certain government assignments in the District of Columbia also provide examples of how previous contact can prepare the interpreter for an assignment. The racial composition of the city is reflected in the composition of its work force, and there are certain assignments where, from experience, we can be relatively sure of several factors which the interpreter will need to know. The first is dress, as most of these assignments are very formal and we receive feedback about interpreters who arrive too casually dressed. We can also anticipate that there will be music and songs at some point during a conference, which we need to arrange for. These are factors, whether cultural or not, we can usually predict and will better prepare the interpreter for the job.

If the interpreter senses that the consumer is uneasy (Step One), she may use one of several methods to identify the problem and its origins. The interpreter tries to understand the client's perspectives based upon direct observations of the client or situation, previous experience with the client or culture, and any dynamics occurring in the environment. Frequently, an interpreter goes to an assignment and the contact person will approach and say, "You must be the interpreter," or "You're from Deafpride, aren't you?" Since this happens so often, we decided to use the model to understand it. When an interpreter is confronted with this response, the first reaction is usually dismay, "Of course, but how did you know?" Sometimes the contact person will even openly say, "Because you are White." One would assume, not unreasonably, that this person had only dealt with White interpreters in the past. Their expectation is that they will be using a White interpreter.

Step Three: Strategy

Once the interpreter has determined the comfort level and identified the source of the problem, she can move on to Step Three of the model which is to decide on a strategy to deal with it. We propose two basic methods of mediation — either confront the consumers directly or do nothing until the assignment is over. To confront a conflict directly is admirable, yet it is not always the most appropriate strategy. Confrontation is a valuable tool, particularly considering the amount of energy required to suppress one's feelings. The diplomacy required to confront effectively is as great as the energy expended. One never knows how the situation will proceed after the issue is confronted.

Another choice the interpreter has is to do nothing at the moment and simply go on with the job. The ability to do this without affecting the interpretation will depend on several factors. Can the assignment reasonably be rescheduled? Is it an emergency? Are the interpersonal dynamics salient to successful communication? Is it a long-term or a one-time assignment? These considerations will help the interpreter determine the most appropriate course of action.

Step Four: Re-Evaluation

The final stage of the model, re-evaluation, is designed to allow the interpreter opportunity to reassess the situation and again determine the comfort level. This is where the interpreter implements her chosen strategy and evaluates its success. If one did nothing but continued with the assignment, what are the options available for afterward? Can advocacy be done possibly by the interpreting service or the local RID? How has the assignment enabled the interpreter to understand better his limits? Will he accept future assignments from the same consumer? Retrospective analysis is valuable for any assignment, regardless of its outcome.

Coordination perspective

Washington, DC has a history of being a predominantly Black city which differs from other metropolitan areas in that it has a well-established Black upper-middle class and middle class, as well as a significant inner-city, lower-income population. According to the 1982 Revised Census of the Office of Planning and Development, 70.3% of the general population in the District of Columbia is Black. In a recent article, Taft (1983) extrapolated the numbers of the Black, deaf population from the general census. She estimated that of the 5,500 deaf residents of Washington, 70.3% or 3,867 are Black. (Whether or not these numbers accurately represent the composition of the hearing-impaired population in Washington is an issue discussed elsewhere in this paper.) Assuming that we can extrapolate in this manner, the proportion of Black interpreters to White interpreters should also be 70.3%. Using the RID's estimate of 149 certified members in the area, 103 would be Black. Deafpride estimates that there are less than fifteen Black interpreters in the entire metropolitan area.

(For this paper, we asked both the RID and BRIDGES (an organization of Black interpreters) for figures on the number of Black interpreters nationally and locally. Neither organization could provide us with even a rough estimate; this demonstrates the need for a thorough demographic study of minority interpreters. This is a second area of concern this paper will address below; namely why in such circumstances is there a dearth of Black interpreters?)

February is Black History Month which is celebrated vigorously throughout the Washington metropolitan area. On the average, 15 to 20 different agencies and organizations will call and request interpreters for their particular events in commemoration of historical events celebrated by Black Americans. Most of these events will be interpreted by White interpreters. The coordinator must deal with countless requests for Black interpreters knowing that few specific requests will actually be filled with Black interpreters. Regardless of how much the coordinator wants to honor the request, in Washington the demand far exceeds the supply. Only a few of the Black interpreters in Washington are certified and most of them maintain full-time positions so they only interpret part-time, usually evenings and weekends.

The question becomes: is it discriminatory to request an interpreter of a specific ethnic and racial background? If one's policy for assigning jobs is by skill of the interpreter first, and if the minority interpreter is not the most skilled interpreter available, what are the referral service's obligations? Could it not be called reverse discrimination by non-minority members? Doesn't the requesting agency have a right to have whatever ethnic interpreter they desire for their dollar?

Another consideration is the feeling of those Black interpreters who may be insulted and offended by being contracted for an assignment on the basis of skin color. Conversely, the White interpreter who accepts a job where a Black interpreter was specifically requested often faces negative cross-cultural dynamics.

A related problem the coordinator must deal with is when there is a request to send someone into a "bad" neighborhood in which the interpreter may be placed in danger. We have requests for police interviews, home visits, clinic appointments and a myriad of other events, which are often in predominantly Black, low-income areas which rarely are visited by Whites. This is not to say that Black interpreters are safe in the same areas; possibly, they are just less noticeable. Racial antagonism is a reality in many areas and the coordinator is naturally concerned about the welfare of any interpreter she has assigned. Many times in these areas the Black deaf person may be uncomfortable with the White interpreter. Sometimes deaf social workers request a Black interpreter because they feel that the deaf client will be able to communicate more freely with someone of a similar racial identity. We have had hospital, police, and court emergencies when the caller notes the client is Black and deaf and specifically requests a Black interpreter. Sometimes they may be correct — some Black deaf persons use regional signs which some interpreters don't know.

The coordinator dealing with requests such as these faces another dilemma; namely, how does one honestly fill them? It is crucial to be open, honest, and to provide as much information as possible to the interpreter since no one wants to be met with "surprises" at the job site. If we are to respect cultural differences and honor consumer preferences, it seems that the situation won't be alleviated until there are enough Black interpreters to go around. Logically, then, our next concern is how to meet the increasing need for Black interpreters.

Recruitment

If increasing the numbers of minority interpreters will alleviate some of the tensions we currently experience, we want to focus on how and who should be addressing this need. Consider the number of interpreters who belong to the ranks of children of deaf parents and once again Blacks are under-represented. The questions become, why are the children of Black deaf persons and siblings of Black deaf children not looking to interpreting as a profession? Is there a general lack of information about interpreting as a profession? Are there no Black role models? Is there no sign communication at home and therefore siblings don't know sign language? We know from a survey of the clients of Project Access that the lack of communication is a characteristic of most homes.

One Black deaf professional we spoke with postulated that deafness may be more of a result of heredity among White families and therefore signing may be more accepted. Deafness among Blacks could be attributed more often to poor medical attention, sudden illness, accidents, or trauma and therefore the deaf person may be the only member of the family who is deaf. Another Black deaf professional we interviewed suggested that White deaf persons were more apt to be involved in the various deafness-related professions; therefore, their children may view interpreting as a viable field. It was also brought out that White deaf persons may take their children with them to interpret more often at various community events; thereby, the children at least learn the process of interpreting early Black deaf persons also share the same obstacles as Black hearing persons to equality of opportunity in this country. Many of the previous suggestions may be applicable to deaf families in general; we cannot be certain until there is definitive research into the matter. However, one thing is clear: there is a lack of professional Black interpreters in the field.

Deafpride interviewed many people while preparing for this paper, and all felt that the RID needs to take action in this area to recruit more minority interpreters. Shirley Childress-Johnson, founder of BRIDGES, states that, although the number of Black interpreters is growing, the idea of an Affirmative Action Plan on a national and local level should be explored. Nationally, the RID should establish a Minority Issues Committee or a Black Caucus within their structure. Locally, RID chapters and interpreter referral agencies should go to area high schools for

Career Day and present information about the field. One concern was that many Blacks who may be interested cannot afford to go to school for two years without support. This concern is obviously not limited to Black persons. Evening programs which would lead to an Associate degree would be helpful for many potential interpreters who are faced with the conflict of working and pursuing an education. Can scholarships or other forms of support be provided? A final resource which must be tapped is the federally-funded interpreter training programs which are charged with the responsibility to recruit and train minority interpreters. Local RID chapters must connect with them and show them how they can best serve area minority populations. In summary, the general consensus was that there needs to be a concentrated outreach effort emanating from the RID to increase minority participation in the field of interpretation.

Conclusion

In Washington, D.C., Deafpride works within a system which presents cross-cultural and cross-racial interpreting opportunities daily. In the majority of cases, our interactions are effective and successful; yet there are still cultural components which need to be respected. We have proposed a model which interpreters can use to determine whether there is a problem in the interaction and whether or not it is culturally related. The model capitalizes upon the ability to introspect as well as observe and analyze cultural information which might otherwise be overlooked. We have pointed out in our examples certain cultural differences which may affect communication if one is not sensitive to one's own values and biases, and also to the values of others. In a coordination role, tactful, and skilled mediation must be used when one is confronted with a request for certain racial or ethnically affiliated interpreters. Finally, the need for more minority interpreters is evident and the RID needs to address the issues of recruitment on a larger scale now more than ever before. Most importantly, interpreters need to look inside and be accountable for their own ingrained biases which may preclude neutrality. The Code of Ethics has effectively eradicated the problems which arise in obvious cases. However, here we deal with the more nebulous incidents which are often unrecognized. Culture is an attitude — it is individual. Interpreters must respect that. As for minority issues in the field of interpretation, it is almost as if we are experiencing a civil rights movement in the deaf community. For the first time, a National Deaf Women's Conference took place in Los Angeles; Black Deaf Advocates has grown to include a nationwide membership; and BRIMS has been established in Washington, D.C. Deafpride encourages the RID to get involved in minority issues at all levels.

APPENDIX
Cross-Cultural Cross-Racial Mediation Model

STEP 1
EVALUATION

Interpreter		Consumer
Comfortable	A.	Comfortable
Uncomfortable	B.	Comfortable
Comfortable	C.	Uncomfortable
Uncomfortable	D.	Uncomfortable

STEP 2
PROBLEM-IDENTIFICATION

Interpreter   Consumer

Background, Beliefs

Significant Experiences
with culture situation
(intensity, duration)

Knowledge of Culture

Expectations

STEP 3
STRATEGY
1. Do Nothing
2. Confront

STEP 4
RE-EVALUATION
1. Reassess Comfort Level
2. Withdraw from Assignment
3. Continue Interpreting

Interpreting for Southern Black Deaf

Anthony Aramburo and Ester McAllister

By starting with the estimated population figures of deaf people in the United States, we can assume that there are approximately 230,000 hearing-impaired people in Louisiana. Of that number, 75,000 would be classified as deaf. In the New Orleans area, we know there are approximately 35,000 hearing-impaired, and 12,000 could be considered deaf. Going a step further, we can assume that some specific percentage of these are Black. For the purposes of this paper, we are focussing on the minority Black Deaf culture who live in Louisiana.

It is rare that Whites ever attend social activities at the Deaf Club in New Orleans. If one asks the reasons, the response is, "That's the way it's always been." Older Black Deaf people seldom interact with White Deaf. Some club members feel it is because the two groups do not share common interests; most people, though, agree that there is a communication problem.

In Louisiana, the Deaf schools were segregated until 1978. When we consider that many Black Deaf adults never associated with Whites until after desegregation, we can easily see why communication has been a problem. The norms of the Black Deaf community and the attitudes of White Deaf were factors in how Black Deaf communicated. Another key to the situation are the differences in language. Blacks did not sign the same as Whites. Another reason is socioeconomic status. Most Black Deaf people worked as janitors or in the trades. On the job, they mainly socialized with other Blacks, whether hearing or deaf. For those who lived in rural areas and stayed home, their limited experience meant they were only able to communicate about what happened within their immediate community.

When we speak of Black Deaf communication or "Black Deaf signs," we do not mean that there is a separate language. We have already said that Black and White Deaf did not grow up in or socialize in the same environment. This created separate ways of signing. Naturally, the school situation had a great influence on how Black Deaf people sign. Eighty-five per cent of the Black Deaf people we surveyed attended the State School for the Deaf on the campus of Southern University, an all-Black university.

The State School for the Deaf (Black) was residential. At the time, teachers used the "Rochester method"; that is, communication was restricted to fingerspelling. Signs were forbidden in the classroom until the early seventies. While students were in class, they fingerspelled their schoolwork. Outside of the classroom, they were able to sign. During free periods and during sports activities, students communicated in signs they had learned from older Deaf students or staff, and also from a few books that were available to them. When sports competitions brought students into contact with youngsters from other Black Deaf schools, signs were copied and exchanged. Also, there were some teachers who were willing to learn more about sign language. These teachers had read books on sign language and began to teach the students to sign in their free time.

Prior to desegregation, then, these were the influences on Black Deaf signing. For instance, it was not until the late 1970's that the team from the neighboring all-White Deaf school was allowed to compete against the State School for the Deaf in basketball activities. When Black team members and other students began to communicate with the White members of the opposing team, all were surprised to learn that they did not easily understand each other. For some of these Black Deaf people, it was the first time they had ever met or talked with a White Deaf person on a social basis.

What is "Black signing" like? Signs themselves, and the order in which sentences are formed are different from White Deaf signing. Another noticeable difference is in non-manual behaviors: facial expressions and head tilts are used differently, and the size of signing space is larger. See Woodward and Erting 1975, and Woodward 1979 for more information on Southern Black signs. ED. When the schools were desegregated, Blacks began to interact with their White Deaf peers. For some, change came easy. For others, it meant frustration and failure.

For the most part, many Black Deaf students were able to learn and adjust their method of communication, and they have acquired the language skills necessary to functioning in the majority Deaf community. For older Black Deaf, who were not in school when the change occurred, learning new signs has come through socializing with younger Deaf. The older Black Deaf did learn this "new" way of signing, but they still remember and use the "old" signs. They go by almost unnoticed by those who are not familiar with them. Through contact with these older Black Deaf, younger members of this community maintain a resource and an identity with the true Black Deaf culture.

This is especially true for those Black Deaf who attended the State School for the Deaf and their children. Remember that this represents a very small percentage of the Black Deaf population. From our interviews with numerous Black Deaf in the New Orleans area, the children of older Black Deaf have a stronger feeling for the Black way of signing, and they recall those signs which used to be the norm. Of those Black Deaf with hearing parents, 92 per cent of those we spoke with said their parents knew no sign language. Most used "home" signs to communicate with family members. Siblings, in most cases, had more abilities in sign than the parents.

What about interpreting for the older Black Deaf or those who still maintain the "Black signs"? In order for these people to function in the majority society (Hearing), it is virtually always necessary to use an intermediary interpreter. The ideal person for this job is a Deaf person who has grown up within the Black Deaf community and who also possesses a good understanding of English. These are people with whom the client can be comfortable. We are not saying that no Hearing person (Black or White) can understand the Black Deaf client.

Our survey shows that the majority of Black Deaf who use an intermediary interpreter are those who had finished the program at the State School for the Deaf before desegregation. The use of an intermediary interpreter is even more important for MLS Black Deaf or for those who had no formal education. These people tend to socialize exclusively among Black Deaf, and their communication skills are based on Black signs. Other Black Deaf, who grew up using Black signs, have now adapted to the signs used by the majority of the Deaf Community. The ability to sign "both ways" is still apparent today. For instance, when older Black Deaf people communicate with Black Deaf age peers, their signing is different from what they use with younger Black Deaf.

In the interpreting situation, these issues are crucial. All of us, in our experience as interpreters, have seen Deaf clients nodding their heads favorably, giving the impression that they fully understand what is happening. It requires a lot of good judgment in those situations to ascertain whether the Deaf client is in fact understanding anything. Although some clients are not willing to admit it, they are doing well to catch even 60 per cent of what is said. Realistically, we cannot blame the Deaf person. Who wants to look dumb or stupid in front of others?

Clients often express their frustrations at not being understood by the interpreter or by the Hearing person. Frustration like this can be readily solved by including an intermediary interpreter in the situation. In New Orleans, for example, we do not have a single interpreter (Hearing) who knows enough of the signs used by older Black Deaf to communicate fluently with them. Therefore, we rely on the intermediary interpreters to ensure that communication is being facilitated adequately.

Interpreting: The Culture of Artful Mediation

Alan A. Atwood and David Gray

When asked, "What does an interpreter do?", most interpreters respond, "Interpreters facilitate communication." In the Introduction to her resource book *Sign Language Interpreting*, Sharon Neumann Solow writes, "The sign language interpreter acts as a communication link between people, serving only in that capacity. An analogy is in the use of the telephone — the telephone is a link between two people that does not exert a personal influence on either" (1981) Emphasis is on facilitating direct communication between the nearing and Deaf with minimal or no interference from the interpreter. Virtually Cry interpreter manual duplicates this view. Consequently, the standard model for interpreting (and the model behind the theme for this convention) shows Deaf culture (D) and Hearing culture (H) connected for communication through the individual interpreter (i).

(D) _____(i)_____(H)

It is our opinion that this model fails on two counts, one prescriptive and the other descriptive. First, the model tells us that while the Deaf and Hearing persons are free to draw upon all their skills and capacities as communicating individuals, the interpreter is restricted to the technical process of facilitating communication. That is, the model prescribes a behavior on the part of the interpreter that suggests the role of the interpreter is to be less a person than the persons who are communicating. People who try to eliminate anything personal from their professional performance experience a loss of self that results in confusion, frustration, anger and a significant reduction of job satisfaction. While the arrangement between Deaf and Hearing communicators described in the model reflects their interests in unimpeded communication, it does not satisfy the basic on-the-job human needs of the interpreter. Additionally, when used as a device for training new interpreters, the model perpetuates the self-concept of the interpreter as "non-person" and causes the new interpreter to experience, from the very beginning of her or his interpreting career, loss of self and isolation from a sense of personal satisfaction at work.

Second, in the same way the Hearing and Deaf persons are representatives of their cultures in communication, the individual interpreter acts as a representative of the culture of interpreting. The model fails in that it conceives of the interpreter as an individual mediating between Hearing and Deaf cultures. By focusing on the individual interpreter, the model directs our attention away from the influence that interpreter culture has upon the individual interpreter and upon the cultures of the Deaf and Hearing. The model denies the existence and presence of interpreter culture and ignores its influence on interpreted communications.

We intend to demonstrate here that interpreters are people who make up a community that is guided, maintained and regenerated by a culture all their own. That is, it is our position that interpreters act as representatives of an interpreter culture that mediates with and between the cultures of the Hearing and Deaf. We propose a new model of interpreting, based on the old model, with the addition of a third force: Interpreter Culture (I),

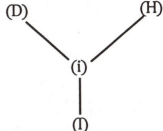

In the following discussion we will describe and elaborate this new model and demonstrate its superiority over the old view.

In a recent series of interviews with interpreters of various skill levels and backgrounds, many described situations and their personal responses that indicate widespread job dissatisfaction and personal conflict. Several typical stressful situations are described below.

Student interpreters often complain that they are being confronted with seemingly impossible requirements for technical skill yet believe they are not getting the training they need to meet these requirements. Many interpreters recount experiences in which they knew one or both clients were not understanding the message of the other; yet, as interpreters, they were bound by the Code of Ethics not to intervene. They were not even able simply to state, "This person does not understand what you are saying." As the so-called communication disintegrated into confusion, these interpreters sensed that they were being held responsible for the communication breakdown and they were prohibited from facilitating the communication. This double bind of not being able to support communication and being held responsible for its breakdown was profoundly dissatisfying and generated considerable internal personal conflict.

Women interpreters have been compelled to interpret obscene jokes in settings where the joke was not a matter of communication between the Hearing and Deaf persons; rather the intent was to force the interpreter to repeat the comments and play the "Let's-embarrass-the-interpreter" game. This amounts to blatant sexual harassment: yet one relatively new but skilled interpreter felt ethically bound to continue the assignment, not intervene or object to the way she was being treated. Later, she was afraid to report the incident for fear of violating the ethic of confidentiality.

Many interpreters feel professionally compelled to block their personal feelings while interpreting, yet find this impossible. The inability to eliminate themselves from their work causes some interpreters to doubt their competence as professionals.

Just before interpreting over the telephone, one interpreter was informed by the Deaf client that, "What I want to talk about is none of your business." The interpreter felt angry and did not want to interpret the call, but was compelled to perform the assignment under very stressful conditions.

Many interpreters are angry that they can discuss interpreting situations with interpreter trainers and coordinators, but cannot discuss them among themselves. They would like to be able to learn from each other and are frustrated that they are not allowed to share their experiences openly with other professionals.

Who is responsible for these negative experiences and feelings? Rather than blame interpreters for the unhappiness they feel, it is important to look for forces at work that are larger than the individual victim. When many individuals experience the same pressure as a group, one should avoid analysis that "blames the victim." That is, one must search for a force or forces larger than the individual person that is acting against the group. Two obvious social forces that influence the interpreter are the world of the Hearing and the world of the Deaf. A hidden but powerful third force rarely discussed by interpreters is the social world of the interpreter.

Much of the pressure interpreters experience from the world or culture of the Hearing stems from four sources: Hearing misunderstanding of the role of the interpreter; technical problems associated with changing communication from one language to another; the general fear among Hearing people of deafness and of Deaf people; and traditional sexist bias that discriminates against women and women's occupations.

Uninformed hearing clients who do not understand the role of the interpreter often mistake interpreter neutrality for hostility or bias in favor of the deaf client. Consequently, interpreters have to develop a set of techniques for educating the hearing client in order to reduce bearing person's anxiety and to educate the hearing person so that the interpreter can proceed without being called on to participate. This takes time and effort and often interferes with the interpreting assignment.

The difficulty of interpreting spoken English into sign language is underestimated by most hearing persons. Hearing persons often expect interpreters to perform unimaginable feats of communication and interpreters find themselves having to interpret language, as well as explain to hearing persons that certain expressions and idioms in English do not have equivalents in ASL. When ethical guidelines prevent the interpreter from explaining to the hearing persons that, "What you said has no meaning to this person," the interpreter can experience tremendous stress with no recourse to resolve it.

Fear of persons with disabilities is a powerful force in the Hearing world. Encounters with Deaf persons can be stressful and it is common for the fearful Hearing person to unload that stress directly onto the interpreter. The necessity of dealing with this extra tension—mediating this conflict between the Hearing person and his/her fear—adds to the already difficult task of facilitating communication. The interpreter has to develop a special set of techniques for dealing with Hearing preoccupation with "wholeness" and the Hearing person's fear of anyone who seems different.

Approximately eighty per cent of interpreters are women and interpreting is characterized by the relatively low levels of pay and prestige that plague the so-called "Women's Occupations." Additionally, women professionals in any occupation feel tremendous frustration from men peers and co-workers who do not take women as seriously as they take men. Women interpreters experience much of this bias on the job when they, as women in a professional environment, are required continually to demonstrate their skill in the face of chauvinistic sexist bias. Again, this only adds to the difficult task of interpreting and the overall effect is to increase the internal stress interpreters feel on the job. Women are sometimes sexually harassed on the job and may have little or no opportunity to defend themselves during the assignment or after the situation is over. Sexist pressure is very powerful and greatly increases interpreter stress.

In all, the pressures peculiar to serving the Hearing culture increase the already difficult task of facilitating communication. These pressures add to the technical requirements and generate conditions of high stress on the job.

Since most interpreters are hearing people, they participate in the general tension that exists between the Hearing and Deaf worlds. The interpreter has to mediate a personal relationship as a Hearing person in the interpreting situation in order to establish trust between her/himself and the Deaf client. All of this takes time and effort that adds to the burden of communication.

Deaf consumers of interpreting services are not always in.formed as to the specific task of the interpreter and may sect the interpreter to perform in a role other than that of neutral facilitator. Some Deaf clients want the interpreter to perform as advocate and, when the interpreter fails to do this, the Deaf person may respond in a negative fashion, thus increasing the problem of interpreting. A Deaf client may place extreme demands on an interpreter whose neutrality prevents her or him from complying. The Deaf client may consider this interpreter neutrality as bias in favor of the Hearing client and may respond in a manner that impedes communication. The interpreter has to work to mediate this conflict.

Interpreting students are encouraged to socialize with Deaf people in order to improve their signing skills; yet, when they approach a level of competency that makes them eligible for interpreting work, they are encouraged to stop socializing with the Deaf community in order to establish "professional distance" from potential clients. This trend among interpreters to socialize for a time and then to abandon their Deaf friends generates significant tension on both sides and tends to increase the level of distrust between interpreters and the Deaf.

Deaf men can be just as sexist as Hearing men and gender-related pressure from the Deaf client is no different from the pressure women interpreters get from Hearing men.

All of this cultural influence from the Deaf world adds to the tension interpreters have on the job and greatly increases stress. The individual interpreter on the job also experiences tremendous pressure from the world of interpretation. Competition is high among interpreters. Freelance interpreters who compete for jobs can easily find themselves at odds with each other over access to work. Employment depends on reputation and peer evaluation is constant among interpreters. The interpreter grapevine is a powerful force; anyone who gets into personal and political contests with another interpreter risks losing prestige in the field. Interpreting in the presence of other interpreters can be particularly stressful, especially when some interpreters feel compelled to comment on one's interpretation either after or during the interpreting situation. Knowing that other members of the audience are waiting for any slip-up compounds the tension the interpreter experiences on the job. Also, the risk to reputation associated with attempting to become certified and failing the evaluation can keep an interpreter from advancing. Lack of confidence — a product of the high stress of interpreting in front of one's peers — can keep a qualified interpreter from seeking the advancement that comes with increased levels of certification. This tension and low self-esteem move in a vicious cycle that drives many good interpreters out of the field.

Additionally, the ethic of confidentiality tends to keep interpreters from openly discussing their experiences in detail and can keep interpreters from finding a way to let off steam or prevent them from learning from the experiences of other interpreters. The lack of training programs available to interpreters makes the local interpreter the primary source of information. Interpreters do not often use one another as resources partly because of the atmosphere of tension that surrounds competition between interpreters.

But the most potent force operating against the interpreter is the lack of identity many interpreters experience. Interpreters report stress, anger and significant loss of a sense of who they are. This lack of interpreter self-consciousness stems from the general absence among interpreters of interpreter cultural consciousness. The loneliness and isolation many interpreters experience is perpetuated by the failure of interpreters to see themselves as a community with a culture. Interpreting is a culture in and of itself. Interpreters make up a community. Sign language interpretation has its own unique history, its own form of language, its own art and its own way of life.

Interpreters today are the products of a unique history that dates back as far as Deaf history. The earliest "interpreters" were hearing members of families with deaf persons and other people concerned about the isolation of deafness. We would call these people "signers" these days; yet their role in mediating and facilitating communication between Deaf and Hearing had a major influence on the Deaf Movement and the rise of Deaf cultural consciousness. As Deaf people moved forward to claim their rights as valuable human beings and the role of the signer became more closely defined, the level of skill and quality of interpretation improved. Early signers took it upon themselves to improve their skills and to establish standards for providing interpreting services to the Deaf. This movement to improve the skill of the interpreter shaped the way the modern professional interpreter goes about the business of facilitating communication. Today, it is not enough to be a signer. One must become skilled at a wide variety of procedures in order to render accurate and reliable interpretation. Interpreters are compelled to perform at a high level of professionalism; yet they often fail to recognize that this professionalism has required many decades of hard work and that interpretation today is founded on a solid heritage.

The capacity to draw upon and express oneself in two entirely different and independent language systems at the same time is unique to sign language interpreting. Interpreters, communicating with one another, switch from spoken English to sign language and back as they move from one vocabulary to the other in search of expression. Sometimes they speak and sign at the same time. These may be in parallel but often the meaning of a word is balanced against the meaning of a sign, with intended meaning hinging on both. Interpreters often pun in one language against the other. And interpreters in noisy bars can keep communicating when the band starts playing. This capacity to communicate in parallel greatly expands the communicative field among interpreters and provides technical means for self-expression in the context of a wide ranging cultural and linguistic system.

Although less than one per cent of RID certificates are Skills Certificate: Performing Arts, this specialization offers significant breadth of ethics that increasing numbers of Interpreters seek. In the 1980 edition of the RID *Introduction to Interpreting*, Stangarone and Kirchner write: "In Performing Arts interpreting one must exhibit a high degree of flexibility and creativity" (p. 80). Interpretive flexibility and creativity are necessary but sometimes risky tools in much professional sign language interpreting; yet they are absolutely appropriate for Performing Arts Interpreting in that they allow the Interpreter to *"function in a manner appropriate to the situation."* Performing Arts interpreters are gaining national notoriety for their artistic expertise in facilitating artistic communication. The theme of this convention, "Interpreting: The Art of Cross-Cultural Mediation," announces to anyone who did not yet know that cultural mediation requires an artist for an interpreter. Interpreter art is good for interpreting and the capacity for self-expression available to the Performing Arts Interpreter is, again, unique among cultures.

The extent to which interpretation is a way of life that influences the total behavior of the interpreter is a question best left to the individual. One's clothing, appearance, friendships, daily schedule and self-esteem are linked to interpreting ethics. Career decisions and personal goals revolve around interpreting. Although interpreting is a relatively small occupation, the world of interpreting is complex and broad-based. In some ways it moves with the Deaf world and in others it moves with the Hearing. But Interpreter Culture is its own way of life and it empowers the individual interpreter, as a representative of the culture, to mediate with and between the cultures of the Hearing and the Deaf.

What is the problem with interpreting? We believe interpreters are not communicating enough with each other. Our solution is that interpreters need to facilitate communication among themselves. This will reduce competition among interpreters and the stress of interpreting. Through communication, interpreters can learn from and support one another.

If interpreters deem it necessary to communicate with one another as a requirement of the profession, then perhaps they can use the new RID Bylaws to give themselves the right to do so. Regardless, interpreters needs to find ways to express their dissatisfaction in order to make interpreting healthy for the interpreter.

Cultural and Psychological Dynamics in Court Interpreting

Daniel H. Pokorny

No interpreting in any setting takes place in a cultural or psychological vacuum.

Among us, one hardly needs a dictionary to confirm the meaning of the word "interpreter," but let's look anyway: "One who translates orally from one language into another. In that simple sentence is a word which describes one of the most complex of human abilities, *language,* because as most social scientists view it, the use of language to symbolize experience and to communicate is man's major accomplishment. The word "communicate" appears prominently linked with language and that suggests that the process of using language (or for that matter of interpreting from one language to another) is commonly done in some group setting. The very root of the word communicate is community, two or more people.

While all this may seem quite simple at first, and might even be shrugged off as irrelevant, understanding the community nature of communicating through language (and so also interpreting from one language to another) will help us to get a clearer picture of environmental group forces which come into play as an interpreter goes about the business of his/her work. A rather sterile look only at the skill of the professional interpreter, without looking at the various settings in which the interpreting is done, can only lead to an ignorance about one of the most powerful influences upon the interpreter' s performance and the community's evaluation of that person and his/her performance.

Freedman *et al.* (1974) note the following about group dynamics:

Someone is sitting alone in a room working on simple mathematical problems. He works steadily and makes a reasonable amount of progress. Then someone else comes into the room and begins to work on similar problems. The two people do not know each other; they do not talk to each other; they have little or nothing in common. Yet the presence of the second person has a profound effect on the first one — he begins to work harder...

A young black man is in a Southern jail, accused of raping a white girl. There is no evidence against him except that he was in the general vicinity of the crime. A crowd gathers outside the jail, builds up, and gets more and more excited and enraged. Members of the crowd start talk of lynching and before long the crowd has turned into an angry mob. It rushes the jail, breaks down the doors, and drags the prisoner from his cell. He is tortured and killed in a sadistic orgy of violence.

These examples are representative of the kinds of effects groups have on their members. People are stimulated and distracted by being in a group. They respond to a wide variety of group norms and pressures. Being in a group or just in the presence of other people causes an individual to behave and think differently from when he is alone. (pp. 170-171)

If we note particularly the second illustration of group behavior, we are struck with the power of the group in connection with a legal situation (someone was in jail awaiting trial) and their following through with an action that was totally irrational, not to mention illegal and despicable!

No interpreter who is involved in a serious legal interpreting situation exists outside of the community of deaf persons who have an interest in the proceedings. A look, therefore, at the group dynamics and at the psychological and social pressures which are involved here will help us to formulate some strategies to cope with the situations which develop.

No matter where the interpreting is done or under what circumstances, there are overtones which play a major role in how the interpreter and interpretation is perceived by deaf and hearing consumers.

To have a point from which to explore the situations, let's just assume for the moment that Myers (1967) description is a clear summary of the situation.

When any man is involved in a lawsuit or a legal proceeding, he may be dragged against his will into court. When he is deaf, he must sit there and watch other people make arguments that he cannot hear, about problems that he may not understand, using a special procedure that he may not comprehend, to arrive at a result about which he may not even be told. He may feel completely lost in court, not understanding what is wrong, what he is supposed to do, and why things must be done in a particular way. (p. 5)

We would have to admit that a rather bleak picture is painted by this author, himself deaf. It implies that a deaf person involved in a court case is quite unable to understand what is going on, and has little experience to help him or her assess the propriety of the proceedings. From this lack of experience, it is entirely possible that conclusions about the proceedings will be drawn which have no basis in fact.

Let me illustrate with two examples from a recent court proceeding held in the St. Louis area. Two deaf men were accused of killing a third deaf man living in their apartment complex. They were arrested and incarcerated in the city jail awaiting trial. Since the two accused of murder had limited English skills, and other psychological problems, the lawyers from the public defender's office decided to seek psychological testing of the two men, with the hope that there might be a ruling in the case that the two were incompetent to stand trial.

To do this testing, a considerable amount of time was needed, and various interpreters were used. As the case was prepared for trial, it was apparent that skillful interpreting was necessary and the attorneys were apprised of this. Their response was to resist attempts by the courts to just hire "any old interpreter," but to seek one of the best qualified interpreters in the country, even if it meant that someone with superior skills had to be brought in at high expense to the court. Obviously, all of this contributed to the length of time that the two men were in the city jail awaiting trial and led to a number of postponements of the trial itself.

How did the community with interest in the trial perceive the matter? In a statement prepared for presentation at a chapter meeting of the St. Louis RID, the father of the victim noted that the interpreters were responsible for the delays! This was, of course, not the case. Interpreters have no power or authority to delay any trial. Indeed, in this very case, the court even issued subpoenas to interpreters, which demanded that they be in the court to interpret at the times required. For an interpreter to delay under those circumstances would be to place himself or herself in contempt of the court!

This misunderstanding led to a general feeling of ill will among those in the St. Louis "deafness community." To suggest that the two men on trial needed to have qualified interpreting services from outside of the community seemed to imply that most of the interpreters in the St. Louis area were incompetent. To search for "super-qualified" interpreters and prepare a defense for the accused required considerable time (more than two years) and this was seen by the community as delaying tactics caused by interpreters.

Working on such a case with those sort of feelings spinning around would naturally influence those interpreting in the case. Not only would such interpreters feel a need (as they always should) to do the best job possible in this situation, but also the need to defend all actions and work, lest they be criticized later. While the feelings do not oppose one another, the mix in the end is hardly conducive to "ideal" interpreting.

In another sense, there is also the feeling of being constantly on display. A courtroom is a public place where anyone may come in and observe the proceedings. Many who watch an interpreter at work, are awed by the mystery and "beauty" of it all. In their untrained eyes, the interpreter can do no wrong and anyone with skills to "talk" with his or her hands most certainly must be able to communicate with all deaf people. Comments made to an interpreter about the wonder of the task might boost the ego for a while, but one soon realizes that the tributes are hollow and so there is little support gained from them; and the interpreter is once more left in the middle of the tension described above.

This fact that the court room is a public place presents yet another problem for the interpreter. When a deaf person is on trial, that person is entitled to the rights and privileges of any other citizen in such a circumstance. One of those rights is that communication between defendant and attorney is confidential and protected. Since sign language is a visual form of communication, if a deaf person wishes to communicate with his or her attorney, he or she must sign to the interpreter who can then whisper the message to the lawyer. Unfortunately, if there are persons in the courtroom who are able to understand sign language, these persons have "access" by sight to this privileged communication.

To prevent such eavesdropping it became necessary in the St. Louis trial to erect a temporary "wall" barrier in the courtroom. When this was done, many in the courtroom audience remarked that they were being denied their ability to view and learn from the proceedings. A feeling of resentment seemed to develop against the interpreters working the case who were now no longer easily visible. (In this case the "wall" only blocked the view of the defense table, but it did make it difficult to see any of the interpreting in the case as well.)

Of course, the question of monitoring the interpretation, so that there be some assurance that the interpreters were doing a good job, also entered into this situation. Notice, however, that the working out of some sound legal principles and procedures resulted in all sorts of emotional responses on the part of many deaf and hearing persons in the community.

It should be evident from the above that there really is a psychological and emotional component involved in any legal proceeding. This component creates, in many instances, a charged atmosphere in which the interpreter must function, an atmosphere which may work counter to the best interests of all involved.

The problem is that most people have little experience in a court of law. Their only concept of what goes on there grows out of what they see on television or read in books. For most this means that there are "good guys and bad guys" and the good guys should always win. Principles of truth and honesty are held by most. Only a fool would come out against truth or honesty or oppose the "good" guys. We all do, after all, support these basic principles, don't we?

So it goes in the reasoning of the general population. Deaf persons usually pick up on such principles and feel the same way about how things should be handled. Unfortunately, while many believe that a court of law is there to support truth and honesty, in reality it doesn't always work that way. A defense lawyer may not be very interested in letting all the truth get out, but wish to suppress as much as possible in order to win his or her case.

Now suppose that a deaf person is on trial for a serious crime and suppose that the deaf community is basically convinced that he or she is guilty of having committed the crime, what sort of feelings will be held by members of the deaf community? Most likely, many will feel that the evildoers should be punished. They are presumed guilty in the minds of most. This position, of course, is contrary to the law, but is generally held by almost everyone who reads a newspaper story about someone who has been accused of a crime. The purpose of the workings of a grand jury hearing usually are unknown to the general public. People feel that someone caught and charged is probably guilty.

It will come as no surprise then, that within the deaf community, many will feel that those accused are guilty even before the trial has begun. To aid such a person (and that is precisely what is assumed is taking place when one is interpreting for the accused) is perceived to be a clever ploy or trick to try to prevent the person s getting his or her just punishment. If taken to its conclusion, then, the interpreters working in such a case are clearly linked to those who are presumed to be evildoers and often seen as setting up obstacles to justice! Here again, with feelings like that floating around, can any interpreter feel that he or she is working in anything less than a very charged emotional situation?

Let us return, however, to the point raised a little while earlier — the system may not be as interested in truth as the general population believes. Saks and Hastie (1978) make this point:

> Probably the most controversy about determining the criminal's state of mind surrounds the legal issue of the insanity defense.... The rationale for the insanity defense against criminal responsibility is that a person who is insane, mentally ill, driven b an irresistible impulse, or unable to distinguish right from wrong lacks the capacity for free choice.

> The criticism is that lawyers are interested not in truth, but in winning — and in the pursuit of victory they are highly selective about what they look for and in the cases they present. (p. 205)

Some of the most famous "deaf" trials are those which have involved the "ability to stand trial" question. This point, closely related to the insanity defense, comes up in two rather widely known trials, one in Chicago and one in Indianapolis. While the details may not fit exactly the situation of those cases, let us assume that part of the problem was communication, or more specifically, communication in the English language. If persons in the deaf community who have skills in ASL look at the situation, they are likely to find it hard to believe that there is a communication problem. After all, *they* have no problem communicating with the person on trial. How could anyone, therefore, suggest such a thing? Their assessment of it could very well be that it's all a plot to suppress the truth and let the deaf person, who is guilty, go free!

So the defense lawyer is trying to prove that communication is limited or impossible and the prosecutor is trying to show just the opposite. Assuming that neither of them are experts in sign language communication, we see that both sides are very dependent on interpreters or experts on deafness. Since interpreters are usually more prevalent, more available and cost less money than experts on deafness, who gets caught in the middle? Right, the interpreter!

Now a professional who usually works harmoniously with his or her peers is cast in a role as a resource against another interpreter! This situation has built into it all sorts of charged emotional and psychological components which could greatly influence the performance of the interpreters in the case and spill over into the deaf community. One who takes a position opposite that held generally by the majority could be viewed by the community as a "trouble maker" who should be isolated and put "outside of the camp."

No longer is there a group of nice people all working together for the common good (as they are used to doing); now you have a fractured and split community in which persons may take sides and pre-judge others.

These points from the St. Louis case may serve to illustrate some of the above ideas. One interpreter (designated interpreter "A") was seated at the table with the defendant and his attorney. Interpreter A was responsible for communication between the attorney and the defendant in private (note comments about "wall" above). Also working in the courtroom were two other "sworn" interpreters (B and C) who, as a team, interpreted all the proceedings of the court for the defendant. If one were to enter the courtroom and observe the situation, one could easily get the impression that the interpreters were "ganged up" on the defendant's side of the room.

Such an observation was made by the prosecutor in this case, who then made a special request of the court that another interpreter (D) be allowed to sit at the prosecution's table and give advice about the nature of the sign language proceedings and to act as an "expert" on deafness. As might be expected, there were objections made by the defense to such a proposal, but in the end the judge did allow interpreter D to sit with the prosecutor and give information.

The case then involved four interpreters! In order to ensure that everyone's rights were protected and no one had an unfair advantage, this seemed to be the only solution. Notice, however, how you now have four people who in most other situations would work together as a team, now cast in the role of keeping tabs on one another and in some instances acting as adversaries. This situation certainly had its emotional and psychological side, influencing all the parties involved. Such feelings were not really a problem for the attorneys who could be arguing with one another in a most hostile-looking fashion and then go out together as friends for happy hour after the court was adjourned for the day!

One final observation needs to be made before we move on to possible ways of coping with such situations. When every word spoken is being recorded by a steno-typist, the words seen to have a *de facto* aura of importance about them. If, in addition, some words have meaning in a legal sense beyond their meaning in normal conversation, the choice of words can become not only important but crucial.

An example of this came up in the St. Louis trial as well. The prosecutor seemed to be trying to create a bad reputation for the defendant. In order to do this, various witnesses were brought to testify about wild parties and such, which had preceded the killing. One such party involved a young deaf woman who had sexual intercourse with one of the defendants at the party. The legal question involved here was whether or not the young woman was *raped*. There was rather a lengthy debate in chambers between attorneys, interpreters and judge. Rape is a word which describes a crime; however, to have intercourse under wild party circumstances is not. Obviously the prosecutor was interested to have the word "rape" spoken during the course of the proceedings and the defense was not. The interpreter was caught in the middle!

Strange proceedings, a highly charged emotional atmosphere, a person's life resting in the balance of every word spoken, and the general misunderstanding connected with legal proceedings, can all lead to interpreter problems. However, the situation is far from hopeless and much can be done to "ease the pain" of interpreting in such settings.

While it may sound simplistic at first, I feel that many of the problems noted above can be solved if interpreters and members of the deaf community become aware of them. It is much easier to succeed against a foe who is known than to fight the unknown.

It is curiously, however, not the case now. There is very little which is being written or done to raise awareness of the emotional and psychological problems which are involved in courtroom interpreting. It is to the credit of the 1965 edition of "Interpreting for Deaf People" that this problem was touched on briefly in the article on interpreting in legal situations. The introductory paragraph to "when the interpreter becomes emotional" is

It sometimes happens that the interpreter may become so emotional during the court proceedings as to make his work ineffective. This could happen if the interpreter knows the deaf persons involved; if the lawyers put undue pressure on the interpreter; or if the general emotional climate gets out of hand during the proceedings. Suggested techniques would include the following:

1. Self-discipline...

2. Reaffirmation of rights...

3. Excuse from the case...

(Quigley and Youngs, p. 52)

Notice that many of the situations involving the psychological and emotional pressures I noted earlier are not mentioned among the difficulties. This will not help to raise awareness of the factors involved and so will not help the interpreter in such a setting to cope with them.

Under the index headings of "emotional" or "psychological" in Myers' book, one finds only a brief note that deaf persons in court are often emotionally or psychologically disturbed. This, too, is not very helpful, since it doesn't address the group dynamics nature of the problem.

In 1970, the Council of Organizations Serving the Deaf (COSD) held a national forum in Chicago on the theme, "The Deaf Man and the Law." A mock trial was held during which a challenge was made concerning the competency of an interpreter (one of the emotion-charged situations I noted earlier). This is the only instance in the whole forum that the emotional and psychological questions of legal interpreting were apparent, but the thrust of the mock trial situation was really to indicate how to handle an interpreter challenge legally.

Judge Rolloff

Mr. Henderson, there is a question being raised as to whether this interpreter 15 really interpreting accurately. (He indicates the interpreter standing beside witness. It was decided prior to trial to challenge some interpreter, to indicate the importance of using a skilled qualified interpreter.)

Q. Now are you really telling us the exact words that the witness stated?

A. Yes, I am.

Q. Are you in any way interpolating what she says and changing it?

A man from the audience (Rev. Pokorny — sic!)

I object, your Honor. She was asked at *what point* did her car enter the intersection. The interpreter said at *what time*.

Mr. Henderson

If Rev. Pokorny would like to request a sidebar and indicate that his expertise is greater, I think that the Court would be willing to listen...

Judge Rolloff

Members of the jury, a question has been raised as to the competency of the interpreter. The Court has an official interpreter and the Court will ask to have her sworn to determine whether the interpreter who was here is competent. (pp. 50-51)

This excerpt clearly shows that there was a great deal of interest in the competency question and the situation of the mock trial was devised to explore that area. What is also clear is that the emotional component of the challenge was completely overlooked in the presentation or the discussions which followed it. However, that it happened at all is a step in the right direction, since this is the only way that interpreters and deaf people will be able to become more familiar with court proceedings and the psychological and emotional stresses of them.

In an article in the *Archives of Environmental Health* (1967) it was noted by Switzer and Williams that deaf people have various life problems. Such problems often center around their being cut off from the mainstream of social experience because of communication difficulties. The authors note that such deprivations are often compensated for by the copying of various social institutions within the deaf "world" itself.

Effectively isolated by his communication problem from sharing meaningfully with most of those with whom he rubs shoulders in the community, in the home, and on the job, the deaf person has sought and created special means to compensate. The chief characteristic of these means is that the communication barrier has been eliminated since all members use the sign language. The result is that deaf people move in and out of the larger culture according to their needs of the moment but always have available a complex of their own resources that enables them to live happy, reasonably balanced, and profitable lives. (pp. 249ff.)

From this we learn that deaf people experience political, social and religious institutions within their own world. A deaf person who is an officer of a deaf club has the opportunity to learn what democracy means and becomes familiar with it. No parallel exists within the deaf world in which a person may learn of the legal and judicial system. There is to my knowledge no deaf court. It would be well, therefore, for schools for the deaf and other training facilities to set up mock trials for students so that this important part of life may not also go unexperienced. The discussions following such a trial should not only deal with the legal terminology and processes presented, but also with the emotional and psychological components related to what was happening.

Finally, no program of interpreter training should be without a unit in the curriculum designed to assist interpreting students to handle the emotional and psychological problems of legal interpretation. RID chapters and the national RID would do well to address this issue also at regional and national meetings so that interpreters become more familiar with the situations and might more easily cope with the problems.

After all, the problem is real and the group dynamics are powerful! In his report on the St. Louis trial, Roberts wrote the following:

> Two psychologists testified for the defense that Spivey had a borderline personality and "atypical psychosis" at the time of Eisenberg's death.

> They testified that Spivey suffers from delusions and has trouble keeping touch with reality.

> Testimony by two state witnesses with expertise in psychiatry and psychology disputed the diagnosis that Spivey had suffered atypical psychosis but agreed he had a borderline personality, which is not considered a mental disease or defect.

> The trial required the use of three interpreters of sign language. Two interpreted the testimony of witnesses and remarks from the judge and attorneys. Spivey and his attorney conferred through a third interpreter.

> In her closing argument Saturday, Judy K. Raker, the assistant circuit attorney, asked the jury to return a guilty verdict to send a clear signal to the deaf community that murder is unacceptable behavior. (p. 15B)

Right or wrong, this last paragraph says quite clearly that legal interpreting is a *group activity*. The circuit attorney saw it as influencing the deaf community a part of which are the many interpreters who had an interest in the case, and other deaf persons who had an opinion about the case. The more we can do to understand and prepare for the group feelings involved in such cases, the better we will be able to interpret them in a professional and expert way for the benefit of all.

The Interpreter as Cross-Cultural Mediator.
How Does a Student Learn to do It?

Judy Liu Cavell and Mary Wells

Introduction

Currently in most interpreter training programs, the emphasis is on language usage and/or acquisition. Within a given curriculum, novice interpreters are prepared to cope with varied language and service settings. Students, however, are not always prepared to cope with the effect rich differences between hearing and deaf cultures will have on them and their performance of the interpreter role. It is one thing to know the cultural differences intellectually. It is quite another to experience and recognize the effects of those differences in everyday life.

While the program at Madonna College requires student participation in Deaf Community activities, faculty have observed that student cultural experiences were often haphazard, incomplete and very stressful. To supplement actual interaction with the Deaf Community, it was necessary to provide a controlled simulated setting which could provide:

1) exposure to a full range of issues specific to cross-cultural situations;

2) a safe arena with a controlled environment to minimize risk-taking; and

3) a reference point for consistent learning.

In addition, aspects of cultural interaction which either facilitate or impede successful communication were identified. These aspects include group structure, stress sources and inter-group dynamics.

This paper describes the simulation experience currently being used at Madonna College, including the simulation process and direct applications to interpreter training.

Background

Madonna College is a private, liberal arts college which offers a four-year Bachelor of Arts degree in Sign Language Studies (SLS). Madonna's program offers students the opportunity to develop ASL skills as well as an understanding of the language and its community. In order to complete the SLS major, students are required to complete thirty-one SLS core credit hours. Students pursuing the B.A. in SLS may choose a concentration in Sign Language Interpretation which requires an additional twenty-two credit hours of coursework at the 400 level.

Students are exposed to the concepts of Deaf culture and community in SLS 100, *Introduction to Sign Language Studies*, a survey course which presents topics of interest in ASL, Deafness, and the Deaf Community. The remaining core courses are for the purpose of ASL skills development.

Because direct contact with Deaf community members is seen as an invaluable tool for learning, students are given assignments within the core curriculum which require documentation of contact hours and/or written or oral reports about the experience. The following is an overview of courses which require contact activities.

SLS 101 — Beginning American Sign Language

Students are required to document fifteen hours of ASL practice time. This practice is to focus on topics of personal interest, i.e., vacation, work, friends, etc. Students are encouraged to seek a practice partner who is Deaf.

SLS 202 — Intermediate American Sign Language

Students are required to attend a social function that requires interaction with Deaf people using ASL. They must submit a written report to the instructor, discussing personal reactions describing the activity.

SLS 231 — Deaf Culture

This is an elective course offered to SLS students which is a survey of factors that contribute to defining Deaf persons as a cultural minority. This course is taught by a Deaf instructor.

SLS 301 — Advanced American Sign Language

Students are required to visit two sites. The first assignment is to visit and observe one of the six designated, local sites which offer educational programming for Deaf students. Students are to write a paper discussing their reactions to the experience focusing on activities observed and communication modes used by teachers and Deaf students. The second assignment is to visit and observe activities at the local Deaf club. Students are asked to describe: the experience, their own involvement, perceived behaviors and reactions by either themselves of the Deaf persons, and perceived cultural differences.

Problem Statement

Curriculum Problems

While these initial cross-cultural experiences are necessary and irreplaceable, some experiential gaps were recognized. Students entering the introductory level interpreting course, Fundamentals of Interpretation and Transliteration, needed to be assured an opportunity for the appropriate kind of experiential base from the beginning of this phase of coursework. Three basic problems were observed.

1. Exposure

Exposure to and recognition of a full range of issues specific to cross-cultural situations could not be assured to students required to attend functions on their own. Nor could faculty guarantee that each student would have the same kind of exposure and experience.

The quality of cross-cultural contacts was inconsistent. Some students tended to hang back and observe, while others plunged headlong into personal contact. Some attended peripheral activities, such as theater events, while others attended functions which provided direct and prolonged interaction with Deaf persons. In addition, many students focused so intently on language comprehension during contact situations, that the cultural aspects were not clear to them.

2. Safe Arena

Students needed a "safe" arena for purposes of experimentation. In field contacts, many students reported feeling intimidated or highly stressed, because they were entering a cultural setting "cold," for the first time, rather like the first day of school, without knowing correct behavior beforehand. They reported feeling confused about what their role should be, and tended to internalize and personalize negative aspects of the contact.

3. Reference Point for Learning

While there existed mechanisms within the curriculum to evaluate personal language skill levels, there was no way to identify or to provide a reference point for interactive skills development within the program. Many students in upper level courses were skilled signers, but lacked "social graces" for cross-cultural facilitation. They did not have a reference point to develop environmental self-feedback.

Cross-cultural problems

In addition to the specific problem areas of the curriculum, it was necessary to identify cross-cultural problem areas which have significant impact on the interpreter role. Three aspects of cultural interaction were identified which may either facilitate or impede successful communication.

1. Group Structure

When people come together from different structures, such as the hearing and deaf cultures, they bring differing perspectives into that

---

setting which affect communication (Higgins, 1980). The structure of groups, organizations and institutions prescribes and organizes the rules of behavior, values and priorities within that structure. Structure determines perspectives that people bring to a situation. Language is one way to express that perspective, but the perspective can be determined, without language present, by observation of the structure and interactive patterns (Gottschalk, 1975).

If a group's structure tends to be formal-, bureaucratic-, hierarchical-, competitive-, achievement- and task-oriented, there are certain ways in which the group's members will look at the world and others in it. If a group's structure tends to be informal-, communal-, network dependent-, process-oriented, it does not mean that group is *less* structured than the first, but *differently* structured, and so the resulting enculturated perspectives will be different than in the first group.

Helping the members of such diverse groups communicate successfully with each other relies on knowing more than language. In addition, an individual interpreter's comfort levels and objectivity levels will vary in each group structure, affecting job performance. If an interpreter is aware of how group structures will affect the communication setting and herself in it, preparation can be more targeted, client and interpreter anxiety levels can decrease, and effectiveness of the interpreter can be enhanced.

2. Personal Stress Sources

Stress, particularly for the novice interpreter, is usually centered around language usage and the service setting. However, there are two sources of stress in the communication setting which are culturally-based:

a) group interaction, and

b) personal conflicts.

Stress stemming from group interaction includes tension which occurs in a setting when the values and priorities of two groups differ. In addition, there is anxiety on both sides when members meet for the first time and know nothing about each other's points of reference.

Personal stress is experienced when those information bases, personal styles, preferences and needs which an interpreter brings to the communication setting lead to misinterpretation or misperception of the interaction cues which either client gives. Interpreter needs for achievement, support, dependency and power are imposed on whatever setting an interpreter enters and may be expressed in a variety of ways besides language, some of which will impede the facilitator role. Moreover, anxiety levels can rise when an interpreter's personal values and priorities conflict with those of one of the groups. Finally, when interpreters do not know the values and priorities of one or both of the client groups, or are not familiar with the service system within which they are performing, there is a feeling of loss of control over the situation and increased anxiety levels.

3. Intergroup Dynamics

The way in which groups interact with each other can facilitate or impede communication. Among the many factors which can influence inter-group dynamics, the simulation game allowed us to focus on three important areas:

a) cultural perspectives,

b) stereotypes and prejudices, and

c) protocols and sanctions.

Cultural perspectives within a group, culture or organization, either for the clients or for the interpreter, involve detailed knowledge of the group and usually are developed in a group's members both prior to and in conjunction with exposure to other, different groups. Enculturation acts as a reference point against which all else is measured and interpreted. Depending on one's enculturation and resulting self-identification, certain environmental cues will be relevant and others will be irrelevant: certain cues will be acted upon while others are ignored as meaningless (Tajfel, 1969).

Stereotypes and prejudices are the generalizations one makes about another group or its members prior to having specific and complete knowledge. They serve a function of group self-preservation and enforce boundaries between groups. They serve to keep non-members distant, as well as to unite group members in common thinking. They are often simplistic categorical labels, which are easily enforced by convergence principles and consensus over time (Tajfel, 1969).

Protocols and sanctions are the rules of a group that govern the extent and quality of interact ion with other groups and determine the limits of access which any outsider(s) will have to that group (i.e., at what level, how frequently, etc.). Protocols and sanctions are most exactly known only by group members. Some astute outsiders can sometimes infer rules by observation or experience, but no outsider knows any group's protocols and sanctions as well as the least astute group member. These also serve to enforce group boundaries and structure and are a means of expressing group perspectives and values (Kramer, 1970).

Game Description

Once the problem areas were identified, it was necessary to have a controlled setting in which learning objectives could be implemented — a simulation which would provide basic cross-cultural experiences to all participants, exposing them to all the problem areas so that learning could be relatively risk-free, consistent and obvious.

For this purpose, a commercial cross-cultural simulation game, BaFa BaFa, was used, with minor adaptations. BaFa BaFa was developed by Dr. Garry Shirtz of Simile II in Del Mar, California. The game was originally designed for use by U.S. Naval personnel and their families who would be stationed in Greece. Its cross-cultural dynamics and group characteristics are quite appropriate to the interface between hearing and deaf cultures, and worked very well for those learning tasks described above.

Basically, participants are first briefed on the purposes of the game, without revealing anything about the cultures involved. Students are then divided into two groups or "cultures," Alpha and Beta, each with a set of rules which governs their behavior as group members. Neither group can reveal its rules to strangers. The Alpha culture is an informal group which values personal contact and intimacy within a sexist and patriarchal structure. Communication is primarily non-verbal. The people are relaxed and very friendly, develop and enjoy friendship, honor and respect their elders.

Friendships, all important to Alphans, are governed by highly structured rules of interaction. The eldest member of the group must approve any interaction with females by strangers. Unauthorized approaches to women are considered to be a challenge to the manhood of all the male members of the group. Woman are considered possessions of the male members of the culture. Violation of the rules of good social conduct are looked on with grave suspicion. Often the person is completely ignored or removed from the group.

The Beta culture is a competitive, aggressive group in which a person is valued by his achievement and ability to acquire in the marketplace. All communication is done in the Beta language which consists of both words and gestures. The people are intense, driven, and respect achievement.

Achievement, all important to Betans, is accomplished within complex card-trading interaction. Additional rules govern acceptable/non-acceptable behavior. When these are violated, the right to conduct transaction is suspended, and the person is ignored.

The groups go to their respective "territories" and receive cultural artifacts. When each group feels comfortable with their own way of behaving, observers are exchanged. The observers try to learn as much as they can about the customs, values and norms of the other group without asking directly about them. When the observers return to their respective groups, they report what they have seen.

Based on information provided by the observers, each group tries to form strategies on the most effective way to interact with the other group. After this initial discussion, the cultures proceed, exchanging visitors who try to interact. After each visitor's turn, the group is briefed and the original hypotheses evolve with this additional information.

Each visitor/observer turn takes about 5-10 minutes, with about five minutes of reporting when visitors return to their groups. The length of time is determined by whether the facilitators think participants have had sufficient interaction with each turn. Some game groups develop more quickly than others, depending on the quality and nature of the participants. Groups with many beginners moved more slowly than those with upper level or older students.

After everyone has had a turn "living" in the other culture, the two groups are brought together for open discussion about their experiences:

1) within their own group,

2) within the culture they visited, and

3) within their personal feelings.

Debriefing continues until all concerns and issues are addressed.

After the game was tested, both a Basic game and an Advanced game were developed. Participants in the Basic game:

1) had never played before and

2) were enrolled in a 200-level sign language course or higher.

Most Basic game participants were preferred to be from 203 and 300-level courses. Experience showed that beginning students (100-level or early 200-level) tended to focus less on cultural aspects and more on the acquisition of signs. When they were put into the simulation, they did not readily "pick up" on cues about themselves and others because they lacked a reference point. However, the older and more experienced students had already completed deaf culture classes, and also seemed to have the right amount of life experience to make the simulation relevant.

Advanced participants:

1) had played BaFa BaFa before and

2) were invited at the instructor's discretion to participate as an advanced student.

All of the advanced students were in 400-level courses, just one or two terms prior to graduation. In addition, all Advanced players were enrolled in interpreter training courses or had completed these classes prior to their second game.

Advanced students were given a briefing separate from the rest of the participants. They were required to be in a group opposite the one they were in for Basic game playing. So, if a person had been an Alpha the first time, s/he would be a Beta the second time. Each advanced student was allowed to see the rules of the first group as a memory-refresher before joining the other culture. Both Alpha and Beta groups were told which of their members had been formerly with the other group, but Advanced students were told that they could not reveal that first group's rules, even if asked, until the final rounds.

Objectives for Advanced participants:

1) students will gain an awareness of intergroup dynamics from a bi-cultural position and learn advanced principles of group structures;

2) students will identify aspects of the bi-cultural position that affect objectivity and perspectives;

3) students will refine their self-feedback process through recognition of personal and environmental cues;

4) students will identify those stresses peculiar to the bi-cultural position and appropriate coping alternatives; and

5) students will identify at least two areas for personal skills development.

Because the game was intended to be a relaxed, experiential learning activity, evaluation of whether learning objectives were achieved was done informally, but thoroughly, through a variety of activities, assuring that all participants received feedback and had an opportunity to provide input to others. Evaluations were integrated into classroom activities and included post-game discussion, personal log entries, classroom projects and testing on related material, classroom discussion on related issues, and individual student counseling sessions.

Discussion

Although the simulation was only an approximation of what happens when hearing and deaf cultures interact, it did provide significant opportunities for learning on two levels, instructive and diagnostic. First, the simulation provided an intensified setting, so that the effects of group self-identification, stereotypes and prejudices, and protocols and sanctions became more obvious, more easily visible within a short time. Classwork could then include basic principles of group dynamics, using the simulation experience as a reference point to make theories more concrete.

Second, because of the intensity of the experience, personal reactions, needs, tolerances, flexibility and other qualities (desirable and undesirable) were made more obvious to individual participants, making self-feedback easier and more clearly defined. In addition, the simulation provided a "safe" environment in which to discover these traits, provide group feedback, and develop personal strategies for coping.

There were two aspects of the game experience which were of special interest to staff. First, the game is well made, so that group development was clear. Growth of stereotypes, loyalties, boundaries and prejudices was obvious. However, the quality of each Alpha or Beta group was modified by the nature of the individuals which comprised it. In one game, Betans were described by Alphans as "descending vultures," while Alphans were "cuddly fuzzy." However, in the next game, Betans were all very mellow, self-confident individuals, resulting in a rather likable Beta group, while the Alphans, composed of more naive, inexperienced persons, appeared quite inaccessible.

Second, the game experience provided a closer relationship between students and staff. Staff found that students increased their use of faculty for feedback and consultation to discuss both career and personally related issues stimulated by the game experience.

Although Basic and Advanced participants experienced the same simulation, both the post-game feedback and classroom applications differed. Specific issues related to the problem areas, learning objectives and classroom application are described as follows.

Basic participants

1. Exposure/Group Structures

The use of a structured game format provided the students with an opportunity to recognize cultural boundaries. Students were given typed instructions about the specific rules of their culture and then allowed time for assimilation. When the rules were understood, students began interacting with group peers, becoming completely enculturated within the group's guidelines. Cultural values were established by the time the first observer was sent to the alien group, and stereotypes were firmly entrenched by the third exchange of visitors. The group, as a whole, could identify behaviors in the visited culture that were similar/dissimilar or liked/disliked, providing clear general cultural distinctions. Stereotypes were strongly reinforced by the group's lack of specific information about the alien culture.

Each group's impression of the other was clearly influenced by its own values and structure. Both observers and visitors looked only at those "clues" in the other group which their own cultural reference defined as relevant. Even when students of one culture tried to facilitate access for alien group visitors, these efforts were often futile, because the visitors had a different point of reference.

Students distinguished cultural differences clearly, but similarities in group structure were more difficult to perceive. For example, Betans frequently misunderstood Alphan touching gestures as truly friendly actions, not recognizing them as the protocol element they were. In the post-game feedback sessions, students' experiences with cultural perspectives and cue interpretation were applied to the interpreting role. Game experiences were used to assist the students in determining the quality of their own objectivity. For most Basic students, the self-feedback process, only beginning to develop, was enhanced by the game experience. An important point was knowing that while an Alphan behavioral cue may seem relevant to a Beta (or vice versa), that cue may actually have a very different meaning, depending on the cultural/structural reference. One must learn to distinguish between one's own reference point and others in a working environment.

Group structure issues were applied to classroom work by introducing the student to structural aspects of service organizations and/or client backgrounds in the interpreting setting. Students were made aware that the structure of the setting affects interpreter performance. Using role play with deaf volunteers, and actual forms and materials from schools, social services, and hospitals, students were able to review various organizational structures and the service processes within those structures to learn how to facilitate communication in those settings.

2. Safe Arena/Personal Stress Sources

During group interaction, both faculty and students recognized conflicts between group values and personal values. Students who were able to distinguish between themselves and the role they were forced to play experienced less stress. Those who were able to adapt to the confines of the group structures and conform as needed reported feeling less stressed, having a more positive experience. However, students whose values remained at odds with a group experienced higher levels of stress and reported feelings of guilt and/or anger directed toward the alien group.

Through both the post-game feedback and related class work, students were able to identify a wide range of both stress behaviors and coping alternatives by sharing personal game experiences with each other. Staff and students provided constructive feedback to each student, so that areas for personal skill development could be identified and addressed. Stress management as well as values clarification elements of the curriculum were then expanded. Game experiences helped students improve their observation and listening skills, fine tuning their awareness of environmental cues related to stress.

A total of fifteen to twenty participants were solicited for each game. This meant that each cultural group had eight to ten members, which became a workable number for the three class hours allotted for the experience. Within an average-sized group of eight to ten persons, no more than two could be Advanced participants.

Prior to the actual game playing, facilitators for each cultural group had to be thoroughly familiar with their group's rules and artifacts. Also, artifacts had to be organized for easy distribution and rooms set up carefully. In addition, game facilitators determined what types of feedback questions and issues would be brought out in the post-game session. This process of determining questions and issues was particularly important for the advanced students (see Appendices A and B).

Learning Objectives

The purpose of the game was twofold: instructional and diagnostic. First, it provided a reference point for classroom instruction on group dynamics and related issues. Second, it provided a means to identify:

a) future issues for classroom learning at an instructor level; and

b) areas for interpersonal skill development at a student level.

For Basic students, the focus of the game was simply to experience it, noting personal reactions and observations. Advanced students, however, were expected to experience the game at a cross-cultural level, applying their observations to the interpreter role in subsequent classwork.

The following learning objectives were set for each group.

Objectives for Basic Participants:

1) students will gain an awareness of intergroup and learn basic principles of group structure;

2) students will identify aspects of cultural and personal differences that affect objectivity and perspectives;

3) students will begin to develop a self-feedback process through recognition of personal and environmental cues;

4) students will identify personal stresses and coping alternatives; and

5) students will identify at least two areas for interpersonal skills development.

3. Reference Point/Intergroup Dynamics

Students reported that often they were unaware of the effects of their own enculturation in intergroup activity until the post-game feedback session, when commonalities and differences were identified and discussed. They were then able to identify potential barriers to group interaction and problems which could prevent communication from occurring.

Facilitators provided input to students regarding behaviors of which they were unaware during the game. Three major areas for personal examination were identified:

A. *Tolerance for Ambiguity*
  The intensity of the game situation provided students with a sense of their own ability to deal with ambiguity and confusion in the cross-cultural setting. Students initially reported feeling hostile, but determined, after discussion, that the hostility was derived from being confused or uninformed, not feeling in control of all elements of the situation.

B. *Adaptability and Flexibility*
  Students who were able to conform to alien group expectations and demand were able to better handle ambiguity and confusion. These students experienced less stress and were more apt to test alternative behaviors and strategies within group structural constraints.

C. *Objectivity*
  Students who were able to separate themselves from the role they were playing could more readily accept differences. Their objectivity allowed them to look at the whole setting, and to begin exploring alternatives for problem solving.

The game experience, combined with feedback, discussion and class activity, provided a simplified explanation to students about:

1) why hearing and deaf groups relate to each other as they do;

2) why Deaf Community history has progressed along certain lines and not along others;

3) why certain Deaf groups are more accessible than others (e.g., younger vs. older, professional vs. blue-collar).

Students were able experientially to increase their understanding of deaf and hearing community structures and "personalities," and to apply this understanding to the interpreter role as cross-cultural mediator.

Using game experiences as a reference point, faculty strengthened existing curriculum related to stress management, ethical issues and cross-cultural facilitation. Activities were designed to help the student develop a repertoire of strategies for:

1) coping with stress,
2) recognizing and working with cross-cultural differences, and
3) increasing self-confidence.

Advanced Participants

1. Exposure/Group Structures

Advanced students reported that group boundaries became more fully obvious to them than the first time they played. In addition, they indicated that they perceived each group very differently from the first time, because of their increased knowledge of both groups. While they observed the development of stereotypes, they did not internalize these generalizations. Rather, they reported being slower to make judgments about the groups, and more able to get professional "distance" from the way groups behaved towards them.

In addition, after close exposure to both groups in two games, they felt they did not identify with either group when the experience was complete, but felt separate and objective compared to Basic participants who still identified as Alpha or Beta even a year after playing the game.

The increased objectivity which resulted from the advanced experience was applied to classroom exercises regarding interpreting settings and observation skills. The most beneficial aspect of this objectivity was that students reported that it was so obvious an experience, that they had achieved a concrete reference point for practical use.

2. Safe Arena/Personal Stress Sources

Advanced students reported that they experienced different stresses and frustrations than in the first game. First, because they had more information about the other group than their peers, there was frustration when they knew that peer actions and judgments were incorrect, and they could not reveal this. Those that gave hints were not even understood by their peers, because the peers did not have sufficient knowledge to make the hints relevant until the last rounds. Also, the strong group identity which developed for their peers created barriers to understanding hints that were contrary to group perceptions. This experience gave Advanced students a clear indication of how well they could tolerate ambiguity and unsolved problems.

Second, there was a special stress experienced by all Advanced participants which occurred because peers knew they had previously been members of the other group. They reported being very conscious of how they appeared to peers.

Facilitators also observed that Advanced students, knowing the rules or protocols of each group, tended to focus more than Basic students on testing the sanctions or limitations within the group. Because of this focus, stress was somewhat higher, since it involved some negative behaviors, like ostracism and boycott. This testing was an essential aspect when applied to the interpreter role as bicultural facilitator.

Stresses for Advanced students approximated closely those stresses which interpreters face daily as bicultural mediators. Students were able to identify a number of important areas for personal attention:

1) personal tolerance levels for ambiguity and unsolved problems;

2) personal qualities of flexibility and adaptiveness; and

3) personal progress in developing a coping repertoire since the first game.

The type and quality of stress was so different for Advanced students that classroom instruction focused intensively on those specific areas described above, fully exploring intergroup stress sources, coping strategies and symptoms of overload. Class assignments required students to attend three different settings with an interpreter, and observe/ analyze what factors peculiar to that setting created stress for the interpreter. By combining game and enhancement activities, students were able to identify stress sources not only for themselves, but for the client groups as well.

3. Reference Point/Intergroup Dynamics

Facilitators observed that Advanced students had better group access behaviors than Basic students. Although Advanced students had prior knowledge of the other group, this knowledge was not sufficient to allow easy access, because of the time lapsed since their first game. When a group had not yet assimilated its rules, its members made access mistakes by not allowing a person to interact who should have technically been permitted to do so. While Basic players were rebuffed by these actions, Advanced players, without exception, showed more persistence and greater flexibility, adaptiveness and creativity in gaining access.

Advanced students tended, again without exception, to be successful in each group by its respective standards. However, for the majority of advanced students, the focus was on accomplishing smooth interaction and group acceptance, not on group values or rewards in either culture. They were, in the words of one "native, easy visitors, or persons who were easier to negotiate with than others. There were also negative tendencies which became apparent to one Advanced student who, instead of using cross-cultural knowledge to facilitate intergroup contact, used it to meet personal needs for achievement and recognition.

Advanced students reported experiencing what they called, "playing a role." They were able, more clearly and definitively than Basic students, to separate their own personality and needs from the role they had to play to get the job done. Some students said they tried deliberately through various strategies, to control the impressions each group had of them. More frequently than Basic students, Advanced students reported being able to pick up on cues from each group that indicated acceptable or unacceptable behavior. In post-game feedback, they received clear messages that how they appeared to others was consistent with how they had wanted to be perceived.

The intergroup dynamics provided a strong reference point for creative problem solving and for self-image aspects of related classwork. Because of the intensity of the experience, those students who tried various strategies for problem solving were able to see outcomes immediately and clearly. As a result, service systems and settings were perceived as more flexible and more receptive to interpreter control when there was a repertoire of alternatives for problem solving to choose from.

Conclusion

The simulation game, BaFa BaFa, is a viable, workable learning alternative. While staff who are untrained in group dynamics can implement this game effectively, results are somewhat more thorough if trained facilitators are involved.

As a learning tool, the use of the simulation game was significant in providing targeted cross-cultural information to students in the interpreter curriculum. In addition, the game experience provided multiple opportunities and concrete information for faculty:

1) to identify areas for further study and personal skill development; and

2) to plan future classroom activities in those areas.

Students can use the controlled game setting as:

1) a reference point to measure personal growth,

2) a means to identify alternative behaviors strategies for problem-solving, and

3) a reference point for facilitating more satisfactory outcomes in the interpreting setting.

Staff should be prepared to be available for consultation and follow-up.

The "safe" arena provided by the game enables students to take risks and make mistakes during initial cultural encounters. Through careful observation, facilitators can provide students with direct feedback. Combined with field experience, the observations and feedback can be used by the student to recognize and control the balance between "self" and "the roles one is forced to play" (Goffman, 1959).

Appendix A
Feedback Questions

1. Beta explain Alpha.
2. Alpha explain Beta.
3. Alpha — How did Beta members appear to you?
4. Beta — How did Alpha members appear to you?
5. Alpha — Your feelings and thoughts when visiting Beta.
6. Beta — Your feelings and thoughts while visiting Alpha.
7. Beta explain Beta.
8. Alpha explain Alpha.
9. Which culture would you prefer to live in and why? (Which values are preferred?)
10. How were observers chosen? How did the group perspective begin? (What is the application to an interpreter's position as cultural mediator?).
11. How did boundaries begin to form? When did you know you had crossed them?
12. How were boundaries maintained (equal pressure from both sides)? When did they feel strongest? When the most visible?
13. How did you feel about the people you knew had been through this before with the other culture?
14. Bi-cultural people, did you perceive your adopted group differently from the first time you played?
15. How was your objectivity affected?
16. When did group boundaries feel strongest to you for your group of origin? For your adopted group?
17. To all, were there any personal surprises, discoveries you want to share? Misconceptions?

Appendix B
Bi-Cultural Feedback Guide
(for Advanced Players)

The following list of questions is a guide to help you obtain self-feedback about your experience. The two groups involved will be referred to as 1) your group of origin and 2) your adopted group, or she group you belong to this evening.

This simulation is designed to give you an idea of very basic dynamics involved when one must go between two different cultures. The more energy you put into it, the more you will learn. There are a few rules to keep in mind.

1. You will be allowed to briefly review the rules of your group of origin just to refresh your memory.

2. You may not under any circumstances feed cues to your adopted group, with the following exception. During the last two exchanges, you may answer questions which either group asks of you, or volunteer information which you consider necessary.

3. Each leader must inform the adopted group you are in that you have played the game before.

Thought Questions:

1. At what point was identity with your former group apparent to you? What triggered that feeling? At what point was identity with your adopted group apparent? What triggered that feeling?

2. Is there a difference in the way you perceive the adopted group now compared to your memory of your last experience? Your group of origin?

3. Was there any point at which you felt emotionally separate from your adopted group? What triggered that feeling? From your group of origin? What triggered the feeling?

4. How was your objectivity affected? How did that manifest itself in your observations?

5. At what points did you feel frustration? What triggered the feeling?

6. What was your role with the adopted group? With your group of origin?

7. Were you able to identify group boundaries more easily than last time?

8. When did group boundaries feel strongest to you for group of origin? For the adopted group? Weakest for group of origin? For adopted group?

9. How did you feel about yourself as you entered, exited each group?

10. At any point did you experience emotion you could not define? Explain. What triggered it?

11. What did you feel when you gave information about the other group?

12. How did you feel when you could *not* give information to anyone?

13. What did you learn about yourself from this experience? (Consider areas of flexibility, adaptivity, structuredness, hostility — tolerance levels, observation skills, risk-taking, etc.).

Section Two
General Issues in
Interpretation and Transliteration

The Role of Message Analysis in Interpretation[1]

William P. Isham

Introduction

In recent years, the field of interpreting has been inundated with new information, much of it based on linguistic research. As more information came to me about American Sign Language and the process of interpreting, the possibility of my ever having the necessary skills to interpret seemed further and further away.

The first inkling I had of help in a practical form was in a class taught by Betty M. Colonomos, [2] who discussed analyzing passages for various characteristics. This I could do, and as I came to understand what each passage meant more deeply, I found that I suddenly had more options. My range of possible ways to produce that passage in another language had grown. From this, I discovered that one obstacle to my own growth as an interpreter had been my lack of listening skills. I had been listening to the words and not the meaning.

I set out to teach myself how to listen properly. What resulted over time is an evolving structure which I extracted from the work of others in areas such as discourse and text analysis, and from discussions with other interpreters. I then assembled this information into a form which suited my needs as an interpreter. I am presently calling this approach to listening "Message Analysis.

Message Analysis is an attempt not only to make theory usable, but also to some extent, to de-mystify this skill we call interpreting. Although at first glance the following information may appear to be more theory, I would like to emphasize that message analysis is a skill. It is practicable. With time and effort, one can improve in it.

Enough of the preliminaries; let's begin.

The search for equivalence

Seleskovitch (1978) presents a strong case against word-for-word translation as an appropriate model for interpretation. Without taking up that discussion here, this paper is based on an equally strong belief in the same principle. The interpreter s task, then, is not the search for the same words in another language, but, in Seleskovitch's own terms, the "search for *equivalents* in two different languages" (p. 84).

Acceptance of this philosophical stand leaves the question, "If not words, equivalents of what?" Message analysis is an attempt to answer this question. In this paper, I present six parameters as initial suggestions of "what to search for," along with a sample text to demonstrate what is meant by each parameter. This will be followed by a general discussion of some techniques for applying message analysis while "on the job."

There are three stages to successfully relaying an equivalent interpretation: identifying what needs to be relayed; searching for equivalents in the target language; and finally, producing them. The search for and production of equivalent interpretations will not be discussed here. The first stage — identifying — is the focus of this paper.

A particular utterance (also to be called a "text") in any given time and place conveys many different things simultaneously. A text can be likened to a many-sided crystal. Each face represents only one part of what a speaker expresses the moment the phrase or sentence is uttered, and taken alone, does not have much meaning. Only by seeing the entire crystal do we fully understand the speaker;[3] this sum of many parts shall be called the "message."

Comprehending another's message is routine for us; we do it without thinking. We are generally unaware that what we understand is actually composed of different parts. As interpreters, we must learn to dissect something most of us never realized was divisible.

Six "faces" of the crystal are important to our task: content, function, register, affect, contextual force, and metanotative qualities. These six parameters are generally useful in analyzing language for a number of purposes. Although there are others, these six are most directly related to the interpreter's task.

Aside from these parameters, there is another aspect — called "context" — which is necessary to understanding any message. Context is not included in the list above, for one must apply the notion of context to each of the parameters. One might say that the context is the pair of glasses one needs to see any part of a message. Therefore, context is our first topic.

Context

Understanding another's message when it is not intended for us is not an easy task. This is because we lack the background information a typical listener would possess. We operate at a disadvantage. Although the kinds of situations where interpreting occurs are those where the speaker and the listener do not know each other intimately, we still are left with a lot of guesswork about our consumers and their relationship to each other. Context is the tool we use to fill in the gaps.

Understanding occurs largely from having background information and prior experience to draw upon. All of us have experienced enjoying a private joke with someone which depends on an experience shared between ourselves and our listener. A third party who does not have that past knowledge will not understand the joke, and will remain unmoved should someone try to explain it. Background information cannot be artificially forced into the present tense. Intuitively we know this to be true, and so when asked for an explanation of our laughter, we will simply say, "You had to be there."

Understanding any utterance one hears is very much like that private joke: there is always some amount of background information required to fully understand the speaker's intention. This background knowledge is called the "situation" by Germain (1979). He defines it as: "...the set of facts known by the speaker and the listener at the moment the speech act occurs." This would include the relationship between the speaker and the listener (i.e., father and son, teacher and student, best of friends, etc.), everything they know about each other's lives, and even everything they know about the world around them: their view of reality itself.[4]

Given enough time, some inferences about the situational context can be made from the discourse itself. Thus, as we join two people in the middle of a conversation, not only can we deduce the topic under discussion, but we can make educated guesses about the relationship of the two people talking. Without knowing anything else about them it is easy to imagine ourselves knowing whether they are family, close friends, or merely acquaintances.

As interpreters, we must listen consciously for these clues we use so automatically everyday. This information provides enormous insight into each speaker's message, and is necessary for analyzing the other parameters. Not only must we listen for situational context to provide us with clues about the message, we must then use the message to help fill out our understanding of the situation. A cycle is formed. Understanding a little of how these people see the world and each other helps us to understand their discourse. The more we understand their discourse, the more we can understand their relationship and the way they view the world.

With this as preparation, we can move to the first parameter, content.

Content

"Content" refers to the facts, ideas, information and other objective material expressed in an utterance. In the sentence, 'Tom has a brown four door," the content relates information about a specific car, its color, and who owns it.

At first glance, content seems to be an easy parameter to handle. It is more difficult than it appears. Listening for content involves many pitfalls, and because understanding seems to come so easily, we may not pay as much attention or give enough energy to analyzing content. From mere habit, we depend too much on the words. The first skill interpreters must master, then, involves breaking an old and trusted habit: we must learn to listen for ideas and not words.

Propositions

A proposition is an idea, thought, or any objectively expressed concept within the discourse. A sentence may include several propositions. Returning for a moment to the first example used in this section, the difference between a sentence and a proposition can be clarified. "Tom has a brown four door," is one sentence, made up of six words and four propositions:

1) there is a car

2) the car is brown

3) the car has four doors

4) the car is owned by somebody named Tom.

Note that the first proposition is not overtly stated, but is implied by the other three.

Paying attention to four propositions instead of one sentence seems to make matters more complicated and not less. In everyday conversation, of course, we hear these four propositions as one unit. Interpreters should do the same, and listen for manageable groups of propositions. Although it may appear we have returned to the sentence level, in fact we have not. Van Dijk (1972) separates the two by saying that propositions *represent* facts, and sentences *express* propositions.

The difference between propositions and sentences is important. A certain set of propositions may be expressed in one sentence in Language A, and require two sentences in Language B. For example, take this sentence: "The man was exhausted after John made him run around the football field." In ASL, these propositions are best handled with at least two and probably three sentences. First, one would depict the man running around the field, and in the second sentence, relate how he was compelled to do so by John. Last, the fact that this left him exhausted could be conveyed. Of course there are other possibilities for combining these propositions. Likewise, there are many samples of ASL sentences which would require two or more separate sentences in English. For these reasons, we should not restrict ourselves to interpreting messages one sentence at a time. Interpreters will help themselves by listening for propositions.

The sample:

After the discussion for each parameter, the following text will be analyzed as an example:

Ladies, ladies...please. My mother always taught me not only that I have a right to disagree, but that I should always be polite when doing so.

Although ideally a spoken text should be heard, it is hoped that we can glean enough from this written version to make the example worthwhile.

First, let us look at the context. The utterance was delivered by Geraldine Ferraro during a campaign speech. She was addressing a fairly large crowd outdoors from a stage. From the beginning of her address, she received loud protest from a group of middle-aged and middle-class women, who were supporters of the pro-life stance on the abortion controversy. At first, their loud protests were gauged to force Ms. Ferraro into discussing the issue, but in time, they resorted to insults about the candidate's personal life. Finally, after trying to ignore their derision, Ms. Ferraro, in a tight but controlled voice, made the utterance we are using as the sample text.

Now having both the utterance and its context, we can look at its content. After getting their attention with "Ladies, ladies...please," Ms. Ferraro presented the following propositions:

1) I have the right to disagree

2) My mother taught me so

3) I should be polite

4) My mother taught me so

5) I should especially be polite when disagreeing

6) My mother taught me that, too.

This is the denotative meaning: the objective, external information. The subjective meaning experienced by the listeners, called connotative, is quite different. Connotatively, other propositions are inferred:

1) Your mothers taught you the same thing

2) Therefore, you should be polite

3) I am being polite to you now, proving my mother taught me well

4) You are not being polite

5) Therefore, your mothers did not teach you well.

Notice that Ms. Ferraro used the term "Ladies" to gain quiet and to attract their attention. By using a term which, to an older generation, connotes gentility and good upbringing, she is foreshadowing the theme of the message to come.

Function

Every time we say something, there is a general purpose behind our words. We intend to accomplish something. Whether it be to entertain, to inform, or to persuade, we communicate because we have a desired result. These purposes, the very reasons we speak at all, are called the functions of the message.

The function of the message greatly influences how something is expressed. If the aim is to convince another that our opinion is correct, certain features are likely to appear in our speech and gesture. We might raise our voices to a higher volume than is necessary for our listener to hear us, or we might stress certain key words, and various hand movements might be incorporated to add emphasis to our conviction.

It is for this reason that Cokely (1983c) stresses the importance of understanding "communicative functions" for students of interpreting. Indeed, any interpreter who works at understanding the function behind the words of the speaker has a great advantage. When interpreters can make their purpose the same as the speaker's, then the choices in delivery will be naturally shaped by that common goal.

The sample:

Ms. Ferraro clearly had one function in mind: to stop the distraction created by the group of protesting women. Her purpose was achieved indirectly, for by making these women look at their own behavior, Ms. Ferraro hoped that they would make their own decision to stop their heckling. A more direct command to "be quiet," no matter how politely put, may have backfired.

In many cases, the speaker's function can be found by asking the simple question, "Why did s/he speak in the first place?" If Ms. Ferraro hadn't needed to stop a verbal onslaught, she wouldn't have addressed the women at all. Any interpretation which expressed Ms. Ferraro's idea but failed to quiet an unruly audience could not be called equivalent.

Register

There are an infinite number of ways to express an idea in any language. In fact, it is impossible to say the same thing exactly the same way twice. We can vary the way an idea is expressed through vocabulary choice, syntax, intonation, facial expression, gesture and the like.

Each of these ways of varying expression can be analyzed for the relative effect it may have on the communication. For our purpose as interpreters, however, we are more concerned with the effects which result from variations of several of these components simultaneously. These variations in the surface structure have been called "linguistic style levels" (Joos, 1967; Cokely, 1983b), and are also commonly referred to as "registers.

One speaks differently when addressing a parent, a close friend, or a teacher. These differences reflect our relationship to the person we are addressing, and the situation we find ourselves in. Cokely describes this phenomena as "social distance":

The particular linguistic style that a person chooses to use is a communicative strategy for creating or maintaining social distance or proximity. That is, since people do not feel equally close to everyone that they communicate with, the style level that a person uses is one indication of the degree of familiarity that s/he feels or wishes to establish. (Cokely, 1983b, p. 4)

In this same article, Cokely provides clear and succinct explanations of the five registers: frozen, formal, consultative, informal, and intimate. (See Cokely, 1983b, for a detailed description.)

The sample:

One excellent illustration of register is to hear the same propositions expressed through language characteristic of different registers. Again, we must make do with a written form and hope that still the point is made. Here is the Ferraro text in three of them: the original in its consultative (or neutral) register, followed by examples of the same propositions rendered first more formally, and then more informally.

Interpreting: The Art of Cross Cultural Mediation

Consultative Register

Ladies, ladies...please. My mother always taught me not only that I have a right to disagree, but that I should always be polite when doing so.

Formal Register

Excuse me, ladies. My mother not only taught me to stand up for my convictions, she also counseled politeness towards those whose beliefs differed from my own.

Informal Register

Hey... hey. Ya know, my mother taught me that it's okay not to agree but the least I could do is be nice about it.

Part of the interpreter's responsibility is to produce an utterance in the target language using the same register. Failing this risks misunderstandings, such as when a listener might think the speaker rude because the interpreter delivered the message too informally. We are not only responsible for the propositions of the message, we are also responsible for how they are expressed.

Changing the register is one way the delivery of a message may change. Altering the affect is another.

Affect

Affect is the emotion and tone conveyed in the text. Affect is perceived by listeners through volume, stress patterns, vocabulary choices and other linguistic and paralinguistic clues given by the speaker.

Affect is nothing new to the field of interpreting. Most of us have received feedback regarding our attempts to relate the affect of the speaker. All too often, however, volume and pitch are the only tools employed to show emotion. Thus, louder speech and changes in intonation are the vehicles which clue our audience in to the fact that the speaker, for example, is angry.

Strong emotion, or lack of it, influences much more than these more obvious indications. Vocabulary choice and syntax may be affected, to varying results and degrees. For example, anger may produce greater eloquence in some, and speechlessness in others. Intense emotion will alter the rate of speech, too, or create new rhythms with the pauses that can come from such things as the hesitancy to express oneself while experiencing deep emotion.

As interpreters, we need not only to be aware that it is our responsibility to convey affect, but to be consciously aware of how this is accomplished in any of the languages we are working with. Knowing how elation is expressed in the source language does not guarantee that these same stratagems can be used in the target language. Finding equivalence in affect does not necessarily mean imitating the delivery of the speaker.

Knowing how to express tone and emotion in a second language is one of the more difficult tasks we must face. One can begin by heightening awareness of the effects of emotion on our native language, and then looking for similarities or differences while conversing in the second language. Mastering this skill will be a flatter of time and effort.

The sample:

This is the most difficult of the parameters to discuss without the benefit of hearing the utterance itself. In fact, without hearing Ms. Ferraro's voice and seeing her gestures, facial expressions or postures, it is impossible to declare anything about her affect one way or another. For the sake of consistency, affect ill be addressed, if for nothing more than exercise. The discussion will be restricted, however, to what can be deduced from the context and a little common sense.

Given the situation, her goal in delivering her speech (gaining votes), and the verbal abuse being directed toward her, it is easy to believe that some anger was involved with her utterance. The desire to speak out directly in her own defense was likely in conflict with the need to behave in socially appropriate ways, resulting in frustration. Finally, there may have been some satisfaction found in having expressed such an effective text.

These are just some of the possible emotions which Ms. Ferraro may have experienced and which may have been evident in her intonation, facial expressions and so on. Likewise, they represent just a few of the possible affects any interpreter will need to be able to convey.

Contextual force

Contextual force is the relative impact (low to high) a message has on its receiver. Hirsch (cited by Horton, 1979) calls it "significance" and contrasts it with "meaning." He points out that, depending on the listener, a particular proposition has a relative impact or charge to it. It is either an emotional topic or it is not; it causes interest or it does not; it stimulates memories of past experiences or it does not.

The utterance meaning, then, is singular and determined by the speaker, while its significance, or contextual force, is multiple in that it changes from listener to listener. Some general claims can be made about social groups, however, that make contextual force more usable for interpreters. When a point about Gertrude Stein is mentioned, for example, the women in the audience will presumably experience a higher contextual force than the men will.

Knowing the context means knowing who our audience is and, in part, what might be important to then. Awareness of the potential impact a message might have to a particular group is important to the interpreter seeking equivalence.

The sample:

The contextual force of Geraldine Ferraro's statement can be assumed to be quite high for everyone who heard it, and especially so for the women to whom it was directed. For the audience in general, many must have been wondering how the candidate would deal with this difficult situation. Some may have been hoping for some kind of retort that would provide an interesting tale at the evening's dinner table. For both of these groups, raised expectations before the utterance contributed to the impact experienced when it finally came.

The high impact the utterance must have had on the group of hecklers is obvious. Ms. Ferraro managed to put down these women, cast doubt on their upbringing, and denigrate their mothers in addition to embarrassing them in front of a large crowd all under the guise of a lesson in politeness. It was a verbal coup.

Metanotative qualities

As an audience listens to a speaker, they not only make judgments about what the speaker says, they are simultaneously making judgments about the person who is speaking. Smith (1978) calls this level of meaning for the listener "metanotative," as opposed to denotative and connotative. Cokely (1983a) explains it thus: "Metanotative qualities of messages and speakers are those non-content characteristics that influence or determine a person's overall impressions of the speaker."

Perhaps the most easily grasped definition is one by Colonomos (personal communication) for what she calls the "speaker's style." Given the same context, content, affect, and register, the speaker's style is everything that makes Speaker A different from Speaker B.

Metanotative qualities of the message are what let us internally answer such questions as "What is the speaker like as an individual? Is he educated or uneducated? Is she friendly? Is she knowledgeable about her topic? Can I trust him?" and so on. Whenever we listen to another, we are forming completely subjective opinions based, in part, on the verbal behavior of the speaker.

As interpreters, our renditions of speaker's messages should reflect their individuality. A dry, monotonous delivery should not be transformed into something interesting by our own cleverness. The target language audience has just as much a rift to know that this man is a bore as those who share his language.

The sample:

By definition, each of us must form our own judgments of speakers subjectively, so it would be a contradiction to state what judgments were made of Ms. Ferraro in this paper. Some of the audience who heard her utterance may have decided that Geraldine Ferraro is witty, while others may have been impressed with her control in such a difficult position. Still other listeners may have thought her cowardly for avoiding the pro-life/pro-choice controversy.

If interpreters can reflect enough of a speaker's unique flavor, then the target language audience will make their own subjective judgments, just as they should.

Message analysis in practice

It would appear that interpreters have enough to do without having to consciously analyze each utterance in the light of these six parameters.

At first, message analysis appears to be more hindrance than help. Yet, message analysis can be used in at least three separate ways, the first of which can be employed by anyone immediately.

The three uses of message analysis to be discussed in brief here are Critique, Identifying Difficulties, and Prioritizing. Although using message analysis requires some practice, it is not as difficult as one might think.

Critique

Any interpreter may begin practicing message analysis by using it after the fact. By reviewing our performance after an interpreting assignment (perhaps with the help of another), we can use the six parameters to help clarify in our own minds where we were and were not successful. Various aspects of our own performance become clear with questions like these: "Were the propositions I provided the target audience equal to those by the original speaker? Was my affect equivalent? Was my register the same, or was I too formal?" By reviewing work done using this structure, we should be able to gain insight into our present level of functioning. At the same time, we are simultaneously solidifying our understanding of each parameter. Likewise, we can offer others feedback of a similar nature. All of us have heard both positive and negative feedback that was too general to be of any practical use ("Your signs were not clear" or "You were wonderful"). Specific input based on identifiable criteria will be refreshing after such well-meaning but useless feedback.

Identifying difficulties

Eventually, as understanding of each parameter is solidified, the next step in using message analysis will most likely take place of its own accord. If your experience is similar to mine, you will not find yourself thinking about each parameter in turn as you are interpreting. Instead, you will suddenly become aware of a particular parameter because it is, at that moment, presenting you with a problem.

That "problem" might be a sudden shift in register that produced laughter in some listeners; or it might be a proposition which presumes context you know your target audience does not have. Whatever the case, the interpreter is suddenly saying to him- or herself: "Oh no. What do I do now?"

This phenomenon of select parameters entering the consciousness of the interpreter while working may imply that, at some level, the brain has in fact analyzed the other parameters and found equivalent phrases in the target language. Whether this is so is an interesting topic for discussion or research. In any case, that this does occur is of tremendous help to the interpreter. It allows us to focus our energy on the "problem," thereby using that energy efficiently. Those few moments that we have between the utterance and our rendition are too precious to be wasted by doing nothing at all, or by trying to accomplish too much. Focusing in on the one or two parameters that are more difficult for a particular text is lag time well used.

Prioritizing

When more than one parameter presents difficulty, it may not be possible to address each of them in the lag time we have provided ourselves. Here, interpreters can prioritize their analysis. There are several possible ways to order the importance of particular parameters for any given text.

First, the interpreter should have some idea of why that parameter is an issue at the moment. It may be that the roadblock lies in the interpreter: s/he does not know a target language utterance which will incorporate a given parameter. Searching for an equivalent is impossible in a subjective sense. If this is the case, there is no point in putting energy into the matter.

It is not message analysis that is judgmental; we are too hard on ourselves already. There is not an interpreter alive who can find equivalents a hundred per cent of the time, and so we should not waste energy feeling badly when we fail. We could be busy analyzing parameters that we *can* handle.

There is another case — when something is not interpretable at all by anyone — where i,e should again drop the issue immediately. This time, the search is impossible in an objective sense: there is no equivalent in the target language. When we have decided this is true, we should waste no time in moving on.

By eliminating the impossibilities, we are left with those parameters of a message which are just plain hard to interpret for any number of reasons. We become acutely aware of an utterance which would be equivalent for all parameters except one, and suspect that with a little more time and creativity, we could find just the answer. Hopefully, after eliminating the "impossibles," whether they are subjectively or objectively so, we only have one left to handle. Focusing all of our available energy on this parameter nay tilt the scales in our favor.

It may be that even after elimination exercises, several parameters are still left which require individual attention. Here, we have to make a decision as to their rank of importance. One guide which is very often helpful is to consider the function of the message, and to concentrate on whichever parameter Bill best further the speaker's purpose. To illustrate, in a classroom the day before the final exam, the *content* of the lecture is of utmost importance. In a campaign speech such as Ms. Ferraro's, where voters are deciding whether or not to trust this potential leader, *affect* and *metanotative qualities* become crucial.

We will always be faced with such decisions, and it is certain that all of us will make both good and bad choices during our careers. Nevertheless, knowing what the issues are and then prioritizing our options will help with these difficult but necessary decisions.

Conclusion

Message analysis provides a structure with which we can understand the speaker's meaning, and thereby search for utterances in the target language which will convey an equivalent message. Consisting of six parameters, each being analyzed in context, message analysis dissects meaning into manageable parts.

Message analysis is a skill. We tend to think of skills as mechanical or physical, but some, like message analysis, are entirely mental: it is learnable and teachable. Practicing message analysis will bring improvement in interpretation. It is suggested that those interested in trying begin by using it to critique themselves after assignments. Eventually, message analysis will begin happening on the job almost of its own accord.

In the search for equivalence, message analysis is the first step. When we become aware of the message as a whole we can hope to interpret the wholeness of the message.

Notes

1) I would like to express my deep appreciation to both Charlotte Baker-Shenk and Betty M. Colonomos for their suggestions and feedback. Any error in fact or understanding is mine alone.
   In addition, I would like to thank the many people who helped by suggesting resources for further investigation, or by either proofreading or critiquing the final draft. (There are too many of you to name here, but hugs are available upon request.)
2) Course title: "ASL to English; English to ASL: Theory and Practice."
3) For convenience in a written paper, all examples will be taken from English. Message analysis, however, is equally applicable to any language, spoken or signed. Terms such as "listener, speaker," and the like are to be understood generically.
4) The situation, of course, can only be fully understood in terms of the speaker's culture. Culture is of such overwhelming importance that it night be said that this paper avoids a central issue. I agree. No matter where I tried to introduce the role of culture in interpreting in general and its place in message analysis in particular, I was unable to do justice to such a complicated topic in the time and space allotted me.

Linguistic Analysis of Historical Change in Interpreting: 1973-1985

Steven Fritsch Rudser

Introduction

The formation of the Registry of Interpreters for the Deaf (RID) marks the formal beginning of the movement to professionalize sin language interpreting in the United States. During the first decade of this movement, many state and local chapters of the RID were formed, a book on the interpretation field was published (Quigley and Youngs, 1965), a national certification program was established (Caccamise, *et al.*, 1980), and interpreter training programs were instituted in a number of community colleges. While the first decade emphasized organizational and institutional development, the second decade, from 1974 to 1984, can be characterized by conceptual development of the understanding of the role and functions of sign language interpreters. This second decade witnessed the proliferation of research proving that American Sign Language (ASL) is a language, and the publication of books and journals on the topic of interpreting.

Many people believe that the understanding of the interpreting task itself has changed very significantly during this period. This belief is supported by a comparison of interpreting and transliterating as they are defined in *Interpreting for Deaf People* (Quigley and Youngs, 1965) and *Introduction to Interpreting* (Caccamise, et al., 1980). The first of these two books defines interpreting as an explanation of another person's remarks through the language of signs, informal gestures, or pantomime" (p. 6). Translating (the task currently referred to as transliterating) is defined as verbatim presentation of another person's remarks through the language of signs and fingerspelling" (p. 7). *Introduction to Interpreting* refers to interpreting as working between American Sign Language and English, and transliterating as working between spoken English and a signed form of English (or non-audible spoken English in the case of an oral deaf person).

The underlying concept which differentiates these explanations is the idea that ASL is a language. The acknowledgement that ASL is a language has had many implications for interpreting. An interesting issue which comes up as a result of these conceptual changes is what interpreters were doing then, and what they are doing now. Or, more precisely, are these changes in the field of sign language interpreting merely semantic, or have they actually changed the way interpreters work?

The Center on Deafness at the University of California, San Francisco had the fortuitous opportunity to address these questions as a result of another project which we are conducting, focusing on the competence of sign language interpreters. This project is based on an earlier research endeavor conducted at the University of Indiana by Stephen P. Quigley and Barbara Babbini Brasel. The Quigley and Brasel project was done in

1973, and involved videotaping thirty interpreters of varying skill levels as they interpreted, transliterated, and voiced prerecorded texts. The subjects for the study were roughly classified according to a five-point scale. A "five on this scale represented native or native-like fluency in sign language, and a "one" represented minimal knowledge of sign language. In addition to the videotaping, the interpreters were given a battery of personality and intelligence tests, with the goal of comparing the interpreters' performance on these tests with their skill in the performance aspects of the test (Strong and Fritsch Rudser, 1985).

Videotaping some of the interpreters involved in the original study, interpreting the same material twelve years later, would make it possible to compare and contrast the interpretations, with an emphasis on the use of ASL and English. If the interpretations were not significantly different, from a linguistic point of view, it could be assumed that the historical change in the conceptualization of the interpreter's task had had little effect on these interpreters. If there were significant differences in the linguistic nature of the two interpretations, it is possible that those differences would be a direct result of the changes in the field.

Methodology

Subjects for this study were selected based on several criteria. Only participants from the group with the highest skills (those who were rated as fives) at the time of the first round were considered. The interpreters must have continued their involvement in the interpretation field during the intervening twelve years. The subjects had to have demonstrated knowledge of ASL in the first round. Though participants in the original study were evenly divided with reference to hearing or deaf parents, only those with deaf parents were considered for this study. None of the interpreters with hearing parents demonstrated enough knowledge of ASL to be included; thus, any differences in their performances between the first and second rounds could easily be attributed to better knowledge of the language, rather than the influence of historical changes on the expectations of the interpreting task. The final criterion was willingness to be involved in the study. Two interpreters, each of whom met the above criteria, were chosen to participate in the study. Each was re-videotaped interpreting the two spoken English segments of the original study. The subjects were instructed to transliterate the first selection, and to interpret the second selection into ASL. They were not told of the specific areas of investigation of the present study.

The English texts that the subjects were asked to interpret and transliterate were each about fifteen minutes long. The rate of speech began at approximately 130 words per minute and increased to about 190. The transliterating text is a lecture on the impact of ego on the ability to speak in public. The text for interpreting was a lecture on child language development in which a story about a small child is embedded. The story comprises about two-thirds of the material, and the lecture the other one-third. The material in both texts is quite complicated, and the speech rate would be considered very fast.

In this paper, I will discuss the results of analysis of the interpreting sections; characteristics of the transliterated material will be discussed in a future paper. This leaves four segments: each of the interpreter's interpreting segments from 1973, and each of their interpreting segments from 1985. These four texts were analyzed for the presence of four ASL features. These are:

1) classifiers and size-and-shape specifiers,

2) rhetorical questions,

3) noun-adjective word order, and

4) non-manual negation.

These four features are not by any means exhaustive or definitive; rather, they are simply four linguistic structures which stand in contrast to English, and which are fairly easy to identify and tabulate.

Results of this analysis were collected, and each interpreter's 1973 performance was compared with her 1985 performance in terms of the presence or absence of these structures in the interpreted task.

Results
Classifiers

Subject A used a total of thirty classifiers in 1973. Within this number were seven discrete handshapes. Twenty-one of the thirty classifiers represented unrepeated combinations of handshapes and movement patterns (e.g., a particular combination which was used in the text only one time); nine were repetitious (e.g., repetitions of one the twenty-one combinations). In 1985, A used classifiers a total of forty-five times. The number of handshapes increased to ten. Thirty-one of the forty-five items were different; fourteen were repetitious.

Subject B used twenty-two classifiers in the first round. Five discrete handshapes were used. Thirteen of the twenty-two classifiers were unrepeated combinations of handshapes and movements; nine were repetitious. In the second round, B used a total of sixty-seven classifiers. The number of hand-shapes increased to eleven. Forty-six of the sixty-seven items were unrepeated; twenty-one were repetitions.

Rhetorical Questions:

Neither subject used a single rhetorical question in their interpretations in 1973; however, both used them fairly frequently in the second round. In 1985, Subject A used a total of ten rhetorical questions, six in the lecture sections and four in the story section. Subject B used thirteen rhetorical questions, nine in the lecture and four in the story.

Noun-Adjective Word Order:

In the first round, there was one instance of noun-adjective word order in Subject A's interpretation, and none in Subject B's. In the later round, Subject A used noun-adjective word order nineteen times, and B used it seventeen times.

The single instance of noun-adjective word order in 1973 is an interesting exception. Subject A signed the phrase ONE VOICE LESS as an interpretation for the English phrase "one less voice asking for something..." This is the only time the interpreter placed an adjective after a noun in the earlier version; however, this word order would also be acceptable in English.

Non-Manual Negation:

There are several facial expressions or movements of the head which signal negation in ASL. These non-manual markers can be combined with a sign of negation, but they also can be made simultaneously with another sign or phrase to establish negation. In the earlier interpretations, neither subject used a non-manual marker alone to negate a sign or phrase. In the 1985 version, Subject B used non-manuals for negation six times. Subject A did not use any non-manuals alone in her 1985 version.

Discussion

For each of the four linguistic features of ASL which were chosen to investigate in this study, there is an increase in the use of that strategy in the later round. Subject A increased the use of classifiers by 50%, went from no use of rhetorical questions to ten, and from one instance of noun-adjective word order to nineteen. Though this interpreter did not use non-manual negation apart from a negative sign, there were numerous instances of changes in the word order, in order to place the negative sign after the sign or phrase it modified. This is also a common means for negation in ASL. In addition, A used other non-manual adjectives and adverbs far more frequently in the second version than in the first. Subject B actually tripled the number of classifiers in the later round. She went from no rhetorical questions the first time to thirteen the second time, and from no instances of noun-adjective word order to seventeen times in the second version. In the original interpretation, she did not use non-manual negation, but used it six times in the second one.

An interesting aspect of this study is the similarity in the number of times the subjects used rhetorical questions (ten and thirteen), and noun-adjective word order (nineteen and seventeen). There is some overlap in where the subjects used these structures, but most of the instances do not appear in the same places in the text. This seems to demonstrate a similarity in style regarding frequency of these grammatical structures. Though each of the interpreters could have employed either of these structures in more places in the text than they did, greater frequency might have been too repetitive. The subjects seemed to agree on how often it was appropriate to use these two grammatical features.

Both interpreters used rhetorical questions more frequently in the lecture section than in the story section. Sixty per cent of Subject A's and seventy per cent of Subject B's rhetorical questions occurred during the lecture part. The lecture material accounts for only one-third of the total text. By contrast, almost all of the classifiers occurred in the anecdotal section: only one of Subject A's forty-five, and two of Subject B's sixty-seven classifiers appeared in the lecture material. The content of the story, because of numerous references to spatial relationships of people and objects, invites the use of classifiers.

It could be assumed that these differences represent changes in only these four linguistic structures. However, preliminary analysis indicates that there are similar increases in the number of instances of other non-manual markers, inflections on verbs, and topicalization. In addition, for both subjects, English mouthing decreased drastically in the second version, and vocabulary choice was noticeably more varied.

Conclusion

It is clear that there is a significant difference in the amount of ASL used in the 1973 and 1985 interpretations by these two subjects. Though there are elements of ASL in the 1973 versions, these are primarily associated with sign choice, facial expression, and body shifts. In the later versions there is ample evidence of the interpreted text exhibiting ASL linguistic features.

In future research, several of the interpreters with hearing parents who scored highest in the original 1973 study will be asked to re-interpret this material, to see if similar development can be seen in their interpreting. In addition, the transliterated texts of the two subjects described in this study will be analyzed for ASL and English features, to see if transliterating has gone through any similar changes over the last decade.

Acknowledgements

This study was made possible in part through grant #G008300146 from the National Institute for Handicapped research to the University of California, San Francisco, Center on Deafness. The author would like to thank Mimi WheiPing Lou, Michael Strong, Michael Acree and James C. Woodward for valuable comments and suggestions. Special thanks are due to the two interpreters who took time from extremely busy schedules to assist in this study.

Throw It Out the Window!
(The Code of Ethics? We Don't Use That Here):
Guidelines for Educational Interpreters

Karen Scheibe and Jack Hoza

SCENE ONE

Scene: Interpreter applying for a job.

Interpreter: I understand you have a position open here for a sign language interpreter. I just completed my interpreter training at St. Paul TVI, and I feel comfortable with my skills and understand the Code of Ethics.

Principal: You know the Code of Ethics that you learned in the Interpreter Training Program? Well, you can "throw it out the window," because we don't use that here!

Introduction

In 1960, with the establishment of the Registry of Interpreters for the Deaf (RID), the RID Code of Ethics was formulated to provide interpreters with a sound foundation for ethical and professional standards. Some interpreters adhere to the Code as literally as possible, while others discard its use because it doesn't seem to fit their work situation. Currently, significant reappraisal of the RID Code of Ethics is taking place nationally regarding its appropriateness and application for educational interpreters. Educational interpreters have a unique position in the educational setting, and experience frustration and concern when attempting to translate these standards into their specialized situations. Additional guidelines are needed to help educational interpreters clarify their role in the educational setting. This paper presents a rationale and model for Guidelines for Educational Interpreters (Appendix A) to be added to the current RID Code of Ethics.

Is the RID Code of Ethics a sound concept for educational interpreters?

Individuals and groups across the nation are currently discussing and assessing the use of the RID Code of Ethics for educational interpreters. The concerns are: that the RID Code of Ethics seems applicable for only the freelance interpreter, that it may not address ethical situations at various educational levels, and that it may not meet the needs of the educational interpreter with multiple roles. The need for guidelines for specific areas such as the educational setting was stated in Caccamise *et al.*, 1980. The Preface to the Code of Ethics states:

> While there are general guidelines to govern the performance of the interpreter/transliterator generally, it is recognized that there

are ever increasing numbers of highly specialized situations that demand specific explanations. It is envisioned that the RID will issue appropriate guidelines for all these situations.

Current reappraisal

The RID has responded to these concerns by establishing an Educational Interpretation/Transliteration Committee. The committee devised and disseminated an Educational Interpreter Survey (Arnesen, 1985), asking interpreters to respond to questions regarding the educational interpreter's job description and current RID Code of Ethics. The results of this survey will be compiled into a "State of the Art" report. *[The Committee's work was presented at the 1985 RID Convention in San Diego — ED.]*

The Iowa State RID established a Task Force on Educational Interpreting and submitted a Code of Ethics with Guidelines for the Educational Interpreter. This task force included recommendations regarding the needs of educational interpreters and a job description — complete with qualifications, salary considerations and responsibilities, and the role of educational interpreters on the educational team (ISRID, 1984).

The Florida RID has presented a proposal for the Evaluation of Educational Interpreters/Transliterators and has proposed a Revised Code of Ethics. The Revised Code of Ethics was developed so that it was possible to have a functional document upon which the Educational Interpreter Evaluation could be based (Dunstall, n.d.).

The National Technical Institute for the Deaf (NTID) prepared a rough draft of a background position statement on educational interpreting — "Educational Interpreting: A National Need for Clarification of Roles, Responsibilities and Standards" (October 1984).

The need to examine and clarify roles, responsibilities, and standards for educational interpreters has been recognized by these groups as well as other individuals, organizations and training programs throughout the country.

The need for Guidelines

Educational interpreters support the concept of a Code of Ethics, realizing the importance of ethical standards in maintaining professional behavior. Educational interpreters strive to follow the current RID Code of Ethics, but often find themselves in complex situations in which their role is vague and confusing. The RID Code of Ethics is viewed as too narrow in focus for educational interpreters who have multiple roles and responsibilities, who are considered a member of the educational team, and who work with children. Educational interpreters' job titles and job descriptions are often that of aide or educational assistant, and these include expanded responsibilities of tutoring, notetaking, devising educational materials, supervision of students, and "other duties as assigned." Educational interpreters and the consumers of interpreting services are often confused by the expanded role, and unique ethical situations arise. When ethical situations occur, the RID Code of Ethics mandates one response and the school district may mandate a different response. The chart to the right provides examples of possible conflicting role expectations:

Educational interpreters are faced with conflicting expectations between the RID Code of Ethics and their job responsibilities as outlined by the school district. Should educational interpreters act "ethically" and follow the RID Code of Ethics or "unethically" and fulfill their job responsibilities? Educational interpreters should not be forced to decide for or against the Code of Ethics. Rather, the Code of Ethics should provide specific guidelines to help them clarify their roles. With these additional guidelines, educational interpreters and consumers of interpreting services will better understand the Code's relationship to the educational setting. Educational interpreters will then be able to use the Code of Ethics and incorporate its ideas and purposes more consistently.

A decision-making process

The RID Code of Ethics with Guidelines for Educational Interpreters is crucial in providing a more complete picture of the roles and responsibilities of the educational interpreter. However, these Guidelines for Educational Interpreters will not be able to address every possible situation. Interpreters must learn to approach the Code as a tool to help them make professional decisions. As problematic situations occur, educational interpreters should employ a decision-making process and investigate the various options, working from the ideal option (close interpretation of the Code of Ethics) to the least ideal. Educational interpreters must become skilled problem-solvers.

Conclusion

Our profession has experienced considerable progress and change since its conception. Currently, we are becoming more sensitive to the needs of educational interpreters. The compelling reasons for adding guidelines to the current Code of Ethics are stated in this paper.

SCENE ONE (REVISED)

Scene: Interpreter applying for a job.

Interpreter: I understand you have a position open here for a sign language interpreter. I just completed my interpreter training at St. Paul TVI, and I feel comfortable with my skills and understand the Code of Ethics.

Principal: I just received a Code of Ethics with Guidelines for Educational Interpreters, and we find that it works very well for teacher, interpreters, and students.

Recommendations

The attached Code of Ethics for Educational Interpreters (Appendix A) was devised to assist educational interpreters in the ethical decision-making process. This set of guidelines is applicable in all educational settings (K-postsecondary). The guidelines and the premises stated in this paper can also be adapted for use by the oral interpreter working in the educational setting. The guidelines can be used in presenting inservices to educational team members, hearing-impaired consumers, parents, and others interested in the role of educational interpreters. It is recommended that educational interpreters designate a supervisor or establish a process for sharing ethical situations with other educational team members.

Rid Code Of Ethics	School District Policies
1. Maintain confidentiality.	1. Educational interpreters are members of the educational team and are asked to share information regarding the academic, social, and emotional progress of the hearing-impaired student during the staff Individual Education Plan (IEP).
2. Remain impartial — not counsel, advise or interject.	2. Educational interpreters are asked to recommend to the student and/or school district additional support services that will ensure the student's academic progress. Educational interpreters often assume tutoring as part of this support service.
3. Accept jobs appropriate to skill level.	3. Educational interpreters are required to interpret in all academic content areas (regardless of knowledge/skill level), to devise educational materials and evaluate student progress (without regard to special training in teaching methods/strategies and child development).
4. Interpret in the language most readily understood by consumers.	4. Often school policies or the student's IEP requires educational interpreters to use a particular sign system for English in which they may not be qualified or they personally feel is not the appropriate language for that student.

Appendix A

Registry of Interpreters for the Deaf, Inc.(RID) Code of Ethics With Guidelines for Educational Interpreters

(In these guidelines the term "interpreting" is used generically to refer to interpreting and transliterating.)

1. Interpreters/Transliterators shall keep all assignment-related information strictly confidential.

   Guidelines for Educational Interpreters:

   A. The educational interpreter may discuss assignment-related information only with other members of the educational team (e.g., interpreters, teachers, supervisors) who are directly responsible for the educational program of the hearing-impaired student(s) for whom the interpreter interprets.

   B. The educational interpreter should report directly to a classroom teacher or a designated supervisor when the interpreter finds it necessary to step out of the interpreter role. The educational interpreter may only step out of the interpreting role to report:

      1) serious behavior which any other school personnel would have to report (such as suspected child abuse, or the breaking of laws or school policies) or

      2) significant academic problems which may require additional support services.

   C. The educational interpreter may provide input for — or may attend — educational team meetings (including Individual Education Plan staffings) to answer questions and address concerns related to a student's communication abilities and needs. The educational interpreter may answer such questions as the following:

      1) Does the hearing-impaired student need interpreting services?

      2) Does the hearing-impaired student attend to the educational interpreter?

      3) How does the hearing-impaired student sign (American Sign Language, Pidgin Sign Language, Manually Coded English)?

      4) How does the student communicate with the teacher, other school personnel, and his peers?

      In these situations, the educational interpreter shall not discuss the student's progress or behavior in the classroom and shall direct questions on school performance to the appropriate school personnel (e.g., teacher, counselor, principal).

   D. If the educational interpreter also works with a student as a tutor, this person may discuss the student's performance in the tutoring session only, but may not discuss the student's performance in a situation in which this person is functioning as an educational interpreter.

   E. The educational interpreter shall *either* interpret *or* participate in I.E.P. meetings, but shall *not* do both.

2. Interpreters/Transliterators shall render the message faithfully, always conveying the content and spirit of the speaker, using language most

readily understood by the person(s) whom they serve.

Guidelines for Educational Interpreters:

A. It is recognized that some hearing-impaired students may not fully understand an interpreter message due to differences in culture, language, or experience. It is appropriate for educational interpreters to clarify bits of information which fit into this category (e.g., hearing-culture jokes, certain English vocabulary which does not translate well). However, this is to be done on a limited basis for the benefit of clear communication — and should not be tutoring per se.

B. The educational interpreter is often asked to use a particular system of Manually Coded English. The interpreter shall consider his/her skills in this system before accepting an assignment.

C. If the educational interpreter disagrees with the school's policy, requiring the use of a particular system of Manually Coded English, the interpreter should discuss this with his/her immediate supervisor or request an I.E.P. conference.

3. Interpreters/Transliterators shall not counsel, advise, or interject personal opinions.

Guidelines for Educational Interpreters:

A. The interpreter shall maintain an impartial role. The interpreter is not responsible for disciplining hearing-impaired students. The student(s) should be allowed freedom to make choices and to learn as independently as possible.

B. For students who are not fully aware of the interpreter's role, the educational interpreter may briefly step out of the interpreter role for the following purposes:

1) The interpreter may give clues needed for successful interaction. For example, when the student mistakenly directs questions to the interpreter, the interpreter may sign, "I will interpret for you, so you may ask the teacher" (or may use subtle body language or eye cues).

2) The interpreter may clarify his/her role in the classroom as situations arise.

C. If the educational interpreter also functions as a tutor, this person may be involved in clarification, review, and reinforcement of concepts presented by a classroom teacher. The interpreter's role during the tutoring session is, therefore, separate and distinct from his/her role during an interpreting situation.

4. Interpreters/Transliterators shall accept assignments using discretion with regard to skill, setting, and the consumers involved.

Guidelines for Educational Interpreters:

A. An educational interpreter should consider the following information about an assignment to determine if his/her skills are adequate for the assignment:

1) the age levels of the students,

2) the content of the various classes (e.g., academic, vocational),

3) special interpreting situations (e.g., assembly programs, field trips, films),

4) the student's English skills, and

5) the student's sign language preference (American Sign Language, Pidgin Sign Language, Manually Coded English).
B. The interpreter should also consider his/her flexibility within the sign language continuum in meeting the needs of the hearing-impaired consumers. Also, the interpreter should consider his/ her competency in the English language as well as in American Sign Language.

5. Interpreters/Transliterators shall request compensation for services in a professional and judicious manner.
Guidelines for Educational Interpreters:
A. It is recommended that educational interpreters be paid according to a salary schedule which includes the following factors:
2) years of interpreting experience (especially in the educational setting);
3) college courses in education; degree in education;
4) Registry of Interpreters for the Deaf (RID) certification; and
5) number of CEU's related to interpreting skills, sign language, deafness, and education.
B. It is recommended that educational interpreters be guaranteed a set number of hours per week and, as a paraprofessional, consultant, or professional, receive the same benefits as other staff members.
C. It is recommended that educational interpreters have a separate category from other staff members, so that their unique skills and expertise are rightfully recognized. Educational interpreters should be classified as paraprofessional or professional depending on this person's role and responsibilities. The following job titles are examples that would be appropriate: educational interpreter, communication facilitator, interpreter/tutor, interpreter/tutor/ notetaker, and interpreter/aide.

6. Interpreters/Transliterators shall function in a manner appropriate to the situation.
Guidelines for Educational Interpreters:
A. The educational interpreter represents an attitude toward deafness and the hearing-impaired students in the mainstream situation, and interpreters must recognize their importance as role models.
B. When the educational interpreter has other duties as well (such as being a tutor or teacher's aide), a clear distinction needs to be made as to which role the person is functioning in at any given time. One suggestion is the wearing of a special smock or jacket to be worn during interpreting, to help clarify and distinguish roles. Another suggestion is that a separate time be established when the student is scheduled for tutoring services from the interpreter.

7. Interpreters/Transliterators shall strive to further knowledge and skills through participation in workshops, professional meetings, interaction with professional colleagues and reading of current literature in the field.

8. Interpreters/Transliterators, by virtue of membership in or certification by RID Inc., shall strive to maintain high professional standards in compliance with the Code of Ethics.

The Role of the Sign Language Interpreter in Psychotherapy

Asa DeMatteo, Daniel Veltri, and S. Margaret Lee

Introduction

The sign language interpreter plays an important role in making the deaf population accessible to hearing people. That is, while the deaf individual may be able to function adequately with hearing persons, communication with a deaf person often seems difficult, intimidating, and cumbersome to the hearing person. Interpreters are often seen as the solution to the hearing person's discomfort. As such, they are seen as a welcome addition. Apparently, they have not been quite as well received in the mental health setting (Stansfield, 1981), particularly in the case of interpreter-assisted psychotherapy. We think there are reasons why they have not been as well received there: use of an interpreter in psychotherapy presents unique problems and raises unique issues.

Our goal here is to present one restricted set of issues relevant to mental health interpreting. In this paper we are concerned with certain aspects of the role of the sign language interpreter in face-to-face individual psychotherapy. Specifically, we deal with issues arising in one sort of individual psychotherapy, namely psychodynamic psychotherapy. In part, we focus on how the interpreter functions within the therapeutic session itself. But we also discuss a role that is thrust upon the interpreter without his or her choosing, namely, that of "transference object."

In particular, we discuss the following:
a) some of the ethical rules and principles governing interpreter practice in any setting,
b) some of the characteristic and naturally occurring processes of psychotherapy, and
c) ways in which standard interpreter ethics present problems for both the interpreter and the psychotherapist in appropriate management of psychotherapeutic processes.

We illustrate our discussion of the conflict between interpreter ethics and psychotherapeutic processes with a case example taken from an actual psychotherapeutic interview.

One of our goals in examining these issues is to offer some ideas and suggestions which we have found helpful in our work and which we believe might be incorporated into standard interpreter practice and interpreter training. We feel, however, that some of our notions are controversial in important ways. Therefore, another of our goals is to offer these notions to the field, i.e., to both sign interpreters and psychotherapists using interpretation services. In this way, we hope the issues will receive more attention and discussion.

Inerpreter ethics

The current RID Code of Ethics (taken from Caccamise *et al.*, 1980) states that, among other things, the interpreter shall:

a) keep all assignment-related information strictly confidential,
b) render the message faithfully, always conveying the content and spirit of the speaker,
c) not counsel, advise, or interject personal opinions, and
d) accept assignments using discretion with regard to skill, setting, and the consumers involved.

Generally, the purpose for these charges to the interpreter seems fairly self-evident. However, the RID Code of Ethics also offers guidelines which expand upon the principles and explain there more fully. For example, the expansion of (a) notes that a trainer shall not reveal the name, sex, age, or other information about the consumer when sharing actual experiences with a trainee. Nor is the trainer to reveal the city, state, or agency relevant to the experience.

The general spirit of the charges under (a) through (d) above is two-fold, it seems to us. First, interpreters need some sort of assurance that they are behaving in an appropriate and professional manner. They also need some sort of protection against inappropriate criticism of the services provided. By faithfully adhering to the RID Code of Ethics and associated guidelines, the interpreter can always be sure of providing appropriate services in a professional manner. Second, the consumer of interpreting services, whether deaf or hearing, needs some sort of protection against intrusions in the communication. The consumer wants assurance that the sort of communication possible is precisely that which would be possible were the two speakers communicating with one another in a common language without the involvement of a third party. Thus, an alternative statement of the guideline under (a) might be formulated as follows: the assignment-related information should remain as confidential as it would have had the interpreter not been present.

It is this notion of the non-intrusiveness of the interpreter that we wish to expand upon here. Relevant guideline statements are these:

(Interpreters) are not editors and must transmit everything that is said in exactly the same way it was intended.... Just as (interpreters) may not omit anything that is said, they may not add anything to the situation, even when they are asked to do so by other parties involved.... The (interpreter's) only function is to facilitate communication.... S/he shall not become personally involved because in so doing s/he accepts some responsibility for the outcome, which does not rightly belong to the (interpreter). (Caccamise *et al.*, pp. 11-13)

Interpreters, then, are not to intrude themselves into the communication in any way. In other words, the interpreter is not to influence the communication process. This is a reasonable charge and one with which we are in full agreement. There is an aspect of the process of psychotherapy, however, which forces the interpreter into the role of intruder. It also suggests that the interpreter influences the process of psychotherapy in significant ways. Indeed, it is the very neutrality and non-involvement of the interpreter that fosters and continues that influence. This aspect of the psychotherapy process is the transference relationship, and it is to an explication and discussion of transference that we turn next.

Transference in Psychotherapy
Psychodynamic Psychotherapy

One of the therapeutic mistakes that novice psycho-therapists frequently make is this: they think of psychotherapy as a setting where the psychotherapist and the client get together for a series of work meetings. During those meetings, the client describes a set of problems, and the psychotherapist provides counsel, advice, and the guidance toward problem-solving strategies. This is not a totally incorrect view of psychotherapy. There are certain clients who need such input (e.g., those with limited intellectual functioning or certain major psychiatric disorders). There are situations which call for such work, (e.g., crisis intervention, suicide prevention). And there are therapeutic models in which such an approach to psychotherapy is appropriate (e.g., behavioral therapies for well-defined problems, certain of the family therapies, etc.). However, for the most part, people (including those who happen to be deaf) have some fairly good problem-solving skills, common sense, and advice networks (e.g., friends, family, church, school personnel, medical service providers, etc.). They use these resources in more or less effective ways to manage and cope with, or solve, the problems that arise in their daily lives. For psychotherapists to imagine that they are a necessary component for the solution of the client's problems is rather arrogant and shows an unfortunate lack of respect for the client.

At the same time, there are individuals who have good problem-solving skills, common sense, and support systems, but who are troubled nonetheless. They continue to have difficulty managing their lives or are troubled by uncomfortable emotions that interfere with their lives in various ways. The question in such cases is this: what is it about these individuals that keeps them from using their "life management" skills effectively? What is it that motivates and supports their troublesome emotional states? More succinctly put, the question is, "Why do they have these problems?"

Another mistake that novice psychotherapists make is to assume that the client simply needs to gain knowledge of the reasons for the problems. The mistaken idea is that with such knowledge in hand, clients can simply correct their errors. They can then go about their lives renewed, refreshed, and armed with the proper skills to manage problems and previously difficult emotions.

Our view is that psychotherapy is much more than advice-giving or revelation of knowledge. We believe that psychotherapy is an extraordinarily complex process. It is a process in which clients establish a richly structured relationship with the psychotherapist and then reorganize their experience of themselves and their environment within the context of that relationship. (It should be noted that there are others who would disagree with our views and beliefs.) The assumption is that people have characteristic ways of perceiving themselves and others, and that these perceptions influence their behavior in powerful ways. A further assumption is that these perceptions have deep motivations and complex historical antecedents which are not accessible to one's awareness (i.e., are unconscious) for various reasons.

The therapeutic model we are speaking of is psychodynamic psychotherapy. It is important to note that this model does not assume that only the mentally ill or psychologically troubled are influenced by factors outside their awareness. It assumes that each of us has a history which crucially influenced our thinking structures as they were developing, and which continues to influence how we feel, behave, and generally operate in the world throughout our lives. Psychological disturbance is defined by the maladaptive nature or personally troubling experience of those characteristic ways of perceiving oneself and one's world. It is not defined by the presence of such unconscious influences.

How does this rich relationship between client and psychotherapist allow the reorganization of experience and perception? It happens in this way: psychotherapy clients bring themselves to that relationship. That is, the ways that the client operates in the world will be reflected in the ways that the client operates within the psychotherapeutic relationship. But there is a difference between the client's relationship with the world and his or her relationship with the psychotherapist. The client's relationship with the psychotherapist is one in which the client can display his or her feelings, thoughts, and behaviors without punishment, without reprisal, without danger — in short, within a safe environment. Because the environment is safe, the client 's view can turn inward in such a way that one can examine oneself in various ways, from various perspectives, and with various personal reactions to the material examined.

It is not just knowledge gained from such examination that makes psychotherapy work. Self-examination—when accurate and comprehensive—is an intensely emotional experience. Why? Personal material is unconscious for very good reasons: it is generally emotionally charged in ways that are unpleasant; may be incongruent with our conscious ways of thinking about ourselves; and is often in conflict, in certain aspects, with what we must do in the world in order to lead our lives in an acceptable and adaptive manner. It can, in short, be quite dangerous to our sense of self.

The job of the psychotherapist is to make that examination of self as free from danger as possible. Safety is needed so that the emotions that occur as the material is examined do not overwhelm or damage the client. It is the emotional content of the material that in part keeps it unconscious; it is the client's experiencing of those emotions within the therapeutic relationship and without damage to the relationship that allows new emotions to develop. Thus, psychotherapists do not simply assist in self-knowledge. They also provide the environment for a corrective emotional experience. That is the stuff of psychotherapy.

Transference

We began this portion of our discussion with promise to give the reader an explication of transference. And yet up to this point we have not used the term at all. Psycho-therapy is such an exceedingly complex activity that it is necessary to lay a foundation for such explication. In fact, it is so complex that our lengthy discussion must be seen as greatly simplified and not at all comprehensive. Nonetheless, the concept of transference is there within our discussion without being named. It is contained in the statement that clients bring themselves — their histories, their motivations, their perceptions, their characteristic behaviors — to the therapeutic relationship. A more formal definition of transference, taken from a standard text in psychiatry (Kaplan, Freedman, and Sadock, 1980), is the following:

Transference is a process in which the (psychotherapy client) unconsciously and inappropriately displaces onto persons in his current life those patterns of behavior and emotional reactions that originated with significant figures from his childhood. The relative anonymity of the (psychotherapist) and his role as a parent surrogate facilitates that displacement to him (or her). The (client's) realistic and appropriate reactions to (the psychotherapist) are not transference. (p. 898)

Transference can involve positive or negative feelings and is experienced by the client as realistic and appropriate reactions to the therapist rather than as distortions in his or her own perceptions. It occurs in any psychotherapeutic relationship and affects the course of psychotherapy in various ways. The difference between the therapy model we have presented (i.e., psychodynamic psychotherapy) and other psychotherapies is that in that model the transference is used as a major therapeutic tool.

In its broadest definition, the concept includes four different types of transference:
a) transference of habitual ways of relating,
b) transference of current relationships,
c) transference of past experience, and
d) transference neurosis (Sandler, Kennedy, & Tyson, 1980).
We shall briefly discuss each of these in turn. However, we will begin with a distinction between transference and what is generally termed the therapeutic alliance.

The therapeutic alliance.
The therapeutic alliance is that part of the client/psychotherapist relationship which is based on the client's conscious and unconscious wishes to cooperate with the therapist, to overcome resistance to the relationship, and for understanding and help with internal difficulties. It involves a basically trusting and positive attitude towards the therapist. And it is this trust which allows the client to tolerate difficult experiences in the therapy (e.g., anxiety, painful emotions, confusion, etc.) in order to attain therapeutic change. It also allows the client to tolerate interpretation of resistance and it counterbalances one of the most common manifestations of resistance, namely, the wish to leave treatment. It differs from transference in that the alliance is more reality oriented. Although it may be colored by neurotic elements and past experience, the alliance is not based on these. Rather, it is based on:
a) a psychotherapist's and client's common goal of helping the client struggle with conflicts, and
b) a more or less clear understanding that the therapist is a professional trained to help people with such difficulties.

The transference, both positive and negative, is what the client and psychotherapist look at in therapy; the therapeutic alliance is what allows the client to look at the transference. With this distinction made, we can return to the four general types of transference.

Transference of habitual ways of relating.

This type of transference is based on early relationships and reflects those relationships in the stylistic aspects of how one relates to other people. For example, one might have a consistent tendency to placate authority figures or, conversely to rebel against authority figures. These stylistic aspects constitute a generalized mode of functioning that is chronic and habitual. They are generally acceptable to the client because they are not so emotionally charged. And, they are also generally not all that disruptive of daily functioning. In this sense, transference of habitual ways of relating is neither helpful nor destructive to the psychotherapeutic process, for the most part. This is because such transference is neither dangerous nor connected to disturbing emotions, and also because it is not specific to the therapist or to the therapeutic relationship. Rather, it is directed to everyone in the client's environment. It nonetheless flavors the therapeutic relationship and usually must be addressed as an issue within the therapy.

Transference of current relationships.

Transference of current relationships occur when there is a "spill over" of emotions and behavior in the therapeutic relationship which are related to current events and relationships in the client's life. For example, a male client might be experiencing difficulty in his relationship with his wife. He may be very angry with her but, for various reasons, be unable to manifest that anger towards her. The acting out of that anger in the treatment sessions is a transference which can occur for various reasons. It can occur in part because the anger is significant in the client's current experience. It can also occur in part because the consultation room provides a safe, confidential, and accepting environment for display of behaviors and emotions that would be unacceptable in his home with his wife.

Transference of past relationships.

This type of transference is one of the most powerful features of psychotherapy. The concept refers to past impulses, wishes, memories, and fantasies that become manifested in the therapeutic relationship, because the work done in treatment revives and stimulates them. Past experience and earlier patterns of emotion and behavior thus stimulated get reenacted in the therapeutic relationship. These reenactments also contain earlier feelings and a repetition of earlier consequences (e.g., depression, trauma, feelings of abandonment, etc.). The therapist, being the target of such transference (or, as we shall term it, the transference object), is seen by the client as being more specifically involved with the feelings, and more specifically the source of the feelings, than in the transference phenomena previously described. An example can be found in our case presentation below where the client, who was looked down upon and discounted by his parents, saw the psychotherapist as looking down on him and discounting him, and responded to the therapist with fury and rage.

Transference neurosis.

Finally, there is the transference neurosis. This is a type of transference that perhaps occurs in its purest form only in psychoanalysis. It is a special case of transference which reflects major conflicts between unconscious elements. For example, an analysand (i.e., a psychoanalytic client) may have an unconscious wish for dependence and nurturance, that is, to be taken care of as an infant would be. A caretaker from the analysand's early childhood, however, may have punished dependent behavior by anger, rejection, and withdrawal of love. The analysand, then, might have an unconscious fear of dependency which is in conflict with the wish and need for dependency. In a transference neurosis, this conflict might be reflected in the following way: each time the analysand reports dependent behavior to the analyst, he or she perceives the analyst as angry and rejecting, and attacks the analyst for not being sufficiently caring and concerned. This perception occurs even though the analyst's behavior has remained unchanged (i.e., the same as when the analysand perceived the analyst as pleased, accepting, and caring). Thus, the transference neurosis is an externalization of major unconscious conflicts acted out within the therapeutic relationship so that the conflict is experienced by the client as being between herself and the therapist. Since this paper is about psychotherapy and not about psychoanalysis, a more detailed account of transference neurosis is beyond the scope of this work.

Related concepts

We have explained what transference is, and have also said a little about how it is used in treatment. There is more to be said, however, and in order to round out our discussion, the balance of this portion of the paper is devoted to three related concepts:

a) the stimulation of transference within the therapeutic relationship,
b) the therapeutic use of transference and the transference reaction, and
c) countertransference.

Stimulation of transference in the therapeutic relationship.

Transference is stimulated within the therapeutic relationship not only because the client brings his or her history and past experience to that relationship, but also because the psychotherapist takes on a particular role. In ordinary relationships, both partners reveal themselves in ever increasing ways and become increasingly reality oriented in their perceptions of each other. An example familiar to just about everyone can be found in the experience of romantic love of the "love at first sight" variety. When two people experience an immediate or nearly immediate attraction for each other, the intense and powerful feelings that surround such attraction are generally quite unrealistic. That is, although the feelings themselves are valid and very real, they are not actually based on objective perception and knowledge of the love object, but rather on the needs, wishes, fantasies, and so forth, of the experiencing individual. Indeed, it is the very lack of objective perception and knowledge that allows such feelings to arise. With increased contact with, and knowledge of, the love object, emotional responses to the object generally become increasingly reality oriented — so much so that the person may come to wonder what it was that he or she ever saw in the other in the first place, or wonder how he or she could have ever felt such love. Such feelings are a kind of transference, a very pleasant kind, indeed, and one which is possible because the transference object is so unknown and ill-defined.

Psychotherapists are also rather ill-defined. They reveal very little of themselves in the way of history, reactive behavior, thoughts, or feelings, except where such revelations can be used therapeutically. They do not take this general stand to be secretive or unauthentic. Rather, they seek to remain somewhat ill-defined precisely because such lack of definition stimulates transference within the client. The more defined and real the therapist becomes, the more objective and reality oriented become the client's perceptions of the therapist. The transference is then diminished, and the therapeutic relationship becomes more like a friendship.

The therapeutic use of transference and the transference reaction.

One night ask why this should be a problem. Why shouldn't the psychotherapist and client be friends? The answer lies in the therapeutic use of the transference. The client is not in the consultation room to better know and understand the therapist; clients are in psychotherapy in order to better know and understand themselves. It is by looking at the transference that the client may come to better know and understand his or her own perceptions, emotions, and history. This is because transference is a reflection of the client's self rather than of the psychotherapist. It is the major tool that both client and psychotherapist use to make sense of the difficulties that brought the client to the consultation room in the first place.

The transference feelings are manifested in what is termed transference reactions. For example, in the case described below, the client had a powerful reaction to a fairly minor error made by the interpreter during the course of an interpreter-assisted therapy interview. The client's behavior was seen as a transference reaction, as an inappropriate displacement of hostile feelings toward the therapist onto the interpreter. The client's reaction, as shall be seen, gave a great deal of information to the therapist. And it also provided material for client and therapist examination that was immediate, spontaneous, emotionally relevant, and profoundly important. By working through the transference (i.e., by experiencing it fully with all of its emotional concomitants, by understanding it, and by mastering those associated emotions), the client is better able to handle such emotions and the events which stimulate them.

Countertransference.

The last concept for discussion here is that of countertransference. This term refers to the transference that the psychotherapist injects into the therapeutic relationship. Although therapists ideally are objective, stable, psychologically intact, and in control of their emotions and behavior, it is nonetheless true that in any psychotherapy there are at least two human beings in the room. Transference is not a reflection of pathology; it is a reflection of one's humanity. And the psychotherapist has a history, an unconscious, and a set of conflicts, too.

True countertransference occurs when the therapist responds to the client and to the therapeutic relationship from an unconscious place. It is troublesome because it can lead to the therapist making interventions that are motivated by his or her own dynamics rather than the therapeutic needs of the client.

Such feelings must be clearly differentiated from the various feelings that arise in the therapist as a response to a particular client. An example of the countertransference reaction might be reflected in, say, the therapist's reacting in a punitive way to some sexual behavior on the part of the client because the behavior stimulates similar, but unacceptable and unconscious, sexual feelings on the part of the therapist. The latter class of therapist reactions are based on a reality based experience of the behavior of the client. For example, the therapist may find him- or herself always feeling disorganized and overwhelmed in dealing with a particular client in ways that aren't a reflection of countertransference or lack of ability, but rather reflects the client's being disorganized and overwhelmed.

In this way, the psychotherapist uses him- or herself as a sort of barometer or testing device. If the psychotherapist reacts in a consistent way to a client, and that reaction is not a countertransference reaction, then it is likely that others in the client's environment have similar reactions. Obviously, such reactions can be very useful and informative.

It should be clear that, owing to their unconscious sources, countertransference reactions are very difficult for the psychotherapist to distinguish from those reactions which are reality based, useful, and therapeutic. That is why responsible and ethical psychotherapists establish an ongoing supervisory relationship with colleagues in which the therapist can share his or her work, reactions, and thoughts for objective review. We will have more to say about ongoing supervision in our discussion of the role of the interpreter in psychotherapy.

Transference in the Interpreter/Client Relationship
Introduction

Although it might not be immediately apparent from our discussion above, the notion of transference relationship and transference object implies something about the interpreter's role in psychotherapy. It suggests that the interpreter, by his or her very presence in the consultation room, might "add to the situation" in important ways.

We have explained how ambiguity and lack of definition in the psychotherapist encourages transference in the client. Interpreters, because they reveal so little personal material in the way of thoughts, feelings, reactive behavior, and history, are quite as ambiguous and ill-defined an object as psychotherapists. Moreover, while the client is encouraged in developing a transference relationship with the psychotherapist by the inherent dependency of being a client in psychotherapy, it must be remembered that s/he is also depending upon the interpreter in crucial ways as well. It would seem, then, that the interpreter is a very likely transference object, perhaps as likely as the psychotherapist. We believe that the interpreter is a very frequent transference object.

Case presentation

We can now turn to a particular case example in which the interpreter in fact did become a transference object and played a significant role in the process of psychotherapy. In presenting this case, we are ourselves violating some of the ethical guidelines of the RID Code of Ethics, because it is known that we work for the University of California Center on Deafness in San Francisco and because we intend to reveal certain aspects of an interpreting situation and of the consumers of interpreting services. The amount of information we reveal, however, is within the limits governing our agency and the practice of psychotherapy, and both psychotherapist and interpreter were staff members of the Center on Deafness and, therefore, subject to that agency's guidelines.

The client in question is a deaf male in his 30's who complained initially of relationship problems in both his personal and professional life. He was seen over a period of several months by a hearing therapist who used the services of a CSC interpreter on staff. As might be imagined, the interpreter had a great deal of experience working in mental health settings.

The client was bright, well-educated, responsible, and generally handled many aspects of his life in an adaptive manner. He had, however, experienced consistent difficulties over a period of two decades because, in his words, "people do not understand deaf people." With exploration of his complaints in some detail over a period of several weeks, it was revealed that he would have angry, at times uncontrolled, temper outbursts in response to what he perceived as "put-downs" or patronizing behavior coming from others, or to violations of his rights.

While he was apparently often correct in his perceptions, his own behavior was frequently excessive, difficult to understand, and frankly intolerable to those around him. As a consequence, he had lost many friendships in the deaf community, had lost important affectional relationships, had lost important training opportunities, and had severe vocational problems. He felt, and was in fact, isolated, uncared for, and unappreciated for his abilities and accomplishments.

The client had a troubled family history. He had been abandoned by his natural mother to institutional care at birth and was placed in foster care at age 17 months. He remained with the same foster family throughout his childhood and adolescence, but he was never treated as an equal member of the family as the foster parents' natural children were. He remembered that he had always felt inadequate, unacceptable, and damaged in his foster parents eyes.

It is likely that such a tenuous position in the family was a source of great distress and pain for the client. It is also likely that he protected himself from such emotional assault. He achieved this sense of being protected by not fully connecting his natural childhood needs for nurturance and dependency onto a set of parents who seemed unwilling or unable to meet those needs.

At the same time, the client was blocked from complete rejection of his foster parents' behavior and emotional separation from them. The family was the only available source of emotional support he had. Thus, he was forced to suppress negative feelings and aggressive drives in order to maintain what little emotional supplies were available from the family.

This situation created in the client a deep sense of isolation and lack of self-worth along with an unsolvable conflict: he had the natural needs of a child and a correlated drive to meet those needs with closeness and dependency. Closeness and dependency with his foster parents, however, were punished by their relative rejection of him and their refusal to provide him a secure place in the family. This in turn created a drive to avoid such danger by distance from, and lack of connection to, others. In short, his childhood was a "damned if he did, damned if he didn't" situation. If he sought connection with his parents, he placed his fragile sense of self in the hands of people who could not be trusted to treat it with respect and care. If he protected his fragile sense of self by refusing connection with his parents, he condemned himself to ever-increasing fragility, for it is only in the acceptance and love from others that a child comes to know and trust his own worth.

This conflict, which was fully outside of his awareness, was played out in many ways throughout his adult life. He would feel unloved and needy and would approach others for support and care; as others moved closer to him, and he closer to others, the unconscious conflict would stimulate deep feelings of danger and threat. He would then experience an impulse to drive the others away, to protect himself through isolation. In terms of the framework developed above, he transferred significant emotional responses connected to the earlier relationship with his foster parents (where such responses were actually adaptive) onto new relationships in his adult life (where such responses most often were maladaptive). He accomplished this "driving away" by his excessively hostile behavior, which assured that others would reject him. He then would physically escape from the situation by running away (i.e., to another job, another school, another state, another relationship, etc.).

The client initially entered therapy in response to a crisis. As the crisis was resolved and he received some support from the therapy, his motivation for serious work and insight development diminished. It became clear that he saw the psychotherapy as an arena in which he could fortify his attribution of his problems to the notion that "people don't understand deaf people." In particular, it was important for him to convince the psychotherapist that all of the other people with whom he had problems were in the wrong and guilty while he himself was innocent, abused, and misunderstood.

The client resisted the interpretation that he himself might be adding something to his difficulties. In fact, when the psychotherapist would suggest ways in which his own behavior might have influenced how others reacted to him, he would claim that the psychotherapist either did not understand the situation or did not understand deaf people. Thus, it was impossible to use the client's prior experiences as a tool to help both psychotherapist and client explore the client's deep, persistent, and pervasive relationship problems.

It was felt that the problem could be addressed only through the transference relationship. The psychotherapist knew that he would make no progress by arguing about the meaning of the client's past behavior. Both psychotherapist and client needed some immediate and tangible experience to examine. The client's transference onto the therapeutic relationship of similar feelings of closeness and fear of that closeness could provide that immediate and tangible experience. The expectation was that as the relationship between the psychotherapist and the client grew, and they became increasingly close, the client would experience a sense of danger and consequently come to feel that the actions of the psychotherapist put him down, patronized him, and violated his rights.

Obviously, it was necessary for the psychotherapist to remain neutral and not to behave in such a way that the client could objectively view as a violation of his rights, as patronizing, or as diminishing of his sense of self. Only by maintaining such neutrality could the psychotherapist assure that such feelings in the client were based on transference, and thus be able to offer him an immediate and safe forum to explore the meaning of those feelings.

Unfortunately, the client's goals conflicted with those of the therapist. Because it was important to the client to present himself as controlled, rational, and pleasant (so that the psychotherapist could see that it was others who behaved incorrectly), he would not allow himself to manifest his powerful negative feelings or to follow his impulse toward angry behavior as he felt himself move closer to the therapist.

The situation continued for several months with little progress made in psychotherapy other than the establishment of a fairly trusting relationship between psychotherapist and client and, incidentally, between interpreter and client. And as expected, as the relationships became closer, they became more dangerous to the client. He would seek to distance himself and change the focus or established procedures of the therapy in small ways that are not important to recount here. Major topics in therapy during this time included plans for a new vocation, the client's living arrangements, and details of the client's history.

During one session at the end of this period, however, the client made a great shift in plans he had been developing over the previous weeks and announced his intention to move to another part of the country. The psychotherapist made a rather minor interpretation of this shift in plans as a way of escaping the difficulties and isolation that had arisen for him in the preceding months. He also pointed out several other times in the client's past when similar events had occurred and served the same purpose in the client's life. The therapist was also attending to another function of such a move, namely, to end the ever closer (and thus ever more dangerous) relationship with the therapist. He did not interpret this function to the client.

The client's face flushed with anger, and he had to pause to regain his control. He then stated that the therapist was mistaken. The psychotherapist sensed that the danger the client had been experiencing was finally surfacing. Thinking that perhaps the opportunity to explore the transference feelings had arrived, he suggested that the client might be angry with his interpretation. The client insisted that he was not angry; he was only pointing out how the interpretation was incorrect and displayed a lack of understanding of deaf people. The session ended with no further progress being made.

At the very next session, the client started off by bringing up the interpretation again. He was in much better control, had formulated some convincing arguments to support his position, and was impervious to alternate ideas. He nonetheless remained agitated and upset. At this point in the interview, the interpreter made a minor error in his signing. The client did not understand the interpreter's communication and asked him directly and in a very angry manner what he was saying. The interpreter tried to clarify his communication; however, the client (perhaps purposefully) had difficulty understanding the clarification. The client then launched into a tirade at the interpreter, telling him that "that's not the way to make that sign to a deaf person." He then asked the interpreter if he had CSC certification.

While there was a miscommunication, and the client was certainly well within his rights to ask for clarification and for a statement of the interpreter's qualifications, his behavior seemed excessive for the situation and sadistic toward the interpreter. It seemed, in fact, precisely the sort of behavior that had brought the client into therapy in the first place. The therapist also noted that the behavior had followed closely upon difficulties the client was experiencing with him. For this reason, the psychotherapist assessed them as being part of transference feelings which really had himself as the object rather than the interpreter. Display of such feeling toward the psychotherapist was too dangerous, so the client displaced them onto the interpreter.

The psychotherapist was placed in a dilemma. He was aware that the interpreter was suddenly involved in the therapeutic process in a way neither he nor the interpreter had planned for. He was also acutely aware of the RID Code of Ethics and its charge that the interpreter not become involved. And finally, he was aware that a significant event had occurred that had been anticipated for months and that might not occur again for several more months. Moreover, there was a great danger of the client terminating therapy: the sudden decision to move was (at least in part) an acting out of the resistance to the growing closeness of the therapeutic relationship. If resistance is not addressed in therapy, there is great danger of premature termination, particularly with a client whose general mode of operation is to run away from difficulties. Exploring the attack on the interpreter with the client would necessarily involve the interpreter in "unethical" ways (particularly since it was likely that the client would want to bring the interpreter into the discussion). But not exploring the event would be counter-therapeutic and not in the client's best interests: not only would it necessarily delay progress in therapy, but it would also collude with the client's resistance and lead to premature termination of the therapy.

Here's what happened: the psychotherapist turned to the interpreter and asked him to sign everything he said. He then said that he was going to do something that might be uncomfortable to the interpreter, and that if the interpreter did not think it appropriate, he should stop him. Then he asked the client how he imagined the interpreter might feel after what had just occurred. The client stated that he had the right to ask about the interpreter's qualifications. The psychotherapist agreed that he had such a right and suggested that he even had in some sense a duty to ensure that his interpreter was sufficiently qualified. But he also pointed out that that was not an answer to the question, which was about the interpreter's possible feelings. The client could not bring himself to answer, but responded with statements such as, "I don't care if it made him angry; if he feels hurt, that's his problem, not mine; he shouldn't get upset if I ask about his CSC." The psychotherapist then said that it seemed that the client imagined that the interpreter might feel angry, hurt, and upset. The client then turned to the interpreter and asked him how he did feel. The interpreter, in violation of his own code of ethics, said that he had felt angry and had wanted to "just get through the session and be done with it." The psychotherapist then, in a supportive manner, said that he was glad that the event had happened because finally there was something that both he and the client were a part of and could look at together.

The general treatment course and the specific event outlined above reflects a complex psychotherapeutic process. That process can be described as follows:

1) the client initially formed a tenuous therapeutic alliance with the psychotherapist which enabled him to discuss painful situations and continue in treatment despite his difficulty in tolerating even gentle confrontation of his beliefs and behaviors;

2) as the relationship between psycho-therapist and client grew more close, the client began to experience strong unconscious wishes to be dependent on and nurtured by the psychotherapist;

3) the dependence wishes in the client activated strong unconscious fears of assault on his self integrity by being rejected and discounted (as he was by his foster parents);

4) the conflict defined by 2) and 3) gave rise to wishes to escape from the relation-ship, to sacrifice his dependency needs in the service of ego integrity (again, as he had with his foster parents);

5) he defended his integrity a) by denial of interpretations made by the psychotherapist and b) by minor attempts to shift the focus and procedure of the psychotherapy. In this way, he could control or escape from the painful aspects of the therapy while maintaining continued (though reduced) contact with the psychotherapist;

6) as his defenses against the psychotherapist/ client relationship failed (i.e., as he grew more dependent on the psychotherapist), he formulated plans to leave the area and thus escape the dangers

of the relationship (a form of transference acting out, limited in this case since usually he would precipitate his own rejection by hostile action prior to leaving);

7) when the psychotherapist interpreted the plan for leaving, the patient lost control of his impulses to act out the transference in a limited way and experienced powerful hostility toward the psychotherapist;

8) direct attack on the psychotherapist would endanger the position the client had taken throughout the psychotherapy, namely, that the problems that he had had in the past were due to the failings of others. Therefore, he directed his transference acting out onto the interpreter.

The test of such an analysis is, of course, in how the psychotherapy proceeded from that point. The psychotherapist said that while he could acknowledge the client's right to question the interpreter's skills, he felt that the client's strong feelings had much more to do with his feelings about the psychotherapist than with the interpreter. He asked the client how he was feeling about him. The client, in contradistinction to the consistent stand he had taken throughout the psychotherapy up to that point, said that he felt the psychotherapist looked down on him, thought himself superior, and expected the client to agree with everything he said and to comply with every suggestion. The psycho-therapist asked him if that was what he had felt about his foster parents, and the client said that it was. He went on to rail against professionals who work with deaf people and how they never understood the deaf person (remember that the interpreter was also a professional working with a deaf person). The therapist asked the client if he felt he was being misunderstood now, and the client said that he did. The balance of the session was spent in examining these feelings. Thus, it turned out that the event described offered the first significant break in the client's resistance and the first substantial movement in the course of psychotherapy.

Case implications

We have offered this extensive description of the case not to train the reader in psychotherapy, but rather to give some sense of the complexity inherent in psychotherapeutic treatment. We have also attempted a description of how the interpreter can become intimately involved with the therapeutic process. It is fine for the psychotherapist and the interpreter to say, following the RID Code of Ethics, that the interpreter will not become involved with the client — in effect, "Thou shalt not transfer onto the interpreter!" But who tells the client? And even bringing this issue up with the client in an effort to limit its consequences would be ineffectual; remember that transference is an unconscious process not accessible to the immediate awareness of the client.

The interpreter, who had a mutually trusting and respectful relationship with the psychotherapist as well as a great deal of experience with and knowledge of psychotherapeutic processes, behaved in a manner absolutely appropriate to the therapeutic needs of the client and to the situation. The feedback that he gave to the client (at the client's request), was authentic and was not punitive, even though it was likely difficult for the client to receive. And his stand toward the client (his client as well as the psychotherapist's) remained helpful and professional in tone throughout the session and, incidentally, in subsequent sessions. However, he had clearly "violated" well-established ethical principles of his profession.

Was it simply that he was very insightful and sensitive — thus able to allow the intrusion on his non-involvement and able to provide accurate and authentic feedback to the client? In part, yes. But more importantly, the interpreter and psychotherapist discussed the case regularly (again, an ethical "violation") and had in fact expected the session described above to present some difficulty. They'd spent a few minutes preparing together for the session, and the psychotherapist had said he expected the client to act out against him in some way because of difficulties in the immediately preceding session (acting out toward the interpreter was not expected). In other words, they had established a working relationship in which the interpreter was seen by himself and the psychotherapist as part of the treatment team, not as an intrusive but a necessary addition to be tolerated. He took the position that interpreting in this psychotherapy setting was unlike interpreting in a classroom, court, medical office, indeed, almost any other setting. He took the setting to be, rather, one in which the best interests of his client nay not be easily discerned and may not be adequately supported by a rigid set of principles seeking to provide protection to his customers in the broadest range of situations possible. He operated as a professional in the best sense of that word.

Interpreter Role, Training and Ethics

We think that there are important points-implied in our discussion of psychotherapeutic processes, of how the interpreter can become involved in those processes, and of an event wherein the interpreter's choice not to maintain an uninvolved stance helped forward the best interests of the client. The points are relevant to:

a) the interpreter's role in any long-term, psychodynamic psychotherapy,
b) the nature of the RID Code of Ethics, and
c) the training of interpreters.

The interpreter as a member of the treatment team

We have suggested that interpreters working in the context of psychotherapy do not really have the choice to be involved or uninvolved. That choice is left to the psychotherapy client, and it is a choice the client may make at an unconscious level. When such involvement occurs, the interpreter's choices are quite limited: a) he can use it in the client's best interests; or b) can deny the involvement occurred. We think the former choice is more appropriate. What is chosen is something that might be termed "controlled unethical behavior." What is avoided is unaddressed countertransference reactions on the part of the interpreter. That is, whenever the interpreter in fact becomes involved with the client, there is a great danger of countertransference reactions which could affect the way the interpreter does the job. By allowing such involvement to be open and available for discussion, one also allows a forum where such counter-transference possibilities can be explored and corrected, if necessary.

Are we suggesting, then, that the interpreter is appropriately seen as a sort of co-therapist who can make interventions and work out the therapeutic issues with the client during a course of treatment? Our answer to that is an emphatic "no." Psychotherapy, when it is really done well, is a powerful and risky business that requires of its practitioners years of training and even more years of experience before they can be said to be top-notch professionals.

Rather, we are suggesting that the interpreter ideally is an adjunct member of the treatment team, which may include a psychiatrist for medication, other medical service providers, a social worker for social service coordination, a vocational rehabilitation specialist, and so forth. The primary coordinator of services, however, must be the psychotherapist. In part, the superordinate status of the psychotherapist is necessary in order to foster a unified and cohesive treatment approach. One person must have ultimate responsibility for the course of treatment. Too, it is generally true that the psychotherapist is privy to the broadest range of information about the client. More important, however, is this: in any course of psychotherapeutic treatment, there are multiple points at which choices for future direction of treatment must be made. Often there are several "right" choices that can be made. In our opinion, however, it is never right or helpful to the client for one member of the treatment team to choose a direction different from another member. We see it as necessary, then, for one person to have the final say — to "call the shots," as it were. If the interpreter is to use her involvement with the client in an appropriate way, it must be under the leadership of the psychotherapist.

This role implies several things: first, it implies that the therapist and interpreter, as well as other members of the treatment team, must have a relationship which provides an opportunity to work out disagreements, to share information, to decide on the direction for treatment, to provide mutual support, and so forth. Such a relationship fosters cooperation and assists the psychotherapist in the leadership role. Second, it implies that the interpreter is subject to the same dangers that the psychotherapist is subject to (i.e., of injecting one's own countertransference issues into the treatment, of managing the transference inappropriately, etc.). Just as the psychotherapist should seek ongoing supervision with respect to these issues, so ought the interpreter. Finally, it implies that the interpreter who chooses to do mental health interpreting ought to share some of the professional values, theoretical concepts, technical vocabulary, and procedural knowledge of the psychotherapist. In short, the interpreter and psychotherapist ought to "speak the same language." (This notion has obvious training implications, which we discuss below.)

There is another obvious answer to the dilemma we have presented. One could not include the interpreter as a member of the treatment team, or as a consistent element in therapy. The psychotherapist might use different interpreters on a revolving basis. That way, a transference relationship between the client and interpreter would have no opportunity to develop. Unfortunately, such moves would introduce a very chaotic and unstable element to the therapy. And part of psychotherapy is precisely to provide a consistent, stable, and safe environment for the client to do his work.

Ethical implications

We think that the RID Code of Ethics needs to be looked at carefully with respect to its appropriateness in dealing with the issues arising in the psychotherapy setting. Each of the statements we outlined at the beginning of this paper is problematic: we have seen that keeping assignment-related information strictly confidential is a knotty issue in a setting where the work done must be discussed with others (i.e., other treatment providers, supervisors, etc.). We have seen that rendering the message faithfully and conveying the content and spirit of the speaker can be a herculean task when some of the content and spirit of the speaker is unconscious and covert. We have suggested that not interjecting personal opinions can be counter-therapeutic in the psychotherapy setting, in certain cases. We would also suggest here that such strict neutrality is destructive to the sort of cooperation and sharing of information between psychotherapists and interpreter necessary for providing the most appropriate services to the client. Finally, we submit that if one does not have appropriate training and experience, or is not willing to take on the unique interpreter role demanded by the psychotherapy setting, then one ought to exclude interpreting in psychotherapy settings from one's practice. Only thus is one using discretion with regard to skill, setting, and the consumers involved.

Training implications

If interpreters are to take such an expanded role in the context of interpreter-assisted psychotherapy, how are they to be trained for that role? We have investigated several interpreter training programs across the country. We found that, in the main, mental health interpreting is not specifically addressed in their curricula, though it may appear as a topic in an ethics course or a multi-topic seminar. It seems as though most interpreters can complete their training and receive certification with no didactic presentation of the special issues relevant to mental health interpreting in general, or interpreter-assisted psychotherapy in particular. We also found that training practica in most programs did not include placements in mental health settings. This means that most interpreters do not receive practical training experience in mental health settings. Obviously, the issues that we have presented in this paper reflect our belief that the standard training most interpreters receive is insufficient to meet the needs of the mental health setting.

We found one shining counterexample, however. That counterexample was the health service interpreting program offered by St. Mary's Junior College in Minneapolis. The St. Mary's program takes practicing interpreters and provides them with advanced training for interpreting in health service settings, including mental health service settings. The curriculum includes an 11-week course in mental health interpreting that covers such topics as theories and techniques of psychotherapy, psychological tests and measurements, psychopathology, epidemiology of mental disturbance, special interpreting techniques, relationship to other service providers, and ethics. Students also receive 30 hours of practicum training in a mental health setting. We were quite impressed with the program and believe it could provide a model for other institutions seeking to provide good interpreter training.

Another means for providing such training is potentially offered by the mental health agencies themselves. Our agency offers in-service training for staff and both a formal and an informal peer supervision network. Members of the interpreting staff regularly participate in training and research activities and discuss cases with the clinical staff. Such activities in any agency could provide the foundation for a more formal in-service training program wherein experienced interpreters are given didactic and practical training in mental health interpreting and ongoing supervision of their work subsequent to the completion of training.

Concluding Remarks

We have attempted to present what we feel are important issues and problems regarding the appropriate functions of the interpreter in the psychotherapy situation. We have also suggested some possible solutions to those problems, all of which point to an expanded role for the interpreter. We do not claim to have offered fully satisfactory solutions, however. Rather, our purpose has been to stimulate discussion of the issues within the separate fields of psychotherapy and interpreting. A comprehensive discussion of the role of the psychotherapist in mental health settings would necessarily address multiple issues, some of which have been addressed by Stansfield (1981):

When therapists need to know information about deafness, language, and communication, should the interpreter comment...?

Should the interpreter be in charge of arranging the seating?

Who should clarify unclear communication from the client?

How should the interpreter handle comments made to him directly by the client?

How can the interpreter deal with his feelings about how the therapist is handling the session?

How should the interpreter assess the client's communication before the session?

It is beyond the scope of this paper to address all of the issues in mental health interpreting, but it is not beyond the scope of the field. We expect that both interpreters and psychotherapists will continue to debate these issues as they have in the past. What we have suggested is that mental health interpreting constitutes a specialty area within the field of general sign language interpreting and, as such, demands special training, experience, and standards of professional practice.

Taking Care of Interpreters at California State University Northridge National Center on Deafness

Debbie Barber-Gonzales, Caroline L. Preston, and Gary R. Sanderson

Introduction

After completing an interpreter training program, the new interpreter is all too often placed on the job with little or no supervision or opportunity for improvement.

The National Center on Deafness (NCOD) Communication Services in noticing this dilemma has set up an extensive array of opportunities for its interpreting staff. These afford the interpreters at the NCOD ways to grow, not only in their skills but professionally and ethically.

Communication Services has developed a program in which interpreters, whether entry level or seasoned veterans, can continue pursuing growth at their own level in a nurturing, safe and relaxed environment.

What follows is a detailed description of various services provided to interpreters at NCOD.

Addressing Special Needs

The Communication Services component of NCOD has established several support groups focusing on the concerns of its staff members and interpreters. These concerns include: Tendonitis, Brachial Neuritis, Carpal Tunnel Syndrome, stress, burnout, role conflict and recognition of outstanding performance.

Physical ailments

The plight of interpreters who have work-related injuries has been an impetus for NCOD to seek out solutions. Inner campus contacts have been made with: the CSUN Student Health Center, the Adaptive Physical Education Department, and the Physical Therapy Department. These have proven to be valuable resources in providing for information regarding these ailments. They have provided our employees with measures for prevention and suggested remedies as a series of exercises, Signercises"
developed by Vanet Yapp, Physical Therapist, CSUN Student Health Center. It is recommended these should be done prior to interpreting and at the end of the day to prevent complications. These "Signercises" have been distributed to all of our interpreters. A hearing-impaired student is currently doing intensive research on Tendonitis and has been instrumental with the support of NCOD, in setting up a weekly, hour-long Tendonitis clinic at the CSUN Health Center. An immediate solution that NCOD provides to the ailing interpreter is a change of their work schedule, allowing for more periods of rest between classes. When interpreters are unable to continue working for a period of time, we recommend that they apply for Worker's Compensation. NCOD will continue to focus on the physical

problems of interpreting in the hopes of providing a more comprehensive support service to its employees.

Stress

Recognizing the need for personnel to interact on a professional level with their colleagues, NCOD sponsored a 'Stress Burnout Workshop" conducted by Kris Vreeland, an interpreter at NCOD. This workshop focused on the various ways of coping with and relieving stress in our professional lives. Participants have expressed a desire to meet on a regular basis in order to establish trust and rapport with their colleagues. During these sessions they discussed ethical procedures in handling situations that arise, and share feelings about functioning as an interpreter. This has led to further discussion regarding establishing support groups on campus supported by the NCOD staff interpreters and thereby limited to the educational setting. As a result, a support group under the auspices of S.C.R.I.D.– San Fernando Valley has been established. The group meets on a weekly basis and is well attended.

Recognition

NCOD is aware that interpreters strive for optimal performance while on assignment. In an effort to recognize those individuals who have exemplified outstanding service, awards are presented annually for "Outstanding Interpreter."

The criteria for the "Outstanding Interpreter" award are:
1) interest in and participation with deaf students at CSUN;
2) ability to work with deaf students;
3) willingness to improve his/her interpreting skills and/or understanding of deaf students; and
4) a good work record and dependability.

The interpreter may nominate himself/herself for the award or be nominated by students, staff or faculty members. A selection committee determines who the recipient of this prestigious award will be. A plaque is presented to the recipient during an "Awards Night" ceremony. At this ceremony, hearing-impaired students are also honored for outstanding achievements in various disciplines.

The honoree's name is added to the plaque designating previous recipients of the award, which is displayed in our offices. NCOD is committed to providing an environment that maximizes optimum working conditions and addresses the needs and concerns of its employees.

Liaison Activities

The NCOD staff functions as a liaison between the hourly employees, faculty, staff and the hearing-impaired students. By encouraging students and interpreters to interact, share feelings and socialize, overall service provided increases in quality. Examples of these kinds of activities are:
1) rap sessions in which students, staff and administrators discuss concerns regarding service, policy and campus life;
2) a graduation reception for graduating students and interpreters hosted by the NCOD's staff, students and administrators to show our pride in their accomplishments;

3) "students vs. staff" basketball, volleyball or softball games;
4) staff members helping to resolve problems between students and employees.

Resources

The NCOD offers its interpreters a variety of resources that are of great benefit to them. These include:

1) the Library on Deafness, which houses the largest collection of deafness related materials on the west coast;
2) a videotape library which houses over 200 tapes, including scenarios in Pidgin Sign English, American Sign Language, foreign sign languages, lectures, historical material, samples of interpreting techniques, linguistics and entertainment;
3) an in-house mini-library of sign vocabulary, interpreting texts, professional newsletters, journals, and university text books (used to prepare for interpreting specific classes and employee projects);
4) extensive vocabulary files germane to the various disciplines taught on campus;
5) the staff of the NCOD, including nationally recognized experts in the fields of interpreting, counseling and entertainment;
6) university staff and professors who work with interpreters in professional seminars and training courses.

Job Performance

The interpreter at the NCOD finds the skills diagnosis program a valuable tool. The following assessment procedures provide an accurate measure of an interpreter's capabilities while promoting a positive rapport between staff and employees.

On-the-job observation/diagnosis

On-the-job observation and diagnosis is available to all interpreters upon request. A copy of the written evaluation is provided with a detailed analysis of skills. Post-performance discussion and recommendations are made to the interpreter. Original copies of all evaluations are placed in the interpreter's file.

Mandatory three-minute videotape evaluation

This is a purely expressive task which is completed each semester. The NCOD maintains video personnel files and data regarding the growth patterns of the interpreter, which then influence the placement of interpreters. This is a technique which makes it possible for all interpreters to be observed and receive feedback each semester.

Raise evaluations

This is a series of videotape evaluations which include professional behavior as well as expressive and receptive areas of skill. A warm-up videotape similar to the actual test is provided, and the applicant may request critique from a staff interpreter. It is at this juncture that the applicant may be advised about readiness for the evaluation and areas for improvement are discussed.

Student evaluations

Each semester, hearing-impaired students have an opportunity to provide input regarding interpreting services. A list of interpreting components Is given to the deaf student and each component is rated on a scale of one (low) to five (high). After all of the evaluations have been submitted, the scores are tabulated and the interpreter receives the averages. This also affords staff members a vehicle for detecting potential problems before they occur.

Skill improvement contract (implementation – fall 1985)

Each interpreter, with advisement from a staff interpreter, will establish areas for specific concentration which will be renewable each semester. A contractual agreement will be drafted by the interpreter, including a personal plan of action to reach his or her goals. NCOD will agree to provide specific learning activities that will reinforce the individual's program. This agreement will be signed by the interpreter and a staff member with the option of changing the goals as needed.

Employee In-Service

In-service training has been an integral part of the NCOD's interpreting services since the program's inception. During the infancy of the program, "in-service" primarily focused on professional behavior, code of ethics and skill building tasks. Pioneering new concepts and techniques for future interpreting training programs, our innovations have led to the present format of employee "in-service" training programs at CSUN.

Individual work

Any interpreter employed by NCOD has the opportunity of having an individual ongoing assessment of their interpreting skills. This training may be very general in nature, or it may focus on one aspect of the interpreting process. Full use of video and audio equipment and other materials is made to maximize the learning experience.

Off-campus workshops

Because of CSUN's central location, workshops offered in the entire Southern California area are always within a two-hour drive from the campus. Interpreters employed at CSUN have access to all announcements of professional workshops and courses and are encouraged to attend. Staff interpreters serve as resources to employees, advising them about appropriate selections of courses and seminars. Upon completion of off-campus training, the interpreter may complete a request for in-service hours which upon approval, will be documented and included in their records. After meeting the requirement of 45 hours of in-service training (among other requirements), the employee becomes eligible for salary increase.

Education interpreting x806

Fondly known as "806," this employee in-service course had its beginnings with the inception of NCOD. One of the enticements of x806 is the fact that the design is always changing to meet the current training demands of the profession. Members of the class have the option of earn-ing the required 45 hours of in-service or credits through the university extension program.

Brush-up workshops

Although CSUN is on a semester system, there are large gaps of time between semesters. Many interpreters feel that they lose their "fine tuned" skills during that interim. One week prior to the beginning of the new semester, brush-up workshops are offered to help interpreters prepare for the heavy interpreting demands that will be placed on them. Frequently the trainers of these workshops are our advanced interpreters and they present prepared projects (see Educational Interpreting x806 Seminar).

Special workshops

The NCOD has hosted numerous special workshops pertaining to the field of interpreting such as:

- Sign-to-Voice Interpreting
- Classroom Techniques for Interpreters
- C.S.C. Preparation
- Individual Diagnosis
- Deaf-Blind Interpreting
- Oral Transmission
- Fingerspelling
- Consumer Feedback
- Stress/Burnout

Coursework for hours

It has been a long-standing policy that in-service credit be given for courses offered at the university which relates to interpreting. Such courses are: Sign-to-Voice, Structure of ASL, Issues in ASL, Practicum, Creative Uses of ASL, and Deaf Culture.

Educational Interpreting 806 seminar

An offshoot of "806," "806-S" is designed for the interpreters who have obtained a more advanced level of skill. Over the years, there has been a higher attrition rate among the advanced interpreters in the 806 classes. In an attempt to challenge these interpreters, 806-S was established. It differs from 806 in that the fundamentals of educational interpreting are well-established, thereby allowing dialogue and exchange of expertise by class members. Participants are required to present a project pertinent to the profession which will be bound and perhaps videotaped for the library. This program has rejuvenated the advanced interpreters and has caused them to increase their motivation toward the inservice program.

Practicum

NCOD is proud to maintain a staff of high caliber interpreters. Along with commanding a "state-of-the-art" salary, another incentive for employment is that many achieve master interpreter status. Master interpreters are observed by the students enrolled in the Special Education Practicum Course, and they provide the students with an opportunity to "apprentice" in the classroom. Realizing the value of such an experience, the interpreters employed by the NCOD have requested the same type of experience be arranged for them. Since the summer of 1984, the Employee Practicum has been underway. This experience has proven to be the most beneficial training provided thus far. An interpreter is assigned to work with a master interpreter at the beginning of each semester. After observing the master interpreter for a short time, a decision is made about how to structure the training program. The usual format of practicum is a rotation of interpreting responsibilities by day (unless the class is long and then the task is divided). The practicum employee is required to take notes while observing and paying close attention to areas that have been pinpointed for concentration. The master interpreter also observes and critiques the delivery of the employee, studying areas of both strengths and weaknesses. For each practicum assignment, there is at least one hour of discussion. At this point a careful analysis is made of the task with comments and suggestions. In-service credit is given for all practicum work. Interpreters who participate in practicum tell us that it is by far the best training experience of their entire career.

"...invaluable to have one-on-one constructive critique...the ability to observe someone with top skills and learn how to incorporate into your own style is a rare opportunity." (Shelly Hoffman)

"...the individual contact is so beneficial —it builds confidence, the feedback is excellent, the 'real' working situation is 'GREAT'...the highlight of this experience is that it is non-threatening, I'm working with someone... and that person is very accessible and personable!" (Roberta Munsey)

"...able to incorporate specific skills, i.e., use of classifiers, conceptual accuracy and lag time.... I sensed immediate improvement and heightened sense of confidence." (Susan Tieman)

"...the most important experience of my interpreter training...it's worth ten classes!" (Margaret Dorfman)

Observation
At any time an employee may observe a master interpreter on assignment. The master interpreter must be available since post-observation is an integral part of the training that the master interpreter and observer are required to meet.

Sign-to-voice practicum
Several faculty members at CSUN are deaf and require services of a sign-to-voice interpreter while teaching classes. In some of the classes, all of the students are hearing-impaired, as well as the instructor. This situation lends itself to the practicum experience.

The employee interpreter and a master interpreter situated in the back of the room can proceed with voicing and discussion without disturbing the class.

Acknowledgement
We thank our colleague, D. Dan Levitt, for his collaboration on this paper.

Attitudes Towards Sign Language

Sheila M. Antosch

Introduction

What are the attitudes of English-speaking Americans and the deaf community towards sign language? This paper is an overview which traces how the reactions and perspectives of two linguistic groups have interacted in American society. Throughout the history of deafness in America, English-speaking educators have cyclically accepted, rejected, and intervened with sign language as an educational tool. Throughout, the deaf community has cherished, protected, and advocated sign language as their natural right of communication, often while succumbing to an imposed stigma on sign language.

What has caused such vehement responses to sign language? This paper offers theories from sociology and sociolinguistics for explanatory clues. In particular, the sociological concepts of deviance, cyclical societal response, and stigma are proposed as possible explanatory frameworks for English-speaking Americans' perspective on sign language. Work from the field of sociolinguistics — especially language deficit theory, the notion of minority languages, and diglossia — serves as the explanatory framework for the deaf community's perspective on sign language.

Some researchers have made careful distinctions about labelling a deaf person as a member of the deaf community. These distinctions are rarely applied to those individuals labelled "hearing." We should briefly examine this unequal application of labels. How is one to know who can be labelled a member of the deaf community? There are three general criteria: common experiences, common language, and participation in community activities. According to Padden and Markowicz (1975), community membership requires a basic identity built on common experiences and expressed in a common language. The crux for achieving membership in the deaf community is the shared experience of being deaf (Higgins, 1980).

To what community do people who can hear belong? There is no single community whose membership depends upon the shared experiences of being able to hear. The common experiences of hearing are so much a part of tacit knowledge that they are taken for granted. Probably very few people who can hear would ever label themselves or their communities as "hearing." Participation in religious, occupational, or residential activities does define communities for people who can hear; participation in the activity of hearing does not. Thus, two of the three criteria for community membership do not apply to people who can hear. To write of the "hearing community" is therefore anomalous.

The only relevant shared attribute among the majority of Americans who can hear is the common language of English, which they assume everyone in America should be able to speak. In this sense, to write of a majority language, English, and a majority culture, American, in contrast to a minority language, American Sign Language (ASL), and a deaf subculture, *does* make sense. Therefore, "English-speaking Americans" is the label I will use for comparing and contrasting groups of Americans who can hear with the deaf community.

Attitudes

English-speaking Americans have two general attitudes toward sign language. First, sign language is viewed as a disability. An example of this attitude is found in educators who advocate oralism and consider the "language of deaf persons a pathological condition" (Stokoe, 1981, p. xxxi). The second general attitude of English-speaking Americans is that sign language is a minority language. However, instead of acknowledging deaf people as a minority group or a "thriving community, the English-speaking majority still often perceives "deaf people as isolated pathological individuals" (Woodward, 1980, p. 105).

Deaf people generally take the attitude that sign language is their natural language. Deaf people, however, are not immune to the English-speaking majority's negative attitudes toward sign language. Consequently, deaf people alternate between two attitudes, considering sign language both as a source of pride and as the basis of a sense of inferiority.

These attitudes of the English-speaking Americans and deaf Americans toward sign language have been in evidence throughout American history. To varying degrees, the attitudes of the two groups have influenced each other. This paper divides and dovetails the historical relationships between English-speaking educators and deaf Americans regarding sign language into four general attitudes:
1) sign language is a disability;
2) sign language is a birthright;
3) sign language is a minority language; and
4) a set of mixed reactions.

Sign language as a disability

At the beginning of the nineteenth century, sign language was respected as an educational tool by a small group of English-speaking educators. The attitudes of this small group probably should not be taken as the norm for the attitudes of the American population as a whole. Yet, educators shape and signal the attitudes of other English-speaking Americans. One example of these educators influence was their success in obtaining legislative support and monies to establish residential and day schools for deaf children. Thus, the attitude of educators and those they influence, especially English-speaking parents of deaf children, will be inferred at least to have been influential over the American public's attitude.

In 1817, Gallaudet and Clerc started using sign language to educate deaf American children. They followed a Signed English approach which stressed the use of "methodological" signs to show English grammar (Lane, 1980b). The Signed English approach of these two educators suggests an attitude that deaf people's sign language was "disabled" and in need of rehabilitation via English grammar. Gradually, methodological signs were cast off as either too cumbersome or ineffective, and American schools for the deaf began to stress ASL rather than Signed English. By 1835, all the teachers in the American Asylum for the Deaf were required to use ASL (Lane, 1980b). Thus, sign language began to be respected as the native language of deaf Americans and was used as the primary language for education in the schools for the deaf for some fifty years after Gallaudet and Clerc's pioneering work (Gannon, 1981).

The attitude that sign language is a "disability" because of a lack of grammar temporarily subsided. At the same time, however, the attitude arose that sign language was a disability because signing deaf people did not speak. The notion that speech is superior to any other mode of language is as old as Aristotle's famous assertion that those who cannot speak are those who cannot think. (See Higgins, 1980.)

American educators were well aware of their European counterparts' preference for oralism. Yet, typical of the pragmatic American attitude was the report from George Day, given to the New York Institute for the Deaf after his 1845 trip to Europe. "The German method (oralism) has advantages for the few; the American method (signs) for the mass" (quoted in Lane, 1980b, p. 145). Although mid-nineteenth century American educators often thought that articulation or oralism was a waste of time, they did not forbid speech training for the deaf. The American proponents of sign language merely insisted that speech could not replace signs as the general educational method, and that speech was advantageous for only a few postlingually deafened students. The European proponents of speech, however, often forbade signs for any purpose whatsoever and declared speech the best educational method for all deaf students. According to oralists, sign language was a disability to be cured.

The Milan Conference of 1880, stacked in favor of oralism (Lane, 1980b), finally legitimized the attitude that sign language was a disability. Although this was supposedly an international conference, the majority delegation, European oralists, represented the smaller number of schools, teachers, and deaf students. The minority delegation, the American educators who signed, represented the greater number. The American delegation also had the only deaf delegate present at the conference (Gannon, 1981).

The final vote of the Milan Conference reflected the attitudes that sign language is both a minority language to be eradicated and a linguistic disability. The declaration labelled speech superior to signs "for restoring deaf-mutes to social life and for giving them greater facility of language" (quoted in Lane, 1980b, p. 155). Thus, by the end of the nineteenth century, the doctrines of oralism treated sign language as a disability, an inadequate form of communication that degenerated superior speech skills (Woll and Lawson, 1981). For the sake of both rehabilitation and integration, sign language was to be suppressed.

The Milan Conference was not the only impetus for the English-speaking American educators' eventual acceptance of oralism. Even before the conference, Alexander Graham Bell in the 1870's attempted to characterize sign language and deafness as pathological conditions (Lane, 1980b).

Bell began his teaching career advocating oralism for the deaf. His later inventions of the telephone and audiometer were attempts to treat deafness with a "prosthesis, with rehabilitation" (Lane, 1980b, p. 150).

Bell apparently held the attitude that sign language creates a separate, and thus unacceptable, minority language community. It is important to note that Bell was close to two postlingually deafened adults, his mother and his wife. These deafened women's native language was spoken English, and they probably felt that deafness had deprived them of their birthright. Thus, Bell's goal was to cure deafness and remove what he and his deafened community" perceived to be the socially isolating use of sign language.

The role of the immediate community in shaping linguistic attitudes can also be seen from the example of Bell's chief opponent, E.M. Gallaudet. A proponent of sign language, Gallaudet, who could hear, was surrounded by congenitally deaf adults, who all used ASL (Lane, 1980b). Because of this intimate community, Gallaudet considered any "course of annihilation for the deaf minority and its language... (to be) anathema" (Lane, 1980b, p. 150).

The deaf community surrounding Gallaudet was less influential, however, than the deafened community surrounding Bell. Oralism became entrenched as the preferred means of educating deaf children. According to English-speaking educators, sign language was the pathological disability causing the linguistic and social deficiencies they perceived in the deaf community: deaf people's lack of speech, poor command of English, clannishness, and exile from the normal hearing world (Gannon, 1981).

Sign language as a birthright

What was the attitude of the deaf community toward sign language in the nineteenth century? While the English-speaking majority was first accepting, then rejecting, and finally suppressing sign language, the deaf community was cherishing sign language as its birthright. In fact, at the first convention of the National Association of the Deaf, in 1880, the deaf delegates deliberately used the term "mute" as an insult to the oralist educators in Milan, who that same year had condemned sign and extolled speech (Gannon, 1981).

The deaf community at the time of the Milan conference was well aware that it was a linguistic minority in need of autonomy. The NAD resolved at its first convention, in 1880, to organize deaf people across the nation in order to address the needs of deaf people as a class. (See Gannon, 1981, p. 62.)

The Milan Conference's rejection of sign language did not leave the self-esteem of the deaf community untouched. Even though deaf leaders continued to praise sign language, a stigma developed around sign language. Oralism all but eliminated deaf teachers (Gannon, 1981), and because signs were outlawed in schools, deaf people began to view ASL as a "stigma of the uneducated, illiterate, and unfit" (Fant, 1977, p. 28). When authority figures in the educational institutions suppressed sign language, a `negative, guilty attitude" concerning the use of signs emerged (Gannon, p. 363). Deaf people's birthright, sign language, had a price: stigma.

Sign language as a minority language

The goal of oralism is not to create a stigma which would isolate deaf people, but rather to integrate deaf people into the general society through common spoken language. This integrative motivation of oralism does not necessarily reflect an attitude that sign language is a pathological disability, but rather the attitude that sign language is a minority language and therefore unacceptable. The "oral majority" truly believe the "welfare of the deaf is best served when they are assimilated into the majority and hence abandon their linguistic traditions" (Lane, 1980b, p.120).

This notion of replacing the minority language with the dominant majority language has been applied by English-speaking Americans to other ethnic groups. As Woll and Lawson (1981) point out, this tendency is probably intensified against the deaf for several reasons. Ninety-five per cent of parents who have a deaf child can themselves hear. Like most parents, the parents of a deaf child want their child to be integrated into the parent's own society, in this case, the dominant society of the culture. The integration of deaf people can most easily be accomplished when they acquire mastery of the dominant language. Most teachers of the deaf are native English speakers, so the integration of the deaf through oralism is further reinforced. Another reason for integrating deaf children through speech is the additional stigma which labels users of sign as "not bright" or "low verbal" (Woll and Lawson, p. 219).

Recently, sign language has become acceptable again to English-speaking Americans. Gannon (1981) lists many factors contributing to this return to the attitude of the first half of the nineteenth century: linguistic research on and validation of ASL as a language, the educational achievements of native signers, favorable media coverage of deaf leaders, and a change in the general public's attitude toward disabilities. This change in public attitude, viewing disabled people as a minority group, has also been influenced by the civil rights movement of the 1960's and 1970's.

Although some linguists now value sign language for its potential to clarify the relationship between language and cognition (Deuchar, 1981), many English-speaking American educators believe that sign language is simply a malleable tool for educating deaf students. Sign language has been "reformed" by both deaf and English-speaking educators who want to make the presentation of the English language clearer to the deaf child. This reformation of, or intervention with, sign language consists of creating various visual English systems (Gannon, 1981). Unfortunately, as Charrow (1975a) points out, these sign systems too often base their signs on phonetic syllables rather than on meaningful morphemes. The result, a phonetic" sign language, may be easier for English-speaking parents of a deaf child to learn, but it is not necessarily easier for a congenitally deaf child to learn. Mastery over arbitrary phonetic symbols is not equivalent to competence in any language.

Besides being easy for English-speaking parents to learn (which may or may not be true), visual English systems remove sign language from the status of a minority language, restricted to a minority group. A deaf student's use of an English system in a classroom of English-speaking students reinforces that deaf student's identification with the majority language, English, rather than the minority language, ASL. This identification or integration of the deaf student into the English-speaking society is the goal of many English-speaking parents for their deaf children.

Other English-speaking Americans have begun to express great interest in sign language as a minority language. Many sign language books have been published since 1963, and enrollment in sign language classes has greatly increased. The chances that a typical English-speaking American will see signing are perhaps greater now than at any other time in American history.

Perhaps the best example of the current attitude that sign language is a minority language worthy of respect and study is the phenomenal increase in the number of trained sign language interpreters. Sign language interpreters no longer are predominantly members of deaf families, but are English-speaking Americans who have learned and developed competence in a minority language, ASL, or mastery of either a signed pidgin or visual English code.

Sign language as a set of mixed reactions

The deaf community in America has reacted to each change and development in the attitudes of English-speaking Americans toward sign language. In contrast to the push for integration with the majority through oralism, sign language has become a pre-requisite for membership in the minority community, the deaf community. In reaction to society's general acceptance of sign language, the deaf community has both expressed pride and experienced a resurgence of stigma. The manipulation of sign language into visual English systems by educators of deaf children has brought mixed reactions from the deaf community. Increasing numbers of sign language classes for English-speaking Americans are regarded with both trepidation and enthusiasm. Nevertheless, most deaf leaders, and probably most of the deaf community, advocate a pragmatic attitude of bilingualism between ASL and English.

Integration into the English-speaking majority through oralism denies a deaf person the self-identification of being deaf, of being a member of a minority group which uses a minority language, ASL. Freda Norman, a deaf actress, describes her experience eloquently:

A teacher said to me, "Teaching the deaf children through the means of oralism is the best method to adopt because the majority is hearing and it is up to the minority like you to join them. Being able to speak is likely to help you people to be accepted into the world."...I wonder now, how valuable it is that we must always try to be like others. My deafness is...myself, it is not something that I must fight against, or hide, or overcome. (quoted in Gannon, p. 355)

Although Norman mastered oral skills, she did not accept integration into the English-speaking world.

Supalla (1984), in an analysis of some early home movies made by a deaf American, Charles Kraul, emphasizes the importance of sign language

---

to the deaf community. In analyzing the films, which date back to 1925, Supalla distinguishes between the stereotype of deafness held by English-speaking Americans and the reality which deaf Americans lived. The stereotype of deafness, according to Supalla, is one of helplessness, isolation, and solitude. In contrast, deaf Americans live in a close linguistic community that protects its own values, lifestyle, and heritage through its language. To Supalla, Kraul's films are important because they prove deaf people in the earlier part of this century were not ashamed of sign language, despite the stigma placed on signs by English-speaking educators.

The current, respectable linguistic status of ASL has a significant effect on deaf people; but a positive attitude is not unanimous throughout the community. Lentz reports on several negative misconceptions about ASL that are "widely held among the deaf population" (1977, p. 239). She feels that these misconceptions are reflections of individual isolation from and loss of identity with the broader deaf community and culture.

Berke (1978) reports a resurgence of the stigma of ASL. Berke's deaf high school students themselves stigmatized ASL and preferred Signed English. According to Berke, such hostile and derogatory attitudes of his deaf students toward ASL stemmed from their perceptions of ASL: its linguistic inferiority to English, its supposed destruction of English skills, and its low social status. ASL may be the way deaf people talk, but it is not the way of success for smart people, or so deaf students believe. What these deaf students seen to have learned is that in America, the English-speaking majority does not overwhelmingly reward those who use a minority language.

Like Lentz, Berke attributes these negative attitudes about ASL to the fact that these deaf students, who are isolated from deaf culture, rarely see any successful ASL-signing deaf adults in the broader deaf community. Yet, if identification with ASL, not hearing loss, is the pre-requisite for entry into the deaf community, then the deaf students' negative attitudes toward ASL will reinforce their exclusion from the deaf community. A vicious cycle of educational isolation, ASL stigma, and community exclusion could develop among younger deaf people.

By interfering with sign language, many English-speaking Americans have shown a lack of respect for the deaf community and for ASL. Kannapell (1977) identifies ASL as the treasure and heritage of the deaf community: "the only thing we have that belongs to deaf people completely" (p. 162). Kannapell reflects other deaf people's worries when she wonders whether teaching ASL to English-speaking Americans will result in an increased domination of deaf people and a disappearance of a group identity among deaf people. Schreiber (1974) echoed these worries and frustrations when he longed for "the good old days" when sign language belonged only to deaf people. Consequently, many deaf Americans are hesitate to share ASL through the numerous sign language classes for English-speaking Americans.

Ironically, the increased interest in sign language classes and widespread exposure of ASL, which causes some deaf leaders to worry, was brought about by the concerted efforts of deaf leaders. The

Communicative Skills Program of the HAD, begun in 1967, had as its avowed goal the improvement of sign language instruction across the nation (Gannon, 1981). This program's resounding success "more than any,thing else helped remove the stigma of using sign language (Gannon, p. 368). Whether or not sign language classes for English-speaking Americans, after having reduced the stigma of signs, will now produce unwanted intrusions into the deaf community is still uncertain.

Most deaf leaders advocate a pragmatic attitude of bilingualism. This tolerant attitude of bilingualism is the position of the National Association of the Deaf which also emphasizes each deaf citizen's right to his or her own communication approach (NAD, 1984). Despite the increased availability of sign language interpreters, deaf people realize that competency in written English is vital for interaction with the majority of Americans. However, any condescension by deaf people toward ASL will only be counterproductive to this practical goal of mastering their second language, English (Kannapell, 1977).

Deaf leaders may advocate the lofty attitude of bilingualism, but the typical deaf person probably still struggles with the stigma of sign language and expects hostile attitudes toward it. Deaf college students in Lentz' class found it difficult to expect or accept favorable comments about ASL from English-speaking Americans.

Theoretical Explanations

Why did these four attitudes toward sign language (disability, birthright, minority language, and mixed) develop? Theoretical insights will be culled from sociological and sociolinguistic theories and then applied to the assumptions and attitudes of the English-speaking majority and the ASL-signing minority. In the first part, English-speaking Americans' attitude that sign language is a disability will be explained by sociological theories: Scheff's (1984) theory of social control, Goffman's (1963) theory of stigma, and Lemert's (1951) cycle of societal reaction to deviance. In the second part, ASL-signing Americans' attitudes about sign language as a birthright, both groups' perception of sign language as a minority language, and deaf Americans' mixed set of reactions toward sign language will be explained by sociolinguistic theories: Trudgill's (1983) definitive criterion, language deficit theory, Lane's (1980b) replacement-versus-dialectization theory, and the theoretical model of diglossia.

Sociological Theories
Social control

Scheff's (1984) theory of social control explains the intensity of English-speaking Americans' attitudes towards sign language. A shared language implies a set of shared expectations. Any violation of these expectations is deviant: it breaks the predictable patterns that allow social interaction to occur with minimal effort and conflict. Disruption of language expectations brings unpredictability to all social interaction into conscious focus, and this unpredictability results in frustration. If the deviance is perceived to be self-willed, then anger and resentment are introduced. This "deep and intense emotional response involving fear, anger and/or embarrassment" results in derogatory labels being given to deviants (Scheff, p. 31).

Sign language can be viewed as a breaking of the shared expectations concerning the use of English in American society. Conformity to shared linguistic expectations by using spoken English or oralism is reinforced. Nonconformity — in this case, using sign language — is negatively sanctioned with "misunderstanding...incomprehension...ridicule...or censure" (Scheff, p. 26). As a result of these negative sanctions, a stigma becomes associated with sign language.

Deaf people communicating in sign language break the predictable patterns and thus maximize the necessary effort and potential conflict involved in any social interaction with English-speaking Americans. A lack of shared linguistic expectations between deaf Americans and English-speaking Americans tends to weaken the common social reality between them. The problem is not merely a matter of patience or tolerance; for many English-speaking Americans, communication with deaf people through sign language is an experience in the collapse of tacit linguistic and social knowledge.

The disability of deafness and sign language itself disrupts the routines and assumptions of everyday verbal interaction (Higgins, 1980). Since most English-speaking people assume all deaf people can easily read lips, or can hear speech with a hearing aid, a communication breakdown is viewed as proof of an additional defect in the deaf person (Levine, 1981). English-speaking Americans may be tempted to assume that the deaf person could have understood and instead chose to be willfully "deviant." However, since English-speaking Americans are themselves frustrated and embarrassed over their own inability to communicate easily, they often stigmatize ASL-signing Americans with derogatory labels.

Stigma

The term "stigma" has been applied to sign language in this paper, but what exactly is it? Goffman defines stigma as an attribute of unintentional and unexpected "differentness that discredits one's social identity (1963, p: 5). Two types of stigma can spoil one's identity: first, the discredited stigma that is visible to all since it arises from physical deformity or tribal membership; second, the discreditable stigma that is invisible to most because it arises from presumably unknown and unperceivable character defects (Goffman, 1963).

This sociological theory of stigma certainly applies to sign language. Signing is an unexpected difference that can possibly discredit a deaf person's social identity in English-speaking society. Sign language is both a discredited stigma that is highly visible, and a discreditable stigma that is invisible until used.

Goffman maintains that "stigma" and "normal" refer not to individuals, but to roles and perspectives in society. The stigmatized are well aware of their own and others' negative perspectives. The stigmatized's own attitudes toward self include: a sense of normality that is not accepted by others; a sense of defilement that is imputed by others but is unpossessed by the self; and a sense of disguise that is precarious at best.

Other people's attitudes toward the stigmatized impute to them sub-humanness, character deficiencies, compensations in behavior, and even potential danger.

The use of sign language and the presence of a sign language interpreter can be considered as stigma because both evoke different social roles concerning the "normal." In addition, the nature of sign language evokes the same attitudes that the stigmatized evoke: sub-humanness, imputed deficiencies, and required compensations. The stigma of sign language is disguised to the extent that English-speaking educators insist on using either visual English systems or oralist skills, as opposed to ASL.

Considering these attitudes, contacts between those in the role of normal" and those in the role of "stigmatized" are filled with uncertainty and exaggeration, if not avoided altogether. When social interaction does occur, commonplace events can become exaggerated into extraordinary feats, and minor failings become embossed as definitive expressions of the "stigmatized difference" (Goffman, 1963, p. 315). These exaggerated failings or feats do not apply merely to the individual person in the stigmatized role. Whenever one member of the stigmatized group achieves or fails, there is a slight transfer of credit or discredit to all members of the stigma group. Thus the stigmatized are praiseworthy or guilty through association with the stigma.

Cycle of societal reaction

In spite of stigma, the general societal attitudes about sign language have changed over the course of American history. What accounts for this change? The cycle of societal reaction to deviance (Lemert, 1951) illuminates some of the causal factors of attitudinal change. Scheff (1984, p. 33) outlines Lemert's cycle as follows:

quiescence	denial of emotional response
exposé	some trigger or "last straw"
reform/repression	hysterical overkill

American attitudes toward sign language follow two complete phases along this theoretical cycle of society's emotional responses to perceived deviance. First, the rise of the cycle, quiescence, was the early English-speaking educators' acceptance of sign language as a teaching tool. Acceptance of sign language, even while requiring English grammar signs, implied a denial of any hostile, emotional response to sign language. The second aspect of the, cycle, expose", had two triggers: the 1880 Milan Conference's condemnation of sign language and A.G. Bell's determination to cure the pathological deaf community of its language. Third, the decline of the cycle, repression in this case, was the hysterical overkill of English-speaking educators enforcing oralism and suppressing sign language.

The next aspect of the cycle, quiescence, was the unquestioning acceptance of oralism by English-speaking parents and educators of the deaf. This group would be the first to deny any hostile emotional response to deaf people; nevertheless, by denying ASL even existed, this group denied any emotional response to sign language itself. Next, the peak of the cycle, expose', had several triggers: linguistic studies of sign language, educational studies of native signers, and the civil rights movement. In short, the expose revealed deaf people to be a separate, minority language group. Finally, the decline of the cycle, reform in this phase, was the overkill of interest in sign language. Educators of the deaf reformed sign language for their own purpose of teaching English. The American public, flocking to sign language classes, reformed their perceptions of sign language.

Sociolinguistic theories

The attitudes about sign language as a birthright, a minority language, and a set of mixed reactions can be illuminated through Trudgill's survey on sociolinguistics (1983). Trudgill defines sociolinguistics as "that part of linguistics which is concerned with language as a social and cultural phenomenon" (p. 32). His text brings to mind many comparisons among minority languages, non-standard dialects, and ASL.

Language: The definitive criterion

First, the attitude that sign language is a birthright for deaf individuals is explained by the self-identification of any ethnic group with its language. According to Trudgill, language is both a "symbol of identity" and also the "defining characteristic of ethnic-group membership." The majority of deaf Americans are not born into deaf families; their mother tongue is not sign language. As Trudgill indicates, however, language is a symbol of group membership. Thus, most deaf people, unlike those people born into an ethnic group, choose to become members of the deaf ethnic group by defining themselves as signers.

Language-deficit theory

Next, the attitude that sign language is a minority language or dialect can be explained by the language deficit theory. Language-deficit theory, as explained by Trudgill, recognizes two distinct linguistic styles: first, the more formal style of middle class children, which may be considered advantageous for academics; second, the more informal style of working class children, which is more advantageous for verbal interaction, such as conversation or narration. American educators of deaf children require the more formal visual English systems in the classroom; yet deaf students may excel in the informal style of ASL outside of the school setting. Furthermore, language-deficit theory claims that non-standard dialect speakers cannot utilize abstract concepts (Trudgill, 1983). This is the same charge that has often been leveled against ASL.

Linguists such as Trudgill, who have tried to apply the language-deficit theory, believe that the suppression or elimination of non-standard styles or dialects is wrong. Psychologically, language is equivalent to a group's identity, and rejecting a group's language is tantamount to rejecting the group itself. Socially, the stigmatization of a non-standard dialect implies that the standard dialect group is more valuable than any other dialect group. Practically, such suppression is fruitless, because users of a non-standard dialect, who prize linguistic solidarity with their peer group, will resist pressures to eliminate their own dialect. Instead of elimination, teachers should help their students understand when and where to engage in appropriate code-switching between dialect styles. Trudgill labels this code-switching "bi-dialectism," and it is the educational approach to non-standard dialect speakers that Trudgill and some other linguists support (pp. 74-75).

ASL is a language in and of itself, not a non-standard dialect of spoken English. The sign language continuum, however, from ASL to the visual English systems, is comparable to Trudgill's discussion of non-standard dialects or styles. Many English-speaking educators of deaf children tacitly assume that ASL is the non-standard dialect of sign language. The presumably standard dialect of sign language, any one of the visual English systems, is more acceptable to many native-born, English-speaking educators and parents of deaf children. If this comparison between ASL and non-standard dialects holds, then Trudgill's psychological, social and practical reasons for not eliminating non-standard dialects clearly apply to the conflict between ASL and the visual English systems. So, too, the linguists' educational recommendation of bi-dialectism is comparable to the educational philosophy of Total Communication. Actually, the practice of bi-dialectism, which is comparable to the NAD's pragmatic bilingual position on communication, could eliminate the attitude that sign language is an inferior, minority language.

Replacement vs. dialectization: Suppression

A different, and negative, comparison between ASL and dialects is offered by Lane (1980b), who argues that the history of ASL has been dominated by the attitude of sign language as a suppressed, not merely inferior, minority language. See Lane's two contributions to this volume for an expanded version of his view. ED. According to Lane and Battison (1978), this suppression was actually a two-pronged effort to annihilate sign language. First, ASL was dialectized so as to eliminate it, by transforming it into a mere "deaf" dialect of English. In essence, this was the method of Gallaudet and Clerc when they used methodological or grammatical signs with native deaf Americans' language. Second, when this sign dialect proved too cumbersome for transmission between English-speaking parents and deaf children, an annihilation policy of outright replacement of ASL was pursued: oralism.

One common attempt to annihilate a linguistic minority is the educational system's practice of replacing a minority group's own language with the standard language of the society's dominant group (Lane, 1980b). Actually, this is the implicit policy of any nation that allows only one official language in its schools. Lane reports that twenty-six American schools for deaf children originally used ASL for instruction, but that by 1907, after the replacement policy of oralism was adopted, 139 American schools for the deaf forbade the use of ASL (Lane, 1980b, p. 131). The educational policy for deaf children now advocates visual English systems; this is a departure from the replacement of ASL and a return to the dialectization of ASL.

Even though ASL may very well be a suppressed minority language, it has neither been completely dialectized into a visual English system, nor completely replaced by oralism. What is intriguing in Lane's comments is the historical shift from the signed English dialect of Gallaudet and Clerc to the dominance of ASL in public schools of the middle 1800's, and then the replacement of ASL by oralism at the turn of the century. This shift is akin to Lemert's cycle of societal reaction to deviance. What is the next phase of the cycle? Since deaf education is now dominated by the dialectization of ASL, the expose of ASL signers as a suppressed linguistic minority may cause a reformation in deaf education. Then ASL could once more become the language of instruction, just as it was in the middle 1800's. Another continuing phase of the cycle would still be possible. English-speaking American society may react in a hostile manner to this projected educational status of ASL, because of either a perceived threat to the linguistic unity of the country, or a conservative resistance to the financial costs of educational reform. If a negative attitude toward bilingual education prevails in the next cycle of societal reaction, will ASL then be repressed by oralism again?

Diglossia

Despite prophetic cycles, the attitudes toward sign language both as a minority language and as a mixed set of reactions can be explained less dramatically, but more realistically, by the linguistic concept of diglossia. Diglossia refers to a linguistic community with two varieties of language, "low" (L) and "high" (H), whose use depends on the formality of the social setting.

Woodward (1978) applies the diglossic model to explain why some deaf people have a mixed set of reactions toward sign language. For example, some deaf people had or still have a negative attitude toward sign language as an ungrammatical, "broken" language. In diglossic language communities, the conversational variety, or "L" form, is viewed as inherently inferior to the formal variety or "H" form. Thus, some deaf people perceive the ASL they use for conversation to be inherently inferior to English. If there is a culprit for this perception or attitude, it is diglossia, not suppression. Also, diglossic attitudes toward appropriate language use can explain why some deaf students may prefer classroom lectures to be delivered in visual English of some sort. According to Woodward (1978), deaf students, as diglossic language users, are likely to expect a formal variety of sign language to be used in the educational setting, and an informal variety, ASL, in the social setting.

If the sign language continuum is diglossic, this has at least three significant implications. First, English-speaking educators alleged interference with sign language is nothing more sinister than the natural tendency of diglossic educators to stress the standardized variety of language in academic settings. Second, attitudes of the English-speaking majority and the signing deaf minority in America are normal and comparable to the attitudes of any other society living with diglossic dialects or languages. Third, if deaf ASL signers define interaction with an interpreter as a formal setting, and hence decline to use ASL, the interpreter will then be hard-pressed to gain fluency in ASL.

Implications for interpreters

This paper does have practical implications for the attitudes and actions of sign language interpreters. Sociolinguistic theories show that language usage patterns are indicative of the user's attitudes toward that language. Generally, deaf people may hesitate to use ASL with English-speaking interpreters, but for three very different reasons.

First, deaf people may restrict ASL to use only among themselves because of a conscious decision to demarcate and maintain the community boundary between "insiders," the English speakers, and "outsiders," the ASL signers, within the broader American society (Higgins, 1980). If this is the case, an interpreter fluent in ASL, or one eager to learn ASL, may not be welcome. Deaf people's right to privacy and exclusivity concerning ASL must be respected even by those professionals who most emphatically need competency in ASL.

Second, deaf people's almost instinctive switch from ASL to a more English style of signing when approached by interpreters may be the result of either unconscious diglossic pressure or conscious bi-dialectical code-switching. The need for and presence of an interpreter may be a subtle social cue to the deaf American that the communication setting is a formal one. To the extent that many interpreting settings are formal, this switch may be most appropriate. Thus, for example, interpreters in church settings should probably balance their signing style between the formality of the setting, which calls for English signing, and the need for clarity, which calls for conceptual signing.

Third, the constant balancing act between ASL and visual English, which characterizes the communication between deaf people and interpreters, may be caused by the minority language user either trying to impress the majority language user or trying to live up to the inevitable expectation: use the majority language. This matching of sign styles, however, may be the result of deaf Americans' fine-tuned sensitivity to the signing levels of others. Whichever the case may be, interpreters should start out with their best ASL signs, expect deaf people to start out with their best English signs, and continue signing until a mutually comprehensible signing style is found (E. Dicker, personal communication).

As for fellow English-speaking Americans, the sociological theories in this paper should clarify the various causes of both their hostile and positive attitudes toward sign language. Understanding the tacit assumptions most Americans make about deviance and stigma should help interpreters realize why they are alternately praised and ridiculed for their work. Interpreters need to be sensitive to the discomfort caused by signing's violation of shared language expectations. This sensitivity should accentuate the interpreters' responsibility to reassure English-speaking Americans about the perceived strangeness of signed communication. This clarification is equally important to the interpreter's responsibility for the transmission of the interpreted message.

Finally, sign language interpreters' attitudes about themselves as users of a stigmatized language can be described by Goffman's sociological labels. In Goffman's theory of stigma, there are two types of "sympathetic others": the "own" and the "wise." The "own" include those with the same stigma, the leaders or role-models of the stigmatized group, and the "stigmaphiles." The latter are professionals whose lives are focussed on stigma activity. The "wise" include the sympathetic normal, the family member, and those who are awarded courtesy stigma so as to serve as a "go-between" for the two worlds (Goffman, 1963). Thus, in Goffman's terms, sign language interpreters are either the "stigmaphiles" among the "own" — the English-speaking lovers of sign language in the deaf community — or are the recipients of courtesy stigma among the "wise" — the signing mediators in the English-speaking society. The difference is subtle, but crucial.

Conclusion

Negative attitudes toward sign language have changed, disappeared, and re-emerged throughout American history. English-speaking educators once perceived signs as a disability to be eradicated through oralism; they now perceive signs as a useful tool for teaching the English language. The deaf community has always perceived sign language as their eloquent birthright even while constantly being stigmatized by it. Now, both deaf and English-speaking Americans hold the seemingly new, but actually 150-year-old attitude that sign language is a minority language.

Will the stigma of sign language as a minority language be any less than the stigma of sign language as a disability? English-speaking Americans may pity the disabled; they rarely tolerate the monolingual user of a minority language. Depathologizing deaf people (Woodward, 1982) from a disabled group who use sign language to a linguistic minority who use sign language may not improve the overall status of the deaf community in relation to the English-speaking majority. Deaf Americans might benefit from a discussion with Japanese, Vietnamese, Laotian, or Hispanic Americans about their status as linguistic minorities. By contrast, English-speaking Americans would benefit from Drake's discussion (1979) of their preference for the assimilationist model, rather than the pluralist model, for any linguistic minority.

At present, most English-speaking Americans still expect minority language users to learn how to speak English. This expectation is unrealistic when it is applied to deaf people using sign language. Not all deaf people can learn how to speak. The pity that the majority of English-speaking Americans feel for the disabled might be transformed into grudging acceptance of sign language as a minority language. If this transformation occurs, then sign language, the deaf community, and sign language interpreters might become the trailblazers for other linguistic minorities seeking acceptance of their minority languages in English-speaking America.

Acknowledgements

The author acknowledges and thanks Rockford College for the use of its facilities and the encouragement of its faculty while she was writing this paper. Special thanks go to Glenda Tellefson for her patient re-typing and constant good cheer.

Closing Address —
The Secret of the Orchard

Harlan Lane

I have been asked to give you my observations on the 1985 convention: it has been five days to remember! I have seen: a lot of hugging, a lot of laughing, a little crying, a whirl of signing, long stretches of speaking, a lot of smiling, a little sleeping, some bouts of drinking, a little dancing, a little stripping. I feel privileged to have been a participant-observer. I have renewed some old acquaintances and made some new friends. Thank you for the warm welcome you have given me, for your generous resolution, for your patience with my questions and with signing, and especially for your candor. Many people here have paid dues for five years to learn as much gossip as I did in just the past few days.

Several speakers have referred to "third culture," meaning the world of interpreters. Well, I like your culture. You hug a lot. You treat visitors from another tribe really well; you even buy them meals and drinks. You communicate about feelings here and now in non-threatening ways. You clearly care about each other and about fundamental human values like self-fulfillment. I have been puzzling over why you are so likeable as a group, so much more likeable than, say, psychologists,

I have concluded that it is because this wonderful organization is full of people who mediate successfully between two cultures. This hard-won achievement has given each of you a priceless gift, perhaps the most valuable lesson to be learned in life, a perspective on one's self, consciousness of self. You have been able to see, as few are privileged to do, that your language, your mores, your values, are merely that — yours. There are other languages, other mores, other values. This has given you humility; it has made you slower to judge and faster to accept; it has enlarged your understanding of the human condition. Thus, you have shared suffering you might have avoided, but you have shared yearnings you might have missed. You are, in short, quite exceptionally existentially alive — and I admire you enormously for it. You have discovered *the secret of the orchard.*

I have made a few observations this past week that seem to arrange themselves under two headings, professionalism and engagement. Nowadays, it is common to ask other people to tell us how to run our lives — doctors, exercise specialists, nutrition experts, couples' counselors, astrological advisors. There was a time when a gentleman wouldn't go near it. But now there are interior decorators, financial advisors, rehabilitation counselors, and especially psychologists; most psychologists spend all their time telling other people, or hinting to them, how to run their lives. So, I thought that perhaps you would excuse this psychologist if, in an act of friendship, I offered some proposals to the R.I.D. (Well, dears, you did ask!) It is your twenty-first birthday, and if Father Psychology, who is about one hundred years old, put his arm around you and spoke to you like a "Dutch uncle," he might say something like this:

I know you have been through some hard years, wondering who you were and what you would become. That's behind you now; you are an adult. Before, you were buffeted by forces often beyond your control; now you must shape your own future. You must decide on your goals and lay down a concrete plan of operation to progress toward each of them. You must have financial goals and intellectual goals, spiritual goals and recreational goals, health goals, and more. The fact that you have little money and little time does not excuse you from this necessary task. Even a handful of people with a few dollars can take the first steps toward the topmost goal.

I submit to my friends in interpreting that professionalism should be one of your major goals. If you want to build a grand professional edifice that will shelter you and generations of interpreters to come, start now on laying the solid academic foundation. Which are the disciplines, committed to the systematic and cumulative acquisition of knowledge, that underpin your profession? There are two groups: cognitive sciences and social sciences.

Cognitive scientists, notably linguists and psychologists, are exploring and have already clarified to an astonishing degree the nature of the extraordinary intellectual skill that you demonstrate every day. They have developed tools to describe linguistic performance and acquisition, theories that relate all the diverse facets of language use and form, a body of knowledge about how languages evolve and bear the imprint of the human mind. How far can your profession continue to grow without substantial knowledge of these methods, theories, and findings? Who will do the basic research on interpreting for you, if you do not pick up these tools and do it for yourselves? Where will the scientifically-grounded innovations in your profession come from, how will you evolve, without sending deep roots down into these underpinning disciplines?

As for cognitive science, so for social science. Who will discover the significant cultural facts that an interpreter must know, who will prepare them so interpreters can incorporate them, who will design the instruments to evaluate that knowledge, if it is not interpreters themselves? No, if interpreting is to continue to grow and improve, if it is to win acceptance in the academic community, if it is to be truly a profession and not a trade, then interpreters must know their foundations as doctors know their anatomy and physiology. If you care enough about your wrist to turn to medical science, don't you care enough about your skill to turn to cognitive science?

At this convention, I have heard many interpreters speak from the podium about their feelings. When I hear someone I like and respect describe how they are conflicted, how they are saddened, how they bear a burden of hurt, then I identify and I feel less conflicted, saddened, isolated, hurt, and I may learn new ways of coping. This is valuable, and so are the astute analyses of the interpreter's tasks and situations that I heard. But these are no substitute for solid scientific grounding. There's hard work to be done. It's all right to be a beginner, as long as you truly begin.

What steps can R.I.D. take to move toward the goal of academic grounding? It could establish a task force on membership development to consider goals. It could organize a panel discussion on that topic at the next convention. It could arrange pre-convention mini-courses. It could incorporate ASL linguistics, bilingualism, cognitive processing, etc., in the next convention program. It could assemble an academic advisory board that would seek, in collaboration with R.I.D. leadership, private or federal sponsors for a university center for research and development in interpretation. It could begin to draw up accreditation guidelines that include solid academic grounding. It could seek foundation or federal support for developing correspondence courses. It could conduct summer institutes with scholarship support and course credit, on the model of the summer institutes that have so enhanced foreign language teaching in the United States and that helped linguistics become a discipline in the decades after the Second World War. It could prepare model curricula for interpreter training programs, and work with university-affiliated interpreters around the country to build those programs little by little. It could prepare proposals under the Rehabilitation Services Administration personnel training program to create master's and doctoral programs in interpretation at one or two key schools. Departments of interpreting or interpreting programs within universities will develop only in the measure as there are doctorate-holding interpreter trainers who are eligible for appointments and tenure.

The evaluation process holds a special place among professionalism goals for your field. There seems to be wide accord among the members that it is crucial, that it needs to be investigated, reformed, and run differently. The task analysis group has done some invaluable hard work. But I believe that solid, standardized, reliable, and valid evaluation on a nationwide scale must meet the high standards set by the Medical College Aptitude Test, the Graduate Record Exam, and the like. This means that the evaluation process needs to be designed in collaboration with psychometricians, linguists and others, possibly under the terms of a special grant obtained from federal or private sources, conceivably with the aid of the Educational Testing Service.

A second set of goals I submit for your consideration comes under the heading of engagement. There may be some among you who accept the self-concept of interpreter-as-machine. But many more do not, believing instead that interpretation by its very nature entails a moral commitment. A computer at the M.I.T. machine-translation project was given for translation into Russian the aphorism, "The spirit is willing but the flesh is weak." According to the famous Slavic linguist Roman Jakobson, what the machine put out was, "The alcohol is ready but the meat is rotten." If an interpreter then, more than a machine, has a moral existence, there are goals you might consider that would reinforce that perception of your profession. Please note as I suggest these goals, that they would also, incidentally, enhance the very field of interpretation itself.

The R.I.D. could well lead the struggle for the acceptance of American Sign Language in the United States. It could publish a glossy pamphlet called "American Sign Language and the American University in 1985" which presents the case for the linguistic and cultural status of ASL. Students all over the country are petitioning their curriculum committees for acceptance of their ASL courses to meet the foreign language requirement; finally, those students and their teachers would have a source of information and a persuasive document. The R.I.D. could work toward requiring accredited schools to accept ASL for the foreign language requirement.

The R.I.D., as part of its program of engagement, could include at the next convention sessions on state law and funding for interpreting that involved state legislators; it could involve officials of international translation organizations; it could sponsor a panel or other forum on the interpreter in the school setting and involve educators of the deaf.

The R.I.D. might give systematic consideration to the development of specialized interpreting: the role of deaf interpreters and their training; interpreters for the deaf-blind; special aspects of interpreting for blacks and language minorities such as Hispanics.

The relation between the R.I.D. and the deaf community bears special consideration. Your organization has had the remarkable, almost unheard-of, wisdom and advantage to incorporate into its very existence some representation of a major consumer group. Psychologists, doctors, and lawyers, for example, do nothing of the sort; they are woefully out of touch with the needs, the satisfaction, and the goals of their consumers. But you may wish to build on that fine beginning. Mount a program to let the deaf community know about the new R.I.D. Recruit former deaf members and new deaf members. Support and strengthen the Deaf Caucus. Take steps to enhance various roles for deaf people within the organization: as MLS relay interpreters; as consumer advocates; as written-English-to-ASL interpreters for video training materials.

The R.I.D. should consider an aggressive outreach program to bring more interpreters into the organization and therefore under the sway of its professionalism and engagement. It might create a recruitment campaign with the goal that every present member bring in a new member within six months. It might ask the membership to come four-handed to the next convention — each one bring one who didn't come in 1985. It might set up regional workshops, heavily publicized, that are training and recruitment events at the same time. It might establish a national hotline (1-800-...) so that anyone anywhere who needs an interpreter or an answer to a question about interpreting can get a referral. It might prepare a brochure entitled "Interpreting, Your Career" and arrange for its dissemination in schools around the nation. Finally, I hope that R.I.D. will put in place some mechanism to consider the plight of interpreting worldwide and the role it can play in fostering it. We have much to offer our colleagues overseas; at this delicate time, they desperately need our help. They will never forget us if we come to their aid, and our lives will be immeasurably enriched. Will R.I.D. aid in establishing a stable international association of registries that will hold regular international congresses?

In brief, R.I.D. is now twenty-one and can care as it never has before about its own welfare — its professionalism — and the welfare of those it serves — its engagement. Your greatest resource for this grand and exciting undertaking is your very diversity. Within R.I.D., there are deaf and hearing, hearing of deaf, white, black, female, and — a few — males; there are free-lancers and full-timers, there are ITP's and old-timers. To find your strength in this diversity within is only natural: the basis of your profession is the diversity outside of your organization. If there were no different cultures, there would be no interpreters. In a world torn asunder with factionalism, enfeebled by the "we" against the "they," R.I.D. stands firm. Its program says: I do not deny your difference. I do not seek to eradicate it. I do not seek to minimize it. I do not tolerate it. I embrace it! You are living the secret of the orchard.

"One day the sun shines on my orchard," Laurent Clerc wrote in his eighty-fourth year, shortly before he died; "another, it does not. The orchard has fruitful trees and unfruitful; even in the same species there are different varieties — everything is variable and inconstant. And we ourselves: we vary in our forms and functions, our hearts and minds. I do not know as you do not know why this should be so. We can only thank God for the rich diversity of his creation and hope that in the future world, the reason for it may be explained to us all."
Thank you, God bless.

References

Alexander Graham Bell Association. 1900. Review, 2.

Allen, T. E. and T. I. Osborn. 1984. Academic integration of hearing-impaired students: Demographic, handicapping and achievement factors. *American Annals of the Deaf, 129,* 100-113.

Allport, G. 1954. *The Nature of Prejudice.* Reading, Massachu–setts: Addison-Wesley.

Altshuler, K. 1974. The social and psychological development of the deaf child: Problems, their treatment, and prevention. *American Annals of the Deaf, 119,* 365-376.

American Heritage Dictionary. 1976. Boston, Massachusetts: Houghton Mifflin Company.

Amir, Y. 1969. Contact hypothesis in ethnic relations. *Psychological Bulletin, 71,* 319-343.

Arnesen, Susan. 1985. Report of the Educational Transliteration / Interpretation Committee. Reported to the RID Convention. July.

Bahr, Howard M., Bruce A. Chadwick, and Joseph A. Stauss. 1979. *American Ethnicity.* Lexington, Massachu–setts: D.C. Heath and Company.

Baker, Charlotte, and Robbin Battison. (Eds.) 1980. *Sign Language and the Deaf Community: Essays in Honor of William C. Stokoe.* Silver Spring, Maryland: National Association of the Deaf.

Baker, Charlotte, and Carol Padden. 1978. *ASL: A Look at its History. Structure and Community.* Silver Spring, Maryland: T.J. Publishers.

Bascom, William R. 1965. Four functions of folklore. In Alan Dundes (Ed.), *The Study of Folklore.* Englewood Cliffs, New Jersey: Prentice-Hall. 270-298.

Basso, Keith. 1979. *Portraits of "The White Man": Linguistic Play and Cultural Symbols among the Western Apache.* Cambridge: Cambridge University Press.

Bender, Ruth. 1970. *The Conquest of Deafness: A History of the Long Struggle to Make Possible Normal Living to Those Handicapped by Lack of Normal Hearing.* Cleveland: Case Western Reserve University Press.

Bergson, Henri. 1911. *Laughter: An Essay on the Meaning of the Comic.* (Translated by C. Brereton and F. Rothwell.) New York: Macmillan.

Berrigan, Dennis. 1983. ASL and me. *Reflector, 5,* 7-9.

Berke, Larry J. 1978. Attitudes of deaf high school students towards American Sign Language. In F. Caccamise and P. Hicks (Eds.) . 173-182. Sage Publications/ Halsted.

Brislin, Richard. 1983. The benefits of close intercultural relationships. In S. Irvine and J. Berry (Eds.), *Human Assessment and Cultural Factors.* New York: Plenum Press. 521-538.

Brislin, Richard. 1981. *Cross-Cultural Encounters: Face-to-Face Interaction.* Elmsford, New York: Pergamon Press.

Brislin, Richard. 1979. Orientation programs for cross-cultural preparation. In A. Marsella, R. Tharp, and T. Ciborowski (Eds.). 287-305.

Brislin, Richard, K. Cushner, C. Cherrie and M. Yong. 1986. *Intercultural Interactions: A Practical Guide.* Beverly Hills: Sage Publications.

Brislin, Richard and P. Pedersen. 1976. *Cross-Cultural Orientation Programs.* New York: Wiley/Halsted.

Caccamise, F., R. Dirst, R. Dominque DeVries, J. Heil, C. Kirchner, S. Kirchner, A. M. Rinaldi, and J. Stangarone. (Eds.). 1980. *Introduction to Interpreting.* Silver Spring, MD: RID.

Caccamise, F. and D. Hicks. (Eds.) 1978. *Proceedings of the Second National Symposium on Sign Language Research and Teaching.* Silver Spring, Maryland: National Association of the Deaf.

Certeau, M., D. Julia, and J. Revel. (Eds.) 1975. *Une Politique de la Langue. La Révolution Francaise et les Patois: l'Enquête de Grégoire.* Paris: Gallimard.

Charrow, Veda. 1975a. Manual English: A linguist's viewpoint. In F. B. and A. B. Crammatte (Eds.). 78-86.

Charrow, Veda. 1975b. A psycholinguistic analysis of deaf English. *Sign Language Studies, 7,* 139-150.

Cokely, Dennis. 1983a. Metanotative qualities: How accurately are they conveyed by interpreters? *Reflector, 5,* 16-22.

Cokely, Dennis. 1983b. Editor's comments. *Reflector, 6,* 3-4.

Cokely, Dennis. 1983c. Editor's comments. *Reflector, 7,* 3-4.

Cokely, Dennis. 1982. Guidelines for instructors in bilingual-bicultural education. *Reflector, 5,* 16-22.

Colonomos, Betty M. 1982. Reflections of an interpreter trainer. *Reflector, 2,* 5-13.

Conrad, R. 1979. *The Deaf Schoolchild.* London: Harper and Row.

Convention of American Instructors of the Deaf. 1909. *Proceedings.* 38-56.

Cook, S. 1970. Motives in a conceptual analysis of attitude-related behavior. *Nebraska Symposium on Motivation, 17.* Lincoln: University of Nebraska Press.

COSD. 1970. *Forum Proceedings: The Deaf Man and the Law.*

Crammatte, F. B. and A. B. Crammatte. (Eds.) 1975. *VII World Congress of the World Federation of the Deaf.* Silver Spring, Maryland: National Association of the Deaf.

Dahl, Ö. (Ed.) 1974. *Topic and Comment: Contextual Boundness and Focus.* Hamburg: Helmut Buske Verlag.

Deregowski, J. 1980. Some aspects of perceptual organization in the light of cross-cultural evidence. In N. Warren (Ed.), *2,* 51-93.

Deuchar, Margaret. 1981. Introduction: Communication aspects. In B. Woll, J. Kyle, and M. Deuchar (Eds.). 163-165.

Dicker, Leo. 1982. *Facilitating Manual Communication for Interpreters, Students and Teachers.* (Revised Edition.) Silver Spring, Maryland: RID.

Dirst, Richard and Frank Caccamise. 1980. Introduction. In F. Caccamise *et al.* (Eds.) . 1-9.

Douglas, Mary. 1968. The social control of cognition: Some factors in joke perception. *Man, 3,* 361-376.

Drake, Glendon F. 1979. Ethnicity, values and language policy in the United States. In H. Giles and B. Saint-Jacques (Eds.), *Language and Ethnic Relations.* Oxford: Pergamon Press. 223-230.

Duncan, J.G. 1984. Recent legislation affecting hearing-impaired persons. *American Annals of the Deaf, 129,* 83-94.

Dundes, Alan. 1973. *Mother Wit from the Laughing Barrel: Readings in the Interpretation of Afro-American Folklore.* Englewood Cliffs, New Jersey: Prentice-Hall.

Dunstall, Carol. n.d. Proposal for the evaluation of educational interpreters/transliterators, and Code of Ethics for educational interpreters/transliterators. Florida Registry of Interpreters for the Deaf.

Ehrlich, Howard J. 1973. *The Social Psychology of Prejudice*. New York: John Wiley and Sons.

Fant, Louie J. 1977. Where do we go from here? In W. C. Stokoe (Ed.). 25-28.

Fant, Louie J. 1972. *Ameslan*. Northridge, California: Joyce Motion Picture Co.

Feinberg, Leonard. 1978. The secret of humor. *Maledicta 2*, 86-110.

Freedman, J., J. M. Carlsmith and D. Sears. 1974. *Social Psychology*. Englewood Cliffs, New Jersey: Prentice-Hall.

Freire, P. 1973. *Education for a Critical Consciousness*. New York: Continuum Publishing House.

Freire, P. 1970. *Pedagogy of the Oppressed*. (Now available in 1983 printing from Continuum Publishing House, New York.)

Fritsch Rudser, Steven. 1980. The Revised Code of Ethics: Some issues and implications. In F. Caccamise, J. Stangarone, & M. Mitchell-Caccamise (Eds.), *A Decade of Interpreting Awareness in a Century of Deaf Awareness*. Silver Spring, Maryland: RID. 58-63.

Fry, William. 1963. *Sweet Madness: A Study of Humor*. Palo Alto, California: Pacific Books.

Fullinwider, Robert K. 1981. *The Reverse Discrimination Controversy: A Moral and Legal Analysis*. Totowa, New Jersey: Rowman and Littlefield.

Gannon, Jack. 1981. *Deaf Heritage: A Narrative History of Deaf America*. Silver Spring, Maryland: National Association of the Deaf.

Germain, C. 1979. *The Concept of Situation in Linguistics*. (Translated by B. J. Wallace.) Ottawa: University of Ottawa Press.

Gerver, David and A. Wallace Sinaiko. (Eds.) 1978. *Language Interpretation and Communication*. New York/London: Plenum Press.

Glickman, N. 1984. The war of the languages: Comparisons between language wars of Jewish and Deaf communities. *Deaf American, 36(6)*, 25-33.

Goffman, Erving. 1963. *Stigma: Notes on the Management of Spoiled Identity*. Englewood Cliffs, New Jersey: Prentice-Hall.

Goffman, Erving. 1959. *The Presentation of Self in Everyday Life*. New York: Doubleday/Anchor Books.

Golovensky, D. I. 1952. The marginal-man concept: An analysis and critique. *Social Forces, 30*, 333-339.

Goode, E. 1978. *Deviant Behavior: An Interactionist Approach*. Englewood Cliffs, New Jersey: Prentice-Hall.

Gordon, Joseph C. 1892. *Notes and Observations upon the Education of the Deaf*. Washington, D.C.: The Volta Bureau.

Gottschalk, Shimon S. 1975. *Communities and Alternatives: An Exploration of the Limits of Planning*. New York: John Wiley and Sons.

Gregory, J. F., T. Shanahan, and K. J. Walberg. 1984. Main-streamed hearing-impaired high school seniors: A reanalysis of a national survey. *American Annals of the Deaf, 129*, 11-16.

Grosjean, Francois. 1982. *Life With Two Languages*. Cambridge, Massachusetts: Harvard University Press.

Gudykunst, W. M. Hammer, and R. Wiseman. 1977. An analysis of an integrated approach to cross-cultural training. *International Journal of Intercultural Relations, 1(2)*, 99-110.

Guthrie, G. 1979. A cross-cultural odyssey: Some personal reflections. In A. Marsella, R. Tharp, and T. Ciborowski (Eds.). 349-368.

Hairston, Ernest, and Linwood Smith. 1983. *Black and Deaf in America: Are We That Different?* Silver Spring, Maryland: T.J.Publishing.

Hall, Edward. 1977. *Beyond Culture.* Garden City, New York: Anchor Books.

Hasenfeld, Yeheskel and Richard A. English. 1974. *Human Service Organizations.* Ann Arbor, Michigan: University of Michigan Press.

Hendricks, W. O. 1976. *Grammars of Style and Styles of Grammar.* Amsterdam: North-Holland Publishing Co.

Herskovits, Melville J. 1948. *Man and His Works: The Science of Cultural Anthropology.* New York: Knopf.

Higgins, Paul C. 1980. *Outsiders in a Hearing World: A Sociology of Deafness.* Beverly Hills: Sage Publications.

Hirschman, Albert O. 1970. *Exit, Voice and Loyalty.* Cambridge, Massachusetts: Harvard University Press.

Hofstede, G. 1980. *Culture's Consequences: International Differences in Work Related Values.* Beverly Hills: Sage Publications.

Horton, S. R. 1979. *Interpreting, Interpreting.* Baltimore: The Johns Hopkins University Press.

Hurwitz, S. 1967. Behavior patterns in the deaf. *Rehabilitation Record, 9,* 15-17.

Iowa State Registry of Interpreters for the Deaf (ISRID). 1984. Interim report of the task force on educational interpreting.

Irvine, S. and W. Carroll. 1980. Testing and assessment across cultures: Issues in methodology and theory. In H. Triandis and J. Berry (Eds.), *Handbook of Cross-Cultural Psychology, vol. 1.* Boston: Allyn and Bacon. 181-244.

Jacobs, Leo. 1980. *A Deaf Adult Speaks Out.* (Second edition.) Washington, D.C.: Gallaudet College Press.

Jahoda, G. 1963. Children's concepts of nationality: A critical study of Piaget's stages. *Child Development, 35,* 1081-1089.

Jarvella, R. and W. Klein. 1982. *Speech, Place and Action.* New York: Wiley & Sons.

Jensema, C. 1975. The relationship between academic achievement and the demographic characteristics of hearing-impaired children and youth. Series R, no. 2. Washington, D.C.: Gallaudet Office of Demographic Studies.

Jones, E. 1979. The rocky road from acts to dispositions. *American Psychologist, 34,* 107-117.

Jones, Phillip. (in preparation.) Questionnaire for Black and Hispanic interpreters: The results.

Joos, Martin. 1967. *The Five Clocks.* N.Y.: Harcourt Brace Jovanovich.

Joseph, Gloria I. and Jill Lewis. 1981. *Common Differences: Conflicts in Black and White Feminist Perspectives.* Garden City, New York: Anchor Press/ Doubleday.

Kannapell, Barbara. 1980. Personal awareness and advocacy in the Deaf community. In C. Baker and R. Battison (Eds.). 105-116.

Kannapell, Barbara. 1977. The deaf person as a teacher of American Sign Language. In W. C. Stokoe (Ed.). 159-164.

Kaplan, H. I., A. M. Freedman, and B. J. Sadock. (Eds.) 1980. *Comprehensive Textbook of Psychiatry/III.* (Third edition.) Baltimore: Williams & Wilkins.

Kerckhoff, A. C. and T. C. McCormick. 1955. Marginal status and marginal personality. *Social Forces, 34,* 48-55.

Klima, Edward and Ursula Bellugi. 1979. *The Signs of Language.* Cambridge, Massachusetts: Harvard University Press.

Kochman, Thomas. 1981. *Black and White Styles in Conflict.* Chicago: University of Chicago Press.

Koestler, Arthur. 1964. *The Act of Creation: A Study of the Conscious and Unconscious in Science and Art.* New York: Dell.

Kramer, Judith R. 1970. *The American Minority Community.* New York: Thomas Y. Crowell Co.

Landis, D. and Richard Brislin. 1983. *Handbook of Intercultural Training* (3 volumes). Elmsford, New York: Pergamon.

Lane, Harlan. 1984. *When the Mind Hears: A History of the Deaf.* New York: Random House.

Lane, Harlan. (Ed.) 1984. *The Deaf Experience: Classics in Language and Education.* (Translated by Frank Philip.) Cambridge, Massachusetts: Harvard University Press.

Lane, Harlan. 1981. Jean Massieu and deaf teachers of the deaf. In F. Caccamise, M. Garretson and U. Bellugi (Eds.), *Teaching American Sign Language as a Second/Foreign Language.* Silver Spring, Maryland: National Association of the Deaf. 4-14.

Lane, Harlan. 1980a. Some thoughts on language bigotry. Paper delivered at Gallaudet College, Professional Day Address. (Available from Department of Psychology, Northeastern University, Boston.)

Lane, Harlan. 1980b. Historical: A chronology of the oppression of sign language in France and the United States. In H. Lane and F. Grosjean (Eds.). 119-161.

Lane, Harlan. 1977. Notes for a psychohistory of American Sign Language. *Deaf American,* 29, 3-7.

Lane, Harlan. 1976. *The Wild Boy of Aveyron.* Cambridge, Massachusetts: Harvard University Press.

Lane, Harlan and Robbin Battison. 1978. The role of oral language in the evolution of manual language. In D. Gerver and H. W. Sinaiko (Eds.). 57-79.

Lane, Harlan and Francois Grosjean. (Eds.) 1980. *Recent Perspectives on American Sign Language.* Hillsdale, New Jersey: Lawrence Erlbaum Associates.

Lawson, Lilian. 1981. The role of sign in the structure of the deaf community. In B. Woll, J. Kyle and M. Deuchar (Eds.). 166-177.

Lemert, E. M. 1951. *Social pathology.* New York: McGraw-Hill.

Lentz, Ella Mae. 1977. Informing the deaf about the structure of American Sign Language. In W. C. Stokoe (Ed.). 239-246.

Levelt, W. 1984. Some perceptual limitations on talking about space. In A. J. van Doorn (Ed.), *Limits in Perception.* Utrecht: VNU Science Press. 323-358.

Levine, Edna. 1981. *The Ecology of Early Deafness.* New York: Columbia University Press.

Levine, Edna. 1956. *Youth in a Soundless World, A Search for Personality.* New York: University Press.

Llewellyn-Jones, Peter. 1981. Simultaneous interpreting. In B. Woll, J. Kyle, and M. Deuchar (Eds.). 89-104.

Lunde, Anders S. 1960. Social factors in the isolation of deaf persons. . . . (Figure). In W. C. Stokoe, *Sign Language Structure: An Outline of Visual Communication Systems of the American Deaf.* University of Buffalo, Occasional Paper 8, of the Studies in Linguistics series. 23.

Markowicz, Harry and James Woodward. 1975. Language and the maintenance of ethnic boundaries in the deaf community. Paper presented at the Conference on Culture and Communication, Temple University, March 13-15.

Marsella, A., R. Tharp, and T. Ciborowski. (Eds.) 1979. *Perspectives on Cross-Cultural Psychology.* New York: Academic Press.

Martineau, William H. 1972. A model of the social functions of humor. In J. N. Goldstein and P. E. McGhee (Eds.), *The Psychology of Humor*. New York: Academic Press. 101-125.

McClelland, D. 1978. Managing motivation to expand human freedom. *American Psychologist, 33,* 201-210.

Meadow, Kathryn P. 1980. *Deafness and Child Development*. Berkeley, California: University of California Press.

Meadow, Kathryn P. 1972. Sociolinguistics, sign language, and the deaf subculture. In T. J. O'Rourke (Ed.) *Psycholinguistics and Total Communication: The State of the Art*. Washington, D.C.: American Annals of the Deaf. 19-33.

Mindel, E. D. and Mackay Vernon. 1971. *They Grow in Silence*. Silver Spring, Maryland: National Association of the Deaf.

Myers, L. 1967. *The Law and the Deaf*. Washington, D.C.: U.S. Department of Health, Education and Welfare.

National Association of the Deaf, Executive Board. 1984. Position on communication and sign language. *NAD Broadcaster, 6(9),* 3.

National Union of the Deaf. 1982. *Charter of the Rights of the Deaf.*

Padden, Carol. 1980. The deaf community and the culture of deaf people. In C. Baker and R. Battison (Eds.). 89-103.

Padden, Carol and Harry Markowicz. 1975. Cultural conflicts between hearing and deaf communities. In F. B. and A. B. Crammatte (Eds.). 407-412.

Poortinga, Y. 1979. The achievements of cross-cultural research: Some critical comments. In L. Eckensberger, W. Lonner, and Y. Poortinga (Eds.), *Cross-Cultural Contributions to Psychology*. Amsterdam: Swets and Zeitlinger. 276-286.

Quigley, Stephen P. and Joseph P. Youngs. (Eds.) 1965. *Interpreting for Deaf People*. Washington, D.C.: U.S. Department of Health, Education and Welfare.

Rainer, J., K. Altschuler, and F. Kallman. (Eds.) 1963. *Family and Mental Health Problems in a Deaf Population*. New York: Department of Genetics, New York State Psychiatric Institute, Columbia University.

Ricoeur, P. 1976. *Interpretation Theory: Discourse and the Surplus of Meaning*. Fort Worth, Texas: Texas Christian University Press.

RID. *Views*. February, 1985. Special Convention Bulletin. 24.

Riegel, Klaus. 1976. The dialectics of human development. *American Psychologist*, October, 689-700.

Riordan, C. 1978. Equal status interracial conflict: A review and revision of the concept. *International Journal of Intercultural Relations, 5,* 161-185.

Roberts, J. 1983. Deaf man found guilty. . . . *Saint Louis Globe-Democrat*, p. 15B. September 12.

Rochester Institute of Technology, National Technical Institute for the Deaf. 1984. Educational interpreting: A national deed for clarification of roles, responsibilities and standards. Background position statement.

Ross, L. 1977. The intuitive psychologist and his shortcomings: Distortion in the attribution process. In L. Berkowitz (Ed.), *Advances in Experimental Social Psychology*, vol. 10. New York: Academic Press. 174-220.

Saks, M. and R. Hastie. 1978. *Social Psychology in Court*. New York: Van Nostrand Reinhold.

Sandler, J., H. Kennedy, and R. Tyson. 1980. *The Technique of Child Psychoanalysis: Discussions with Anna Freud*. Cambridge, Massachusetts: Harvard University Press.

Scheff, Thomas J. 1984. *Being Mentally Ill: A Sociological Theory.* (Revised ed.). N.Y.: Aldine Publishing Co.

Schein, Jerrold and M. Delk. 1974. *The Deaf Population in the United States.* Silver Spring, Maryland: National Association of the Deaf.

Schowe, B. 1979. *Identity Crisis in Deafness.* Tempe, Arizona: The Scholars Press.

Schreiber, Fred C. 1974. And the cons. *Gallaudet Today,* Winter, 5-6.

Seleskovitch, Danica. 1978. *Interpreting for International Conferences.* Washington, D.C.: Pen and Booth.

Shirtz, Garry. n.d. BAFA BAFA: A Cross-Cultural Simulation Game. Del Mar, California: Simile II.

Sicard, R. A. 1790. *Second Mémoire sur l'Art d'Instruire les Sourds et Muets de Naissance.* Paris: Knapen.

Simpson, George E. and J. Milton Yinger. 1972. *Racial and Cultural Minorities: An Analysis of Prejudice and Discrimination.* New York: Harper and Row.

Smith, R. 1978. The Message Measurement Inventory. Bloomington, Indiana: Indiana University Press.

Solow, Sharon Neumann. 1981. *Sign Language Interpreting: A Basic Resource Book.* Silver Spring, Maryland: National Association of the Deaf.

Stagner, Ross and Charles M. Solley. 1970. *Basic Psychology.* New York: McGraw Hill.

Stangarone, James and Suzie Kirchner. 1980. Section H: Performing arts. In Caccamise, *et al.* (Eds.). 78-82.

Stansfield, Millie. 1981. Psychological issues in mental health interpreting. *RID Interpreting Journal, 1,* 18-31.

Stokoe, William C., Jr. 1981. The study and use of sign language. In M. Sternberg (Ed.), *American Sign Language: A Comprehensive Dictionary.* New York: Harper and Row. xi-xxxvii.

Stokoe, William C., Jr. (Ed.) 1977. *Proceedings of the First National Symposium on Sign Language Research and Teaching.* Silver Spring, Maryland: National Association of the Deaf.

Stokoe, William C., Jr. 1970. Sign language diglossia. *Studies in Linguistics, 21,* 27-41.

Stonequist, Everett V. 1961. *The Marginal Man.* New York: Russell and Russell.

Street, David, R. Vinter, and C. Perrow. 1966. *Organization for Treatment.* New York: The Free Press.

Strong, Michael and Steven Fritsch Rudser. ms. An assessment instrument for sign language interpreters.

Supalla, Ted. 1984. The films of Charles Kraul. Lecture delivered at Harper Junior College. Palatine, Illinois.

Sussman, Alan. 1976. Attitudes toward deafness: Psychology's role, past, present, and potential. In F. B. and A. B. Crammatte (Eds.). 254-258.

Switzer, M. and B. Williams. 1967. Life problems of deaf people. *Archives of Environmental Health.* August, *15,* 249ff.

Szanton, D. 1966. Cultural Confrontation in the Phillipines. In R. Textor (Ed.), *Cultural Frontiers of the Peace Corps.* Cambridge, Massachusetts: MIT Press. 35-61.

Taft, Brenda. 1983. Employability of Black Deaf persons in Washington, D.C.: National implications. *American Annals of the Deaf,* 453-456.

Taft, R. 1977. Coping with unfamiliar cultures. In N. Warren (Ed.). *Vol. 1.* 121-153.

Tajfel, Henri. 1969. Social and cultural factors in perception. In G. Lindsay and E. Aronson (Eds.), *Handbook of Social Psychology,* Second Edition. Reading, Massachusetts: Addison-Wesley. *Vol. 3.* 315-394.

Taylor, D. and V. Jaggi. 1974. Ethnocentrism and causal attribution in a

South Indian context. *Journal of Cross-Cultural Psychology, 5,* 162-171.

Triandis, H. 1977. *Interpersonal Behavior.* Belmont, California: Wadsworth.

Trifonovitch, G. 1973. On cross-cultural orientation techniques. *Topics in Culture Learning, 1,* 38-47.

Trudgill, Peter. 1983. *Sociolinguistics: An Introduction to Language and Society.* Middlesex, England: Penguin Books.

Trybus, R. J. and M. A. Karchmer. 1977. School achievement scores of hearing-impaired children: National data on achievement status and growth patterns. *American Annals of the Deaf, 122,* 62-69.

Tyler, S. A. 1978. *The Said and the Unsaid: Mind, Meaning and Culture.* New York: Academic Press.

Useem, J. and R. Useem. 1955. *The Western Educated Man in India.* New York: Dryden Press.

Useem, J. and R. Useem. 1967. The interfaces of a binational third culture: A study of the American community in India. *Journal of Social Issues, 21(1),* 130-143.

Vander Zanden, James W. 1966. *American Minority Relations.* New York: Ronald Press Co.

van Dijk, T. A. 1977. *Text and Context: Explorations in the Semantics and Pragmatics of Discourse.* London: Longman Group Limited.

van Dijk, T. A. 1972. *Some Aspects of Text Grammars: A Study in Theoretical Linguistics and Poetics.* The Netherlands: Mouton & Co. N.V.

Veditz, G. 1933. The genesis of the National Association of the Deaf. *Deaf-Mutes Journal, 62(22),* 1 June.

Warren, N. (Ed.) 1977. *Studies in Cross-Cultural Psychology.* (Two volumes.) London: Academic Press.

Warren, Rachel B. and Donald E. Warren. 1977. *Neighborhood Organizer's Handbook.* South Bend, Indiana: Notre Dame University Press.

Watson, Peter. (Ed.) 1973. *Psychology and Race.* Chicago: Aldire Publishers.

Wolk, S. and T. E. Allen. 1984. A five-year follow-up of reading-comprehension achievement of hearing-impaired students in special education programs. *Journal of Special Education, 18,* 161-176.

Woll, Bencie, James Kyle, and Margaret Deuchar (Eds.). 1981. *Perspectives on British Sign Language and Deafness.* London: Croom Helm.

Woll, Bencie and Lilian Lawson. 1981. British Sign Language. In E. Haugen, J. D. McClure, and D. Thomson (Eds.), *Minority Languages Today.* Edinburgh: University Press.

Woodward, James. 1982. *How You Gonna Get to Heaven If You Can't Talk With Jesus? On Depathologizing Deafness.* Silver Spring, Maryland: T. J. Publishers.

Woodward, James. 1980. Sociolinguistics: Some sociolinguistic aspects of French and American Sign Language. In H. Lane and F. Grosjean (Eds.). 103-118.

Woodward, James. 1979. *Signs of Sexual Behavior.* Silver Spring, Maryland: T.J. Publishers.

Woodward, James. 1978. Some sociolinguistic problems in the implementation of bilingual education for deaf students. In F. Caccamise and D. Hicks (Eds.).183-210.

Woodward, James. 1973. Some observations on sociolinguistic variation and American Sign Language. *Kansas Journal of Sociology, 9(2),* 191-200.

Woodward, James, and Carol Erting. 1975. Synchronic variation and historical change in American Sign Language. *Language Sciences, 37,* 9-12.

Worswick, C. and H. Hamilton. (Eds.) 1982. *Roots of Racism: Book One.* London: Institute of Race Relations.

Table of Contents